CORPORATE SOCIAL RESPONSIBILITY (CSR) PRACTICES

Toward Economic, Environmental, and Social Balance

CORPORATE SOCIAL RESPONSIBILITY (CSR) PRACTICES

Toward Economic, Environmental, and Social Balance

Edited by
Nilanjan Ray, PhD
Abhijeet Bag

AAP APPLE
ACADEMIC
PRESS

First edition published 2022

Apple Academic Press Inc.
1265 Goldenrod Circle, NE,
Palm Bay, FL 32905 USA
4164 Lakeshore Road, Burlington,
ON, L7L 1A4 Canada

CRC Press
6000 Broken Sound Parkway NW,
Suite 300, Boca Raton, FL 33487-2742 USA
2 Park Square, Milton Park,
Abingdon, Oxon, OX14 4RN UK

© 2022 Apple Academic Press, Inc.

Apple Academic Press exclusively co-publishes with CRC Press, an imprint of Taylor & Francis Group, LLC

Library and Archives Canada Cataloguing in Publication

Title: Corporate social responsibility (CSR) practices : toward economic, environmental, and social balance / edited by Nilanjan Ray, PhD, Abhijeet Bag.
Names: Ray, Nilanjan, 1984- editor. | Bag, Abhijeet, editor.
Description: First edition. | Includes bibliographical references and index.
Identifiers: Canadiana (print) 20210260769 | Canadiana (ebook) 20210260831 | ISBN 9781771889759 (hardcover) | ISBN 9781774638781 (softcover) | ISBN 9781003146414 (ebook)
Subjects: LCSH: Social responsibility of business. | LCSH: Strategic planning.
Classification: LCC HD60 .C74 2022 | DDC 658.4/08—dc23

Library of Congress Cataloging-in-Publication Data

Names: Ray, Nilanjan, 1984- editor. | Bag, Abhijeet, editor.
Title: Corporate social responsibility (CSR) practices : toward economic, environmental, and social balance / edited by Nilanjan Ray, PhD, Abhijeet Bag.
Description: First edition | Palm Bay, FL : Apple Academic Press, 2022. | Includes bibliographical references and index. | Summary: "This volume, Corporate Social Responsibility (CSR) Practices: Toward Economic, Environmental, and Social Balance explores the management concept whereby companies integrate social and environmental concerns in their business operations and in their interactions with their stakeholders. This practice also benefits the company and helps it to reach its strategic goals. This volume takes interdisciplinary and multidisciplinary perspectives to exploring a multitude of themes in CSR, including corporate social responsibility in conjunction with employee quality of life, globalization, industry sustainability, environmental accountability, academic spin-off, education, empowerment of women, corporate reputation, expenditures for CSR purposes, and more. The chapter authors consider the impacts and outcomes along with the emerging challenges of incorporating CSR in an organization's business strategy. This volume is an important academic journey into some of the most relevant yet under-studied issues of today. It helps to provide an understanding of those issues in a broader perspective of analysis. This volume will be a valuable resource for faculty and students in business as well as for industry professionals, researchers, and others"-- Provided by publisher.
Identifiers: LCCN 2021032550 (print) | LCCN 2021032551 (ebook) | ISBN 9781771889759 (hardback) | ISBN 9781774638781 (paperback) | ISBN 9781003146414 (ebook)
Subjects: LCSH: Social responsibility of business.
Classification: LCC HD60 .C67325 2022 (print) | LCC HD60 (ebook) | DDC 658.4/08--dc23
LC record available at https://lccn.loc.gov/2021032550
LC ebook record available at https://lccn.loc.gov/2021032551

ISBN: 978-1-77188-975-9 (hbk)
ISBN: 978-1-77463-878-1 (pbk)
ISBN: 978-1-00314-641-4 (ebk)

About the Editors

Dr. Nilanjan Ray

Nilanjan Ray, PhD, is an Associate Professor and Centre Coordinator, Centre for Research of Business Analytics, Department of Management, School of Business and Economics, Adamas University, West Bengal, India. He has 10 years teaching experience at the university level and six years of research experience. He has guided over 50 postgraduate student projects. Dr. Ray has published over 60 research papers in national and international refereed, peer-reviewed journals and proceedings and has edited eight research handbooks published by Springer, IGI-Global USA, and Apple Academic Publisher/CRC Press. He is also a reviewer for the *Tourism Management Journal of Service Marketing, Journal of Business and Economics*, and *Research Journal of Business and Management Accounting*. He is an editorial board member of several journals as well. He has also chaired a technical session at the IJAS Conference 2012 at Harvard University, USA. Dr. Ray is a life member of the International Business Studies Academia and a fellow member of the Institute of Research Engineers and the Doctors Universal Association of Arts and Management Professionals (UAAMP), New York, USA. Dr. Ray obtained a certified Accredited Management Teacher Award from All India Management Association, New Delhi, India.

Abhijeet Bag

Abhijeet Bag is an Assistant Professor in the Department of Commerce, Cooch Behar Panchanan Barma University, West Bengal, India. He formerly worked at Adamas University and Serampore College as an Assistant Professor. Presently he is pursuing a PhD from the University of Calcutta, India. He awarded his MPhil and MCom (Accounting and Finance) from the University of Calcutta. He has also qualified UGC NET and WBCSC SET in the year 2017. Mr. Bag is a life member of the Indian Accounting Association Research Foundation and Commerce Alumni Association, Calcutta University, India.

Contents

Contributors

Fernando Almeida
Faculty of Engineering of Oporto University, INESC TEC, Porto, Portugal

George Kofi Amoako
Marketing Department, Faculty of Management, University of Professional Studies,
P.O. Box LG 149 Legon Accra, Ghana

Effie Kwansema Ansah
Accra Institute of Technology, P. O. Box AN-19782, Accra-North, Ghana

Kwesi Amponsah-Tawiah
Department of Organisation and Human Resource Management, University of Ghana Business School,
Accra, Ghana

Rebecca Baah-Ofori
Faculty of Information Technology and Communication, University of Professional Studies,
P.O. Box LG 149 Legon Accra, Ghana

Abhijeet Bag
Cooch Behar Panchanan Barma University, Cooch Behar, India

Sandip Basak
Department of Commerce, Heramba Chandra College, Kolkata, India

Kwasi Dartey-Baah
Department of Organisation and Human Resource Management, University of Ghana Business School,
Accra, Ghana

Priyanka Das
Department of Commerce, Maharaja Sris Chandra College and Research Scholar,
Department of Commerce, University of Calcutta, Kolkata, India

Shounak Das
Department of Commerce, University of Calcutta, Kolkata, India

Sourav Kumar Das
Assistant Professor, School of Business and Economics, Adamas University, West Bengal, India.

Yaw A. Debrah
Swansea University, University of Wales, Cardiff, United Kingdom

Nand L. Dhameja
FMS Manav Rachna International Institute of Research and Studies (MRIIS), Faridabad, India

Dr. Chandrani Dutta
Khudiram Bose Central College, Kolkata, India

Sumi Karmakar
Department of Commerce, University of Calcutta, Kolkata, India

Sharmila Kayal
Adamas University, Barasat 700126, Kolkata, India

Sahita Mitra
Department of Commerce, Heramba Chandra College, Kolkata, India

Ferhat Mohsin
FMS Manav Rachna International Institute of Research and Studies, (MRIIS) Faridabad, India

Ruma Saha
Manipal University Jaipur , Rajasthan, India

L.G.E.A. José Luis Soriano Sandoval
Maestría en Negocios y Estudios Económicos, Universidad de Guadalajara, C.P. 45100, Jalisco, Mexico

Satyaveer Singh
Former MIS Expert, Asian Development Bank under India Technical Assistance Project 7625

Gladys Narki Kumi Som
Central Business School, Central University Accra Ghana, P.O. Box 2305 Tema, Greater Accra, Ghana

José G. Vargas-Hernández
Department de Administration, University Center for Economic and Managerial Sciences, University of Guadalajara, Jalisco, Mexico

Subah Singh Yadav
Baroda Academy, Bank of Baroda, Jaipur, India

Editorial Board

Abbreviations

AGI	Association of Ghana Industries
BIST	Borsa Istanbul
BSE	Bombay Stock Exchange
CEO	chief executive officer
CFCs	chlorofluorocarbons
CFO	chief financial officer
CFP	corporate financial performance
CPSEs	central public sector enterprises
CSR	corporate social responsibility
CTO	chief technical officer
DSRE	Deposit Scheme for Retired Employees
EFA	environmental financial accounting
EFA	exploratory factor analysis
EFR	family responsible enterprise
EMA	environmental management accounting
ENA	environmental national accounting
EPS	earning per share
ESR	socially responsible enterprise
FP	financial performance
GDP	gross domestic product
GDPR	general data protection regulation
GEA	Ghana Employers Association
GER	gross enrolment rate
GHBC	Ghana Business Code
GNCCI	Ghana National Chamber of Commerce and Industry
HUL	Hindustan Unilever Ltd
IICA	Indian Institute of Corporate Affairs
ILO	International Labour Organization
IMC	integrated marketing communication
IoT	internet of things
IUDs/IUCDs	intra-uterine contraceptive devices
JSW	Jindal South West
KVP	Kisan Vikas Patra

MCA	Ministry of Corporate Affairs
MNCs	multinational corporations
MOHFW	Ministry of Health and Family Welfare
MPKBY agents	Mahila Pradhan Kheriya Bachat Yojana Agents
MSG	management study guide
MSMEs	micro, small, and medium enterprises
NGOs	nongovernment organizations
NSE	National Stock Exchange
NSS	National Sample Survey Report
NSS	National Savings Schemes
NVG	National Voluntary Guidelines
OECD	Organization for Economic Co-operation and Development
PAT	profit after tax
PCAV	voluntary environmental compliance program
PPF	Public Provident Fund
PSI	Population Services International
ROA	return on assets
ROE	return on equity
RTE	Right of Children to Free and Compulsory Education
SAS	Standardized Agency System
SHE	safety, health, and environment
SME	small and medium enterprises
SSA	Sub-Saharan Africa
STPS	Secretary of Labor and Social Prevention
SVI	Search Volume Index
TERI	The Energy and Resource Institute
TTO	Technology Transfer Office
USR	University Social Responsibility
VIF	Variance Inflation Factor
WBCSD	World Business Council for Sustainable Development
WCED	World Commission on Environment and Development
WHO	World Health Organization
WTO	World Trade Organization
YMCA	Young Men's Christian Association

Acknowledgments

DEDICATION

This edited volume is dedicated to my father, the late Nirmalendu Ray.

ACKNOWLEDGMENTS

First and foremost, I would like to thank my parents, the late Sri Nirmalendu Ray and Smt. Rina Ray, for their unending inspiration and for standing beside me throughout my career and for writing this book. I would like to especially thank to my doctoral supervisor and my teachers Dr. Dillip Kumar Das, Associate Professor and Head of the Department, Department of Tourism, The University of Burdwan, India, for guiding me for developing the applications for this project, for giving me the freedom to manage my projects, for providing the necessary time and resources toward the applications and databases.

I acknowledge my indebtedness to all the members of editorial advisory board and technical reviewers of this volume. I am also grateful to all the authors whose valued contributions have enriched the volume. I wish to thank the officials at Apple Academic Press for their invaluable efforts, great support and valuable advice for this project toward successful publication of this book.

— **Dr. Nilanjan Ray**

DEDICATION

This book is dedicated to my father, the late Biswanath Bag, and my mother Mrs. Basanti Bag, with love.

ACKNOWLEDGMENTS

I would like to express my sincere and heartfelt gratitude to my teachers Prof. Dr. Ashish Kr. Sana, Head, Dept. of Commerce, University of Calcutta; Dr. Sarbapriya Ray, Head, Dept. of Commerce, Vivekananda College; and Dr. Nilanjan Ray, without whose motivation and guidance I would not have initiated and completed the project.

I am thankful to all the members of the publishing team.

— Abhijeet Bag

Preface

Corporate social responsibility is a management concept whereby companies integrate social and environmental concerns in their business operations and interactions with their stakeholders. CSR is generally understood as being the way through which a company achieves a balance of economic, environmental and social imperatives ("triple-bottom-line approach"), while at the same time addressing the expectations of share-holders and stakeholders. In this sense, it is important to draw a distinction between CSR, which can be a strategic business management concept, and charity, sponsorships or philanthropy. In times past, "social responsibility" was related to philanthropic practices.

Strategic CSR involves choosing philanthropic activities that will also benefit the company and help it to reach its strategic goals. Caring corporate community service activities can enhance consumers' perceptions of the business and attract more customers. A restaurant may choose to support the arts to grow its business from the after-theatre crowd. Morale may increase if employees become involved in meaningful corporate volunteer programs, which can increase job satisfaction, which, in turn, can decrease turnover (Lantos, 2002).

This initiative presents itself as a serious academic journey into some of the most relevant yet understudied issues of today. The understanding of those issues, however, requires a broader perspective of analysis as well as invoking interdisciplinary and multidisciplinary perspectives of discussion.

CHAPTER 1

Corporate Social Responsibility, Labor Development, and Quality of Life of Workers

JOSÉ G. VARGAS-HERNÁNDEZ[1*] and
L.G.E.A. JOSÉ LUIS SORIANO SANDOVAL[2]

[1]*Department de Administration, University Center for Economic and Managerial Sciences, University of Guadalajara, Jalisco, Mexico*

[2]*Maestría en Negocios y Estudios Económicos, Universidad de Guadalajara, C.P. 45100, Jalisco, Mexico*

Corresponding author. E-mail: jvargas2006@gmail.com

ABSTRACT

In recent years in Mexico, private and public institutions have implemented mechanisms to encourage companies to adopt practices focused on Corporate Social Responsibility (CSR); however, there has been a certain level of disbelief in society about the benefits generated based on the practices of social responsibility implemented by the companies and especially on the quality of life of the collaborators, so that the analysis is performed, through a descriptive analytical method that can better describe the phenomenon and detect if in reality the strategies implemented, on the practices of CSR in Mexico.

1.1 INTRODUCTION

This chapter aims to identify and analyze the application of Corporate Social Responsibility (CSR) practices and establish the relationship with labor development and the quality of life of workers, within their working environment, in Mexican territory. The above is established based on the following lines of research: (1) Quality of life and sustainable development, (2) Sustainable social and local development, (3) Strategies, quality and sustainable development, and (4) Economics, strategy, and sustainable development of organizations.

It identifies a complex problem regarding the effectiveness of social responsibility practices and their positive impact on the quality of life of workers. Various factors can be involved in the process, such as corruption, incompatible models, disinterest, or simply by ignorance of the factors that generate a misinterpretation and/or application of CSR. Although it is known, the verification of the effectiveness of these practices, as marketing tool (Fernández, 2005).

Efficacy to improve the quality of life of workers is put to trial, although there are no indicators of development evaluation for workers working in companies that adopt social responsibility practices, one of the objectives of this work, is common to listen, the company bought the certification! Walmart is certified as Socially Responsible Enterprise (ESR) and pay very little! My company is said to be socially responsible and treat employees very badly! What is happening? Various news in Mexico circulate, signaled to companies certified in Social Corporative Responsibility (SCR) with acts of contamination, discrimination, and corruption. Contrary to the practices established by the SCR, an example is the news published by Excelsior in 2013 in the state of Jalisco, where a company certified with SCR practices, abused of labor abuse of workers (Excelsior, 2013).

In terms of the environment, it is not the meaning of the company Cloralex that implements SCR practices. The organization Womens Voice for earth has verified how some gases that contain chlorine, such as chlorofluorocarbons (CFCs) and HCFCs, destroy stratospheric ozone. It has also stated that the chloroform contained in Clorox can cause cancer (Womens Voices, 2011). These questionings are not exclusive to Mexico. In the documentary The Hidden Side of Google can visualize the discontent of workers within a leading company in social responsibility practices (Roland, 2015).

Therefore, the purpose of the study is to serve the design of strategies for the improvement and/or solution of the development of the quality of life of workers with respect to companies that implement social responsibility practices, since there are no studies that analyze the impact on workers' quality of life, if not only the economic viability of the company (Öberseder, 2011).

1.2 BACKGROUND

The CSR is understood as the active and voluntary contribution to social, economic, and environmental improvement by companies, with the objective of improving their competitiveness, and its added value, according to the Ministry of Economy (SE, 2016). For the International Labor Organization, the social responsibility of the company is the set of actions that companies take into account so that their activities have positive repercussions on society and affirm the principles and values by which they are governed, both in their own internal methods and processes as well as in their relationship with other actors (ILO, 2007, p. 53).

The origin and evolution of the concept has six phases (Bhaduri, 2016):

1950–1960—Period of introduction of CSR in the academic field and corporate philanthropy as CSR

1970s—Period of rapid growth in the concept of CSR

1980s—Period of stakeholder theory and business ethics

CSR of the 1990s

2000 onwards—Empirical work period to investigate determinants and Consequences of CSR in corporate strategy

The concept of CSR has been studied from the economic, social, and environmental point of view. Within an economic approach, there are two main aspects of study, first is the productivity in relation to the CSR model based on indicators of productivity in workers and the second is the profitability as marketing techniques for consumers. This point is studied in depth and validated. In this approach, the economic benefit is taken as the most important variable of study.

Social responsibility takes sustainability into consideration. Several authors agree, such as Haneke et al. (1998) in a definition ad literam "development that satisfies the needs of the present generation without compromising the ability of future generations to meet their own needs."

Within the social perspective, studies are justified by productivity indicators tending to economic issues. However, there are no studies that verify the truthfulness of improving the quality of life of workers in relation to the establishment of CSR practices in the company that they work, which in turn, can influence the productivity of the workers and therefore in a decrease welfare in the society that ends in economic repercussions for the Mexican economic environment. From an environmental point of view, there are economic, environmental, and an example, the Kuznets environmental curve (Correa et al., 2005) that directly affect the company as a structure, the viability of legal framework in Mexico and its incentives toward the company, which also tends to be conditioned by economic factors.

As pollution vs. economic growth is a debate within the environmental sciences and economics. In addition to the above, the concept has also been studied from the biological point of view, which focuses on minimizing pollution regardless of economic costs or viability within the current economic system, tends to be more utopian (Gudynas, 2009).

Sustainable development has become more a discourse than a resource, a way and a method of reconfiguring society and preserving nature and life itself (Salinas, 2007). The technical problem of this is to obtain an acceptable estimate of the social cost and externalities to bring the tax (or subsidy) in line, which raised the need to carry out, in collaboration with other specialists, environmental impact assessments that would serve as a basis for the desired pecuniary estimates. Even though the obligatory partiality and arbitrariness of such assessments has served most often to provide benign estimates of the social costs that justify state authorization of damages (Cruz, 2006).

Although the issue of CSR is not new, the line that investigates the impact of the application of CSR practices on workers has little depth of theoretical and methodological research, since research on the subject focuses more, the profitability of the company and its effectiveness as a marketing theme.

Certified models known in Mexico, Family Responsible Enterprise (EFR), ESR, Including Company (DEI), the three above, are programs operated by the Federal Ministry of Labor and Social Prevention (STPS) (PROFEPA) and at the state level, exclusive of the state of Jalisco, the Voluntary Environmental Compliance Program (PCAV), in addition to ISO 26000 in Social Responsibility and ISO 14000 focused on the environment, and lastly the A8000 certificate focused on the practices of corporate social development.

Do these certifications actually work? What do they work for? An example is the Family Responsible Company model, 5 years after its implementation, what benefits have been achieved? Does the quality of life of the workers actually increase?

An example more attached, is the Family Business model, which was replicated in Mexico through the program of distinctions awarded by the Secretary of Labor and Social Prevention (STPS). This program was developed by the business school of the University of Navarra, Spain, where through assumptions and theories of competitiveness and productivity in workers, justify the importance and feasibility of its implementation.

However, there are no studies that demonstrate the evaluation of the model, once it has been implemented. The most attached to this is the IESE Family Responsible Employer Index developed by the same University of Navarra and analyzes the level of implementation of the Responsibility Familiar Corporate and its impact on people and organization. However, their studies do not take into account Mexico, so there is a lack of information regarding the feasibility of implementing these practices in Mexico and creates doubts, whether or not true these practices work as they say on their website.

The objectives of this analysis are to identify the variations that exist between the application of CSR practices within the company and the quality of life and development of workers. Hierarchize the importance of the most relevant factors within the application of the CSR. Provide information that serves to design strategies for the improvement and/or solution of the development of the quality of life of workers with respect to companies that implement social responsibility practices. Establish links between CSR and the welfare of society.

1.3   JUSTIFICATION

The phenomenon of social responsibility is essential within the strategic planning of a company. However, in Mexico, this phenomenon is little studied and it is assumed that the implementation of social responsibility practices, will obtain positive results, but these results, few times are analyzed and evaluated. Therefore, some degree of disbelief in Mexican society is perceived on the benefits of these practices. In addition to the above, some news and the null results of the evaluations related to the CSR models to reinforce the hypothesis that the implementation of these models are not working for the companies, from the point of view, of the improvement in the quality of life of the workers.

1.4 THEORETICAL-CONCEPTUAL REVIEW

The problem lies in the following way: To what extent do employees who work in companies with CSR practices improve their quality of life? Is there a relationship between the development and improvement of the quality of life of employees and the model of CSR? What factors intervene? Do SCR practices actually work to improve social welfare?

The political factor is an important variable, since it can influence directly or indirectly the way in which companies adopt the SCR practices. The theoretical limits of the problem are based on the assumptions in which companies adopting SCR practices have external certification issued by third parties, whether governmental or non-profit institutions.

The Geographic delimitation is Mexico, since it is where the problematic is identified and it is viable in questions of resources for the analysis. In addition, it can be a unit of comparison, with respect to the other countries, since they share characteristics (at country level) that can influence the study, such as culture, legal structure, and applicable models.

The object of study and/or observation units, will focus on individuals working in certified companies and individuals who do not work in certified companies.

1.4.1 CORPORATE SOCIAL RESPONSIBILITY

Social welfare is also a task for multinational corporations. The Ministry of Economy (SE, 2017), through the National Contact Point, has the mission of promoting CSR, through the Guidelines for Multinational Enterprises of the Organization for Economic Co-operation and Development (OECD). These guidelines are a set of principles and standards that seek to ensure that the operations of multinational enterprises: develop in harmony with public policies, strengthen trust between business and society, improve the climate for foreign investment, and increase the contribution of multinational companies to sustainable development. OECD member countries regularly review the guidelines to ensure that their content is updated and reflects global changes.

In this section, it develops the theoretical concepts to be used within the work, as well as the set of ideas, background and theories that support the research in order to make clear each of the terms that are mentioned and can understand the perspective from where to leave. So far only the main theme has been referred to in a superficial way. It is up to here to define what has at first been described as social responsibility. From this point, it is referred to this as CSR.

In some companies (if not most) when referring to social responsibility practices they use the term socially responsible company, whereas in the scientific literature there does not seem to be a difference between CSR and socially responsible companies, rather than as an adjective on the part of the second to indicate that they make use of this type of measures. Therefore, both terms will be understood as equal.

In most of the concepts within the world of research, there is a great debate to have a single definition that serves as a basis, and CSR has different (Azmat and Ha, 2013), although the study of this topic is not new since it has been developed for decades. It has not been possible to reach a consensual definition by the guild (McWilliams et al., 2006). In this chapter, it is used as reference but does not have absolute definitions, the ones supported by Ramasamy and Yeung (2009) and Mcguire (1963, p. 144). The idea of social responsibility means that the corporation not only has economic and legal obligations, but also certain responsibilities toward society that go beyond these obligations.

In addition, Davis (1973, p. 313) goes further since it explains what should not be the ESR: Social responsibility begins where the law ends. A company is not socially responsible if it simply meets the minimum requirement of the law because this is what any good citizen would do ... Social responsibility is a step forward. It is the acceptance of a company from a social obligation beyond the requirement of the law.

There are different theories of CSR; however, Garriga and Melé (2004) focused on four main aspects: To reach the main objective of the company using CSR, maximizing shareholder value and gaining a competitive advantage based on the resources and capabilities for long-term benefits. In addition, using the power with where it counts as a company in a responsible manner, refers to implementing activities that help society through altruistic acts where the same company is taken as a citizen more involved to support a community.

Another aspect addressed by Garriga and Melé (2014) was the integration of social demands based on the way the company manages their relationships with their stakeholders. To take the CSR as a company policy that goes beyond the law is a measure adopted before a demand of the public opinion. Finally, the company must focus on doing well for a better society, that is, consider human rights, labor and care and respect for the environment, everything revolves around a more ethical approach.

The work conducted by Lizarzabur and Del Río (2016) combines the approaches proposed by Garriga and Melé (2004), as well as the main points of each approach. They were also able to identify the main researchers who have developed CSR and locate them in some of the aspects that the model mentions. This is how RSC understands many terms and, therefore, it has not been easy to reach a consensus in its definition.

Already with a clearer picture of what CSR is about, there are still some terms that need to be defined in order to continue with the development of ideas. Companies should take into account different perspectives according to their needs to take choosing appropriate strategies for it is necessary to know the different theories that help to understand the organization in its different edges. Mahoney (2012) talks about five blocks that make up the organizational economy, they are:

1) Behavioral theory where the main variable at stake is uncertainty because the company is an organization composed of people and these are full of limitations. Although Adam Smith talks about the rational individual and his choices, trying to maximizing his own benefit, in practice it is not as simple as Simon (1957) says about limited rationality, which is given by limited resources available, asymmetric information, and different cognitive abilities. Although the individual is rational, sometimes the problems often exceed their abilities.

2) In addition, the theory of transaction costs where Coase (1937), Williamson (1979), and Arrow (1974) explain that there are certain mechanisms, which allow a company to grow, one of which is the costs associated with the moment of realization. Some operations, either internally or externally, and opportunism plays a key role within this block, as long as greater opportunism can be generated, transaction costs will be greater (Vargas-Hernández, 2014).

3) The third block refers to the theory of property rights. Mahoney (2012) refers to this as an important point that should be obtained well-defined and correctly allocated rights to create wealth.

4) In block of agency theory, Peng (2012) clearly explained the problems, which can occur between the principal and agent because of the divergence of interests on the part of one and another, where

transaction costs are generated, usually caused by the principal's interests to maximize the value of their long-term actions, while agents seek to maximize their own profit (Vargas-Hernández, 2014).

5) Finally, the theory based on resources and capabilities, where Penrose (1959) emphasizes the internal resources and management capabilities of the company in relation to its growth. Through the study by Mintzberg et al. (1997) using the five forces developed by Porter is how they perform a company strategy analysis and thus improve their performance.

1.4.2 QUALITY OF LIFE

For the World Health Organization (WHO), quality of life complements the following factors, such as physical, psychological, facets of pain, energy, discomfort, sleep, rest, medications, mobility, reflection, feelings, work capacity, social support, opportunity to acquire financial loans, transportation, spirituality, and among others less relevant. However, the main ones are those mentioned above and from which you can get to build indicators in order to evaluate their implementation and its efficiency (WHO, 2017).

1.4.3 WELL-BEING INDEX

For the OECD, welfare rates focus on improving people's well-being in order to achieve better policies for a better life. It is complex to talk about the concept of well-being since it is multidimensional and covers various aspects of life that has to do from housing, income, life-work quality, and health-related competencies.

The most recent evidence on welfare is the 11 dimensions of life suggested by the OECD, which follows standards from the various points mentioned above related to the welfare issue, as was the initial hypothesis, the countries with the highest Gross Domestic Product (GDP), tend to have higher welfare indicators than those with lower GDP, which can be concluded that if there is a strong relationship between GDP and the welfare of each country, where the most relevant points are focus on pollution and employment (OECD, 2014).

1.4.4   SOCIAL RESPONSIBILITY MODEL

Porter (2006) mentions the importance of the social responsibility model, and states that governments, activists, and the media have become experts in holding corporations accountable for the social consequences of their actions. In response, CSR has emerged as an inescapable priority for business leaders in all countries.

Since the efforts of CSR are often counterproductive for two reasons: first, independent of each other and second, companies are pressured to adopt social responsibility practices in a generic way without giving them an opportunity to adopt the practices in an organic way and more appropriate for their individual strategies. So the fact that CSR approaches are so disconnected from strategy is why many companies see this approach as an additional cost and yet as Whole Foods Market, Toyota, and Volvo have done. Practices can be a powerful source of innovation and competitive advantage.

So Michael Porter (2006) proposes a fundamentally new way of looking at the relationship between business and society that does not address corporate growth and social welfare as a zero-sum game. They introduce a framework that individual companies can use to identify the social consequences of their actions. To discover opportunities that benefit society and themselves, strengthening the competitive context in which they operate. To determine which CSR initiatives to address and to find the most effective ways to do it. Perceiving social responsibility as an opportunity rather than as a damage control or public relations campaign requires a radically different thinking—a mindset—the authors warn, which will become increasingly important to competitive success.

1.4.5   VARIABLES TO MEASURE THE PERFORMANCE OF SOCIAL RESPONSIBILITY

According Alcabés (2005, pp. 158–160), there are 10 variables to measure the performance of a company in order to know how socially responsible are:

a)   Structures of payments for salaries. The employees of the organization representing the essence of the company. The greater the number of well-paid workers, the higher purchasing power and, consequently, the economic movement of the country will be encouraged.

b) Generation or declining employment. It refers to acquisitions or mergers. It is estimated the total number of employees at the beginning of the year, plus the total of persons engaged in the same, minus the total of people who stopped working in the company.

c) Preservation of the environment. The company calls itself from number 1 to 5 for the quality of the environment in the development of its operations. The degree of pollution in the air, water, and soil as a result of their production processes and/or their waste is measured.

d) Concern for occupational health of its personnel. It is measured by the number of diagnosed cases of occupational diseases in the period and the number of accidents attributable to failure of the means of prevention or protection.

e) Level of customer satisfaction with the products or services of the company. An enterprise should measure the degree of acceptance of their products or services through the level of sales and growth curve over time. It should be clarified whether the market competition is high or there is oligopoly.

f) Intensity of competition. It should be measured if there are (in the market) many or few competitors.

g) Use of natural resources of the country or domestic inputs. This variable will explain how the organization contributes to the generation of jobs and foreign exchange savings for this domestic production must be competitive and required quality.

h) Share of exports in total production value of the company. When exports contribute to national development, to job creation, the use of natural resources and domestic inputs.

i) Net income as a percentage of shareholders' equity or the owners invested in the country. When a company dedicates a percentage of its profits to investment in its country of origin, the organization makes clear its commitment to national development.

j) Contribution of the company works or actions for the benefit of national communities. This variable includes those direct actions or contributions from the company or works programs to benefit communities in the country.

1.5   REVIEW OF THE EMPIRICAL READING

It was mentioned above that, within the social perspective, studies are justified by productivity indicators (tending to economic issues). However, there are no studies that prove the truthfulness of improving the quality of life of workers in relation to the establishment of practices of CSR in the company that work, which in turn, can influence the productivity of the workers, and therefore, in a decrease welfare in the society that ends in economic repercussions for the Mexican economic environment.

Although the issue of CSR is not new, the line that investigates the impact of the application of CSR practices on workers has little depth of theoretical and methodological research, since research on the subject focuses more, the profitability of the company and its effectiveness as a marketing theme.

In Mexico, there is very little information on the subject of social responsibility, but it is possible to identify the null documents referring to the evaluation of established practices of CSR.

CSR is used to differentiate products within the competition, as explained by McWilliams et al. (2006) since by means of a vertical differentiation one product is preferred to another, so it happens when the desired product which has characteristics of CSR is better than the other that does not have them. For example, the case of Honda, where many of its consumers prefer the hybrid Accord instead of the conventional model even though they have to pay much more for the first one, this is because of the characteristics that make up the hybrid is to be less polluting what is more valuable to the customer. In developed countries, CSR is increasingly a marketing strategy in order to gain trust and consumer loyalty, use different communication tools such as certificates, reports, everything to announce that they are doing internships of social responsibility (Azmat, 2013).

To date, most of the research that carried out on CSR has been in developed countries. In the case of developing or emerging economies, the study of CSR is very useful. The justification for doing so, is that these economies represent a market in full expansion, which turns out to be a very lucrative business for companies, where social and environmental crises are most accentuated. In addition, the impact on society of economic aspects such as globalization, investment, and entrepreneurial activities has drastic repercussions, whether positive or negative.

The problems of developing countries with respect to CSR are very different from those in developed countries. The main aim is to improve living conditions through private sector participation (Jamali and Mirshak, 2007). That is why Visser (2008) proposes, based on Carroll's initial model of CSR, to make modifications and to exchange the priorities of each level of the pyramid in which economic responsibility remains the most important pillar within the emerging countries, because of the amounts of money that governments have for companies to set up in their territory, in addition to the jobs it generates, however, for the same reason of wanting to retain what governments have achieved. To overlook some ethical, environmental, or social risks in order to retain companies.

The second block is the philanthropic responsibility where more than an act of good faith is a necessity and where companies need to improve the conditions of the community to operate in a good way. Legal responsibilities have a lower priority, as Peng (2012) explains. Usually in the emerging countries, there are weaker institutions which encourage companies to settle as there is less pressure from the government. For developing countries, the lowest priority is ethical responsibility, says Visser (2008), as corruption still largely affects business activity, although there have been cases such as South Africa that with its CSR inclusion report managed to cover issues social, ethics, security, among others, is still an exception to the rule.

In Latin American and Caribbean countries, the most associated problems are social and not environmental problems, as can happen in developed countries, because the emerging countries have more problems than developed countries, such as poverty, lack of medical care, housing problems, and education, as governments fail to meet these needs, the societies of the population, civil societies pressure companies to cover government inefficiency (Schmidheiny, 2006).

According to the Mexican Center for Philanthropy (Cemefi, 2017), there are several reasons to apply CSR to companies, because they have positive effects on them which can be measured by means of quantitative and qualitative information. Some of them extracted from the same portal (Cemefi, 2017):

1) Loyalty and less turnover of the stakeholder groups.
2) Improvement of relations with neighbors and authorities.
3) Contribution to the development of communities and the common good.

4) Increased visibility among the business community.
5) Access to capital by increasing the value of its investments and its long-term profitability.
6) Better informed business decisions.
7) Increased ability to receive financial support.
8) Improvement in financial performance, reducing operating costs by optimizing efforts, and making resource use more efficient by focusing on sustainable development.
9) Improvement of the corporate image and strengthening of the reputation of the company and its brands.
10) Increase in sales and reinforce consumer loyalty.
11) Increased productivity and quality.
12) Improvement in the skills to attract and retain employees creates loyalty and a sense of belonging among the staff.
13) Reduction of regulatory oversight.
14) Teamwork is promoted and made more efficient.

Some studies, such as the one by Vasal (2009) carried out in India, where they sought to analyze the relative performance of the equity portfolio of companies that execute social responsibility practices, finding that there is a positive but statistically non-significant return. This type of results has influence on the shareholders. While in other countries like Bangladesh (Azmat, 2013), it tries to explain the difficulties of the Asian country and how CSR with the government could help to improve the supply chain.

1.6 CONCEPTUAL FRAMEWORK

The concept of well-being is very complex since each individual has a different perception of reality and therefore, the definition established by the OECD, for that institution, welfare is taken up, is considered as the priority of an individual to be happy, so that to elaborate the welfare index, 11 indicators were developed, which are: housing, expenditures, employment, community, education, environment, civic commitment health, satisfaction, safety, and work life balance. The latter is the most important for the study, since the hypothesis focuses on the fact that the balance of life.

Work does not improve, with the "Social Responsibility Practices" of a company certified in this model. As a result of the study, the OECD (2017) defines it as finding the right balance between work and the daily life of each person, without but it is a challenge faced by all workers. In general, families are the most affected, since the ability to successfully combine work, personal commitments and family life is important for the whole family. In this respect, governments can support facilitating means of well-regulated legal frameworks that can support workers in this regard.

Based on the above, the questionnaire was developed and later complementary aspects such as those defined below (OECD, 2017) are taken into account since the time devoted to leisure and personal care, in addition, the more people work, the less time they will have to dedicate it to other activities, such as personal care or leisure. The quantity and quality of free time are important for the general well-being of people and can generate additional benefits for physical and mental health. A full-time employee at the OECD devotes on average 62% of the day, about 15 h, to personal care (eating, sleeping, etc.) and to leisure (social life with friends and family, hobbies, games, computer and television, etc.). A shorter work schedule for women does not necessarily equate to more leisure time, since leisure time is approximately the same for men and women in the 20 OECD countries studied.

On the other hand, are the definitions by the Business School of the University of Navarra, which refer to the following:

a) Promote Corporate Family Responsibility that facilitates satisfaction and results.
b) To promote the flexible and responsible leadership that favors the commitment and the family and labor enrichment.
c) Promote the adoption of flexible policies that enhance motivation and customer orientation.
d) Provide the tools and diagnostics needed to create flexible and enriching environments."

In addition to the above, the following points are added (Business School University of Navarra, 2017). The factors that affect productivity are multiple and are related to each other. Among the variables that facilitate productivity, IFREI focuses on two key factors: people commitment and motivation, and management policies and strategy. Rotation and lack of commitment have negative consequences that affect the company's results:

a) Lower productivity

b) Loss of experience
c) Greater rotation
d) Deterioration of the environment and the working environment
e) Non-perception of the emotional salary
f) Lack of commitment to the company
g) Increased stress and associated diseases
h) Smaller creativity and initiative
i) Difficulty attracting and retaining talent

There are also other significant direct costs:

a) Absenteeism
a) Cost of selection for replacement
c) Cost of training a new employee
d) Cost of replacing the replacement time

All of the above takes the view that there is a suspicion that social responsibility practices in Mexico do not improve the quality of life of workers and their professional development, perhaps because of their poor implementation, because they grant the certificates to companies, without a true verification of the practices or simply because the CSR model, does not work to improve the quality of life of workers.

1.7 RESEARCH METHODS

A quantitative and qualitative analysis is used, through surveys applied to workers working in a company in Jalisco, with certified practices of social responsibility, where the answers are used to analyze previously created indicators, to identify the relationship between variables and the factors that can intervene.

The questions are taken from the OECD welfare indexes, specifically from the Work Life Balance Indicator, since the model of the University of Business of Navarra, Family Responsible Employer Index IFREI, model that is taken up by the STPS in Mexico and that ensures its positive impact on this indicator, so it is decided to return to this indicator as a basis for the questions. The questionnaire is applied to workers who work in companies with certificates of "Socially Responsible and Family Responsible Company," since they are the certificates that return to these CSR models.

Therefore, the following questions were used:

a) Do you have knowledge that your company has certification in social responsibility? R = yes/no
b) How many hours do you work a week?
c) What kind of benefits do you get compared to another company, if you get them?
d) Do you think that you are satisfied with the company's social responsibility practices? R = Very Satisfied, Satisfied, Satisfied, Satisfied.
e) Do you think the company deserves the certificate?
f) In addition to the previous questions, the age and sex of the interviewed worker were registered, so that the questionnaire was presented to the interviewees.
g) Any additional comments, complaints or suggestions?
h) R = Yes/No

The questionnaire was applied to 50 people employed in a company located in the state of Jalisco with certificates of CSR anonymously.

1.8   RESULTS

The most relevant results showed that workers are not satisfied with the social responsibility practices applied by the company, in addition to the fact that most do not know the policies of the company as a whole and did not have the knowledge that the company was with a current certification in CSR.

This is of the utmost importance, since it demonstrates a failure in the implementation of the social responsibility actions since one of the objectives is to make known to the internal members of the company and in general to the stakeholders, the activities that are implemented within the company. It is identified that the area of human resources operates the policies and fully knows the activities of the employees.

Continuing with the results, it can be observed that the respondents have a certain levels of disagreement with the way in which the certificate is granted to the companies, since the majority disagrees with the award of the certificate to the company for the practices, and who mention that the company has never implemented some social responsibility practices that are indispensable for the granting of the certificate, even 27% of the respondents mention that the company works outside the law, which would automatically turn the company into a null candidate to acquire or even participate in certificate programs, related to social responsibility.

Specifically, the hours of work, in the majority of interviewees, show that companies are within the limit of allowed hours of work, so that although companies carry out CSR activities, the workload is not taken into account. Account in most cases limits the positive impact on the quality of life of workers.

In terms of gender equity, the results presented remarkable benefits, since the respondents say that the treatments for men and women are the same within the CSR policies detected in the company.

1.9   CONCLUSIONS AND RECOMMENDATIONS

It can be concluded that the practices of social responsibility within the company are not well founded in Mexico, since the CSR models are not adapted to be applied satisfactorily in the companies located in Mexico, since they try to apply exactly as in other countries with dubious benefits, so it is necessary to make adjustments and adapt it to the Mexican environment, always respecting its laws and regulations in labor matters.

With respect to the impact of workers' quality of life, a positive impact is identified as it ensures that most employees do not obtain relevant benefits that increase their quality of life, apparently the institutions that are dedicated to certifying such practices in Mexico, fail to apply their audit tools efficiently, as it leaves much doubt as to how they award the certifications to the companies participating in the programs.

In this sense, the most essential aspect of CSR should be the main focus, to raise the quality of life of workers, leaving aside the current priorities, such as marketing benefits and environmental care, which only increase the discourse of companies, but it is not taken seriously the common benefit of all individuals, since the pursuit of common benefit, is the true objective of CSR policies.

In order to reinforce policies, it is necessary to follow the policies implemented by the company and to carry out an evaluation analysis every year, in order to detect possible improvements, errors and tangible direct benefits to improve the quality of life of workers.

In Mexico, CSRs have had very little evaluation, which limits credibility and creates uncertainty in society, so it is important for current projects to implement their evaluation.

KEYWORDS

- **corporate culture**
- **diversity**
- **social responsibility**
- **business administration and business economics**
- **marketing**
- **accounting**
- **personnel economics**

REFERENCES

Alcabés, N. La empresa socialmente responsable: Una propuesta de autoevaluación. *Universidad ESAN*; Recuperado de: Perú, 2005; jefas.esan.edu.pe/index.php/jefas/article/view/176/167

Arrow, K. *The Limits of Organization*; W.W. Norton and Company: New York, NY, 1974.

Azmat, F.; Ha, H. Corporate Social Responsibility, Customer Trust, and Loyalty-Perspectives from a Developing Country. *Thunderbird Int. Busi. Rev.* **2013,** *55* (3), 253–270; doi:10.1002/tie.21542

Bhaduri, L. La importancia de la responsabilidad social empresarial, Evolucion del concepto. *Negocios y entorno* **2016,** *32* (4), 7–17.

Centro Mexicano para la Filantropía (Cemefi). *CEMEFI, Servicios*; Recuperado de, 2017; https://www.cemefi.org/

Coase, R. The Nature of the Firm. *Economica* **1937,** *4* (16), 386–405; Doi: 10.2307/2626876

Correa, F.; Vasco, A.; Pérez, C. La curva medioambiental de Kuznets: evidencia empírica para Colombia. *Semestre económico* **2005,** *8* (15), 13–30.

Cruz, C. Valoración de bienes y recursos ambientales y naturales: el problema de la medición. *Registro Colombia* **2006,** *21* (2), 11–17.

Davis, K. The Case For and Against Business Assumption of Social Responsibilities. *Acad. Manage. J.* **1973,** *16* (2), 312–322; doi:10.2307/255331

Excelsior. *Empresas que abusan de jornaleros eran "Socialmente Responsables"*; recuperado de: México, 2013; http://www.excelsior.com.mx/nacional/2013/06/13/903900#view-1

Fernández, D. ¿Existe disponibilidad a pagar por responsabilidad social corporativa? Percepción de los consumidores. *Universia Bussiness Rev.* **2005,** *7* (3), 38–53.

Garriga, E.; Melé, D. Corporate Social Responsibility Theories: Mapping the Territory. *J. Busi. Ethics* **2004,** *53* (1/2), 51–71; Recuperado de; http://www.jstor.org/stable/25123282

Gudynas, E. La ecología política de la crisis global y los límites del capitalismo benévolo. *Iconos de Ciencias Sociales* **2009,** *6* (36), 53–67.

Haneke, D.; Glosw, R.; Hernand, S. Medio Ambiente y desarrollor sustentable. *Revista Sustentable LDC* **1998,** *3* (2), 18–24.

Jamali, D.; Mirshak, R. Corporate Social Responsibility (CSR): Theory and Practice in a Developing Country Context. *J. Busi. Ethics* **2007,** *72* (3), 243–262. DOI: 10.1007A10551-006-9168-4.

Lizarzaburu, E.; Del Brio, J. Responsabilidad social corporativa y reputación corporativa en el sector financiero de países en desarrollo. *GCG:Revista De Globalización, Competitividad & Gobernabilidad* **2016,** *10* (1), 42–65; DOI: 10.3232/GCG.2016.V10. N1.02

Mahoney, J. *Chapter 6: The Theoretical Building Blocks of Organizational Economics: Economic Foundation of Strategy*; Sage: Illinois, EstadosUnidos, 2012.

McGuire, J. W. *Business and Society*; McGraw-Hill: New York, 1963.

McWilliams, A.; Siegel, D. S.; Wright, P. M. Guest Editors Introduction: Corporate Social Responsibility: Strategic Implications. *J. Manage. Studies* **2006,** *43* (1), 1–18. DOI: 10.1111/j.1467-6486.2006.00580.x.

Mintzberg, H.; Quinn, J.; Voyer, J. Capítulo 4: Análisis de estratega a nivel empresa. In *En el proceso estratégico*; Pearson, Ed.; Hispanoamérica, 1997.

Öberseder, M. Why Don't Consumers Care About CSR? A Qualitative Study Exploring the Role of CSR in Consumption Decisions. *J. Busi. Ethics* **2011,** *104* (4), 449–460.

OCDE. *How's Life? 2015: Measuring Well-being*; OECD Publishing, 2014. DOI: 10.1787. how_life-2015-en.

OCDE. *Índice de Felicidad*; EU, Recuperado de: New York, 2017. http://www. oecdbetterlifeindex.org/es/topics/work-life-balance-es/.

OIT. *Organización Internacional del Trabajo, ¿Quiénes somos?* Informe, P.53, Recuperado de, 2007. http://www.ilo.org/inform/online-information-resources/research-guides/ lang--es/index.htm.

OMS. *Referencia y definiciones*; recuperado de: EU, 2017. http://www.who.int/es/.

Peng, M. *Global Strategy*; Thomson South Western: Cincinnati, Estados Unidos, 2012.

Penrose, E. The Theory of the Growth of the Firm; John Wiley and Sons: Nueva York, EstadosUnidos, 1959.

Porter, M. Strategy and Society: The Link between Competitive Advantage and Corporate Social Responsibility. *Harv. Busi. Rev.* **2006,** *84* (12), 78–93.

Ramasamy, B.; Yeung, M. Chinese Consumers' Perception of Corporate Social Responsibility (CSR). *J. Busi. Ethics* **2009,** *88* (Supplement 1), 119–132. DOI: 10.1 007/ sl 055 1 -008-9825-x.

Roland, S. *The Hidden Side of Google*; Francia, 2015; 68min.

Salinas C. El desarrollo Sustentable. *en Memorias del Segundo Congreso de In- vestigación sobre Sustentabilidad y Calidad de Vida, UAEM* **2007,** *2* (2), 12–21.

Schmidheiny, S. A View of Corporate Citizenship in Latin America. *J. Corp. Citizenship*, Sprinf 2006, 21–24.

SE. *Definición de Responsabilidad Social Empresarial*. Recuperado de: México, 2017b. https://www.gob.mx/se/articulos/responsabilidad-social-empresarial-32705.

SE. *Punto nacional de contacto*; Recuperado de: México, 2017b. https://www.gob.mx/se/ articulos/responsabilidad-social-empresarial-32705

Simon, H. A. *Models of Man: Social and Rational*; John Wiley and Sons, Inc.: New York, 1957.

Vargas-Hernández, J. G. *Capítulo VIII. ¿Cómo los agentes y como los administradores confunden las cosas? Teoría de la agencia. Gestión estratégica de organizaciones*; Elaleph: Buenos Aires, Argentina, 2014.

Vasal, V. Corporate Social Responsibility & Shareholder Returns—Evidence from the Indian Capital Market. *Indian J. Ind. Relations* **2009,** *44* (3), 376–385. Recuperado de http://www.jstor.org/stable/27768210.

Visser, W. *Corporate Social Responsibility in Developing Countries.* In *The Oxford Handbook of Corporate Social Responsibility*; Crane, A., McWilliams, A., Matten, D., Moon, J., Siegel, D., Eds.; Oxford University Press: Oxford, ReinoUnido, 2008; pp 473–499.

Womens Voices. *Los hechos sucios de las compañías con certificados de sociablemente responsable*; PDF, México, recuperado de, 2011; http://www.womensvoices.org/wp-content/uploads/2011/12/Dirty-Secrets-Fact-Sheet-spanish.pdf.

CHAPTER 2

A Study on the Relationship between CSR Spending and the Firms' Profitability of Select Indian FMCG Companies

PRIYANKA DAS

Department of Commerce, Maharaja Sris Chandra College and Research Scholar, Department of Commerce, University of Calcutta, Kolkata, India

E-mail: daspriyanka640@gmail.com

ABSTRACT

This empirical study examines the impact of Corporate Social Responsibility (CSR) spending on firm's profitability of top three FMCG companies from the Nifty FMCG Index listed in National Stock Exchange (NSE). Data have been collected from secondary sources, that is, money control and the annual reports of the selected companies for the period of 5 years from 2014–2015 to 2018–2019. Correlation, simple regression, and multiple regression analysis have been conducted to analyze the relationship. The variables Earning per Share (EPS) and Return on Assets (ROA) have been considered as the proxy for firm's profitability and CSR has been considered as the proxy for CSR spending. Empirical results revealed that CSR has a positive and statistically significant impact on the profitability measure (EPS) of HUL, negative, and statistically significant impact on profitability measure (ROA) of ITC Ltd and Britannia Industries Ltd, respectively. Data so collected have been analyzed using Stata14 software.

2.1   INTRODUCTION

Over the course of last decade, there has been a visible shift in the focus of Corporate Social Responsibility (CSR) activities from charity and classical philanthropy toward more direct engagement of business in mainstream development and concern for disadvantaged groups in the society. The inclusion of CSR has been an initiative taken by the government of India to synchronize business goals and activities with development strategy of the country. As per the new companies Act, 2013 in Section 135, Schedule VII, CSR is mandatory in India with effect from 1 April 2014. Under the said Act, those companies that have a net worth of 500 crore or more; or turnover of 1000 crore or more; or net profit of five crore or more, have to spend 2% of their average profit of last 3 years.

The companies enjoy many benefits by contributing toward CSR like improved financial performance (FP), lower operating cost, enhanced brand image and reputation, increased sales and customer loyalty, product safely, material recyclability and greater use of renewable resources (Richa Gautam, 2010). CSR has been considered as a significant factor for profitability as most of the firms believe that expenditure in CSR activities may enhance the profitability. And if the firm's profitability improves then firms can further spend much more for CSR activities than before. CSR activities also help in maintaining long-term relationship with their stakeholders and hence can attract a good number of employees and provide a suitable working condition which would result in improved productivity and ultimately affect the profitability of firms. CSR activities also have the advantage to build a good relationship with investors that would help the business houses to attract huge amount of capital and investment from them.

This study, therefore, attempts to examine the relationship between CSR spending and firm's profitability of the top three FMCG companies in India listed in the National Stock Exchange (NSE).

2.2   REVIEW OF LITERATURE

Following are some of the earlier literatures which have studied both at the Indian as well as at the International level:

Menezes (2019) examined the impact of CSR spending on the firm's FP of the top ten companies for CSR spending for a period of 5 years. For this study, three variables are taken into consideration such as ROA, Earning per Share (EPS), net profit along with CSR spending. Independent pooled OLS regression, fixed effect and random effect method were used. The findings showed that net profit had a significant relationship with the CSR Spending whereas ROA and EPS had no impact.

Selcuk (2019) tried to investigate the impact of CSR engagement on firm FP in a developing country, Turkey, and to analyze the moderating role of ownership concentration in the CSR–FP relationship. Non-financial public firms listed on the Borsa Istanbul (BIST)-100 index for the period 2014–2018 have been selected as the sample data. Empirical results using an instrumental variable approach showed that CSR had a positive relationship with FP and also this relationship is negatively moderated by ownership concentration even when endogeneity is controlled for.

Hou (2019) aimed to examine the relationship between CSR and corporate FP (CFP) in Taiwan. Using CSR awards as a social responsibility indicator, this study found that socially responsible firms can achieve financial results superior to those of firms which do not pursue CSR initiatives. The Google Search Volume Index (SVI) was used as a specific proxy for firm visibility. It was observed that SVI had a positive influence on the CSR–CFP relationship.

Bafna (2017) investigated the impact of CSR on the FP of companies using annual data ranging from 2014 to 2016 in India. Correlation analysis and regression analysis have been used in this study to find the relationship and the impact on the variables. The results reveal that CSR had a positive significant influence on net profits of the company. However, CSR shows only a slight correlation but no significant influence with EPS and return on assets (ROA) of a company.

Resmi et al. (2018) investigated the impact of CSR on FP of Agribusiness Industries of Bangladesh, using a sample of four renowned Agribusiness industries for the period of 3 years from 2015 to 2017 through purposive sampling method. Regression, correlation was used for analyzing the data and results discussion. The results revealed that return on equity (ROE) and net income had significant impact on FP favoring those firms that do CSR, whereas ROA and EPS have no significant impact on FP.

Garai (2017): The main objectives of the Garai's study are to know the relationship among CSR, firm's profitability, shareholders' value, firm's value, and the impact of CSR on firm's profitability. I used correlation to know the nature of relationship among the variables and regression to measure the impact of CSR on firm's profitability. The study showed that there was no significant positive relationship among the variables and the CSR has no impact on firm's profitability.

Lin et al. (2009) attempted to measure the impact of CSR on FP, our sample was extracted from the top 1000 (by sales revenue) Taiwan-based companies as evaluated by Common Wealth Magazine. For each company, financial data were retrieved from the Taiwan Economic Journal Databank from January 2002 to December 2004. The results revealed that CSR does not have much positive impact on short-term FP, however, there exists a remarkable long-term fiscal advantage.

Bhunia and Das (2015) examined the impact of CSR on firm's profitability of seven Maharatna Companies in India for the period from 2004 to 2013. Correlation, simple regression, and multiple regression have been used for this study. Empirical results indicated that CSR affect the profitability in case of Gas Authority of India Ltd and negatively in case of rest of the companies under study.

2.3 OBJECTIVE OF THE STUDY

The main objective of this empirical study is to analyze the relationship between CSR spending and profitability of the top three FMCG companies in India.

2.4 RESEARCH HYPOTHESIS

The following hypothesis has been developed to know the relationship between CSR spending and firm's profitability:

H_0: There is no linear relationship between CSR spending and firm's profitability.

H_1: There is linear relationship between CSR spending and firm's profitability.

2.5   RESEARCH METHODOLOGY

Sample selection: For this empirical study, we have selected top three out of 15 FMCG companies from the Nifty FMCG Index listed in the NSE. The companies are arranged on the basis free float market capitalization method. As on 31st March 2020, the top three companies were Hindustan Unilever Ltd (HUL), ITC Ltd, and Nestle India Ltd. but sufficient data were not available for the Nestle India Ltd., so Britannia Industries Ltd. has been considered in the sample.

Study period: The present study has been conducted for the period of 5 years from 2014–2015 to 2018–2019.

Model Specification: Two simple regression model one between EPS and CSR, one between ROA and CSR and one multiple regression model among CSR, EPS and ROA have been used were, CSR has considered as the dependent variable and EPS and ROA have been considered as the independent variables to find out the association between CSR spending and Firm's Profitability of the selected FMCG companies in India.

Multicollinearity has been tested by using Variance Inflation Factor (VIF) which indicates whether an independent variable has a strong linear relationship with the other independent variables. Another measure to assess the multicollinearity is Tolerance statistic which is reciprocal of VIF. VIF values less than 10 (some researchers prefer it to be less than 5) and tolerance statistics greater than 0.10 indicates no multicollinearity problem in the dataset.

The base model is as follows:

$$Yit = a + bXit + e_{it}$$

where Yit is the dependent variable of ith company at period t;

a is intercept b is regression coefficient;

Xit is the independent variable of ith company at period t;

e_{it} is error term.

Simple Regression Models:

$EPSit = a + b*CSRit + e_{it}$

$ROAit = a + b*CSR_{it} + e_{it}$

Multiple Regression Model:

$CSRit = a + b1*EPSit + b2*ROA_{it} + e_{it}$

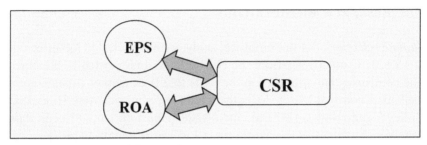

FIGURE 2.1   Conceptual framework.
Source: Author's compilation.

2.6   DATA ANALYSIS, FINDINGS, AND DISCUSSIONS

2.6.1   EMPIRICAL RESULTS OF HINDUSTAN UNILEVER LTD

The Correlation Matrix shows the degree and type of association between the dependent variable and the independent variables and also among the independent variables themselves. Table 2.1 shows that there exists a very strong and positive relationship between CSR and EPS whereas moderate but positive relationship between CSR and ROA of HUL.

TABLE 2.1   Correlation Matrix.

	CSR	EPS	ROA
CSR	1.0000		
EPS	0.9168	1.0000	
ROA	0.5074	0.7789	1.0000

Source: Author's computation using Stata.

TABLE 2.2   Simple Regression between EPS and CSR.

Dependent variable		EPS
Model	Coefficient	Probability
Constant	2.687872	0.629
CSR	0.1892393	0.028*
$R^2 - 0.8405$	F- statistic – 15.81	Prob – 0.0284**

** significant at 5% level.
Source: Author's computation using Stata.

It is evident from the above Table 2.2 that the coefficient of CSR is 0.1892393, which implies that an increase in CSR by 1% will r esult in an increase in EPS by 0.1882393% and it is statistically significant at 5% level. R^2 value of 0.8405 represents 84.05% of the variation in EPS, which is explained by the independent variable CSR.

TABLE 2.3   Simple Regression between ROA and CSR.

Dependent variable		ROA
model	Coefficient	Probability
Constant	26.45137	0.011*
CSR	0.0458214	0.383
$R^2 - 0.2574$	F-statistic – 1.04	Prob – 0.3829

** significant at 5% level.
Source: Author's computation using Stata.

Table 2.3 shows that 1% increase in CSR will lead to 0.0458214% increase in the ROA even though the result is not significant even at 10% level. And only 25.74% variation in the ROA can be explained by CSR.

TABLE 2.4   Summary of Multiple Regression.

Dependent variable		CSR
Model	Coefficient	Probability
Constant	141.9996	0.174
EPS	6.425478	0.035*
ROA	−5.821418	0.174
R^2		0.9492
F-statistic		18.69
Probability of F-statistic		0.0508**

** significant at 5% level.
Source: Author's computation using Stata.

Based on the results of multiple regression as evident from Table 2.4, the coefficient of EPS is 6.425478, which means that 1% increase in EPS would increase CSR spending by 6.425478% and it is statistically significant at 5% level. Whereas, 1% increase in ROA would result in 5.821418% decrease in CSR spending but it is not statistically significant.

However, as much as 94.92% variation in the CSR is jointly explained by the EPS and ROA.

Therefore, in case of HUL, the impact of CSR on EPS is positive and statistically significant.

TABLE 2.5   VIF and Tolerance Statistic.

Variable	VIF	Tolerance statistic (1/VIF)
EPS	2.54	0.393254
ROA	2.54	0.393254

Source: Author's computation using Stata.

Table 2.5 shows the results of VIF. All the independent variables are found to be less than 10, even less than 5 (as recommended by some researchers); also the tolerance statistic which is the reciprocal of VIF is observed to be greater than 0.10 for all the independent variables. Hence, it may be concluded that there is no problem of multicollinearity in the dataset of HUL.

2.7   EMPIRICAL RESULTS OF ITC LTD

The correlation matrix in Table 2.6 shows a very strong but negative relationship between CSR and ROA and strong but positive relationship between CSR and EPS of ITC Ltd.

TABLE 2.6   Correlation Matrix.

	CSR	EPS	ROA
CSR	1.0000		
EPS	−0.7121	1.0000	
ROA	−0.9882	0.7275	1.0000

Source: Author's computation using Stata.

TABLE 2.7   Simple Regression between EPS and CSR.

Dependent variable		EPS
Model	**Coefficient**	**Probability**
Constant	19.17731	0.032*
CSR	−0.0327504	0.177
R^2 − 0.5071	F-statistic − 3.09	Prob − 0.1772

Source: Author's computation using Stata.

Simple regression between EPS and CSR in Table 2.7, shows that an increase in CSR by 1% would result in 0.0327504% decrease in EPS and the result is statistically insignificant.

TABLE 2.8   Simple Regression between ROA and CSR.

Dependent variable		ROA
Model	**Coefficient**	**Probability**
Constant	30.7366	0.000*
CSR	−0.042999	0.002*
R^2 – 0.9766	F-statistic – 125.00	Prob – 0.0015*

Source: Author's computation using Stata.

In Table 2.8, the coefficient of CSR is −0.04299, as result in increase in CSR by 1% will lead to decrease in ROA by 0.04299% and it is highly statistically significant at 1% level. And 97.66% variation in ROA can be explained by CSR.

TABLE 2.9   Summary of Multiple Regression.

Dependent variable		CSR
	Coefficient	**Probability**
Constant	705.7005	0.005*
EPS	0.3140157	0.935
ROA	−22.95272	0.024**
R^2		0.9767
F-statistic		41.84
Probability of F-statistic		0.0233**

Source: Author's computation using Stata.

It is evident from the Table 2.9 that, since the coefficient of ROA is −22.95272, an increase in ROA by 1% would result in decrease in the CSR by 22.95272% and it is statistically significant at 5% level. As high as 97.67% variation in the CSR is jointly expressed by the independent variables together, and only 2.23% of the variation remains unexplained.

In case of ITC Ltd, CSR and ROA has a linear relationship which shows a significant negative impact on ROA.

TABLE 2.10   VIF and Tolerance Statistic.

Variable	VIF	Tolerance statistic (1/VIF)
EPS	2.12	0.470808
ROA	2.12	0.470808

Source: Author's computation using Stata.

In Table 2.10, VIF of the independent variables being less than 5 and Tolerance statistic greater than 0.10 confirmed no multicollinearity problem in the dataset of ITC LTD.

2.7.1   EMPIRICAL RESULTS OF BRITANNIA INDUSTRIES LTD

In case of Britannia Industries Ltd, Table 2.11 represents a very strong but negative relationship between CSR and ROA. However, the relationship between CSR and EPS is very week but positive.

TABLE 2.11   Correlation Matrix.

	CSR	EPS	ROA
CSR	1.0000		
EPS	0.1382	1.0000	
ROA	−0.9987	−0.1466	1.0000

Source: Author's computation using Stata.

TABLE 2.12   Simple Regression between EPS and CSR.

Dependent variable		EPS
Model	Coefficient	Probability
Constant	58.11099	0.046*
CSR	0.2455894	0.825
R^2 – 0.0191	F-statistic – 0.06	Prob – 0.8246

Source: Author's computation using Stata.

In case of Britannia Industries Ltd, CSR does not impact EPS significantly. As low as 1.91% variation in EPS is explained by CSR as represented in Table 2.12.

TABLE 2.13   Simple Regression between ROA and CSR.

Dependent variable		ROA
Model	**Coefficient**	**Probability**
Constant	27.72836	0.000*
CSR	−0.3204746	0.000*
$R^2 - 0.9973$	F-statistic − 1122.21	Prob − 0.0001*

Source: Author's computation using Stata.

Results of simple regression between ROA and CSR revealed that CSR negatively affects the ROA. In Table 2.13, the coefficient of CSR being −0.3204746, 1% increase in CSR would result in 0.3204746% decrease in ROA and the result is highly statistically significant at 1% level.

TABLE 2.14   Summary of Multiple Regression.

Dependent variable		CSR
Model	**Coefficient**	**Probability**
Constant	86.712	0.001*
EPS	−0.0046899	0.840
ROA	−3.115858	0.001*
R^2		0.9974
F-statistic		383.88
Probability of F-statistic		0.0026*

Source: Author's computation using Stata.

Table 2.14 posits that the coefficient of ROA is −3.115858; hence, 1% increase in ROA would lead to 3.115858% decrease in CSR spending of Britannia Industries Ltd which shows high statistical significance at 1% level. The combined effect of the independent variables together can explain 99.74% of the variation in the CSR.

Hence in this company, CSR has a significantly negative impact on ROA even though its impact on EPS is not significant.

TABLE 2.15 VIF and Tolerance Statistic.

Variable	VIF	Tolerance statistic(1/VIF)
EPS	1.02	0.978516
ROA	1.02	0.978516

Source: Author's computation using Stata.

In the above Table 2.15, the dataset of Britannia Industries Ltd is also free from multicollinearity problem as the VIF of the independent variables are less than 5 and Tolerance statistic much greater than 0.10.

[* significant at 1% level]
[** significant at 5% level]
[*** significant at 10% level]

2.8 CONCLUSION AND RECOMMENDATIONS

The empirical findings of the study highlights that CSR and EPS are positively and very strongly correlated in case of HUL but CSR and ROA are very strongly but negatively correlated in case of ITC Ltd and Britannia Industries Ltd, respectively. Simple regression analysis also reveals that CSR has a positive and statistically significant impact on EPS with 95% confidence interval in the case of HUL. Whereas CSR has a negative and statistically significant impact on ROA with 99% confidence interval in the case of ITC Ltd and Britannia Industries Ltd, respectively. In Multiple regression analysis, CSR was considered as the dependent variable and the two profitability measures, that is, EPS and ROA have been considered as the independent variables. Results posit that EPS has a positive and significant impact on CSR at 5% level in case of HUL. While in case of ITC Ltd and Britannia Industries Ltd, ROA has a negative and statistically significant relationship with CSR at 5% level and 1% level, respectively. The test results of VIF confirm no multicollinearity in the dataset of all the three FMCG companies. So, we may conclude that there exists a linear relationship between CSR spending and Firm's profitability measure, that is, EPS for HUL and ROA for ITC Ltd and Britannia Industries Ltd, respectively.

KEYWORDS

- **NSE**
- **FMCG**
- **CSR**
- **correlation**
- **regression**

BIBLIOGRAPHY

Bafna, A. A Study on the Impact of CSR on Financial Performance of Companies in India. *Int. J. Eng. Technol. Sci. Res.* **2017,** *4* (12), 325–331.

Bhunia, A.; Das, L. The Impact of Corporate Social Responsibility on Firm's Profitability-A Case Study on Maharatna Companies in India. *Am. Res. J. Human. Soc. Sci.* **2015,** *1* (3), 8–21.

Das, N. G. *Statistical Methods Combined Edition (Volumes I & II)*; Tata McGraw Hill Education Private Limited: New Delhi, 2012.

Garai, S. Impact of Corporate Social Responsibility on Firm's Financial Performance with a Special Reference of RIL. *Int. J. Appl. Res.* **2017,** *3* (1), 38–41.

Hou, T. C. T. The Relationship between Corporate Social Responsibility and Sustainable Financial Performance: Firm-level Evidence from Taiwan. *Willey- Corp. Soc. Respon. Environ. Manage.* **2019,** *26* (Csr.1647), 19–28.

Lin, C. H.; Yang, L. H.; Liou, Y. D. The Impact of Corporate Social Responsibility on Financial Performance: Evidence from Business in Taiwan. *Technol. Soc.* **2009,** *3* (1), 56–63.

Menezes, G. Impact of CSR Spending on Firm's Financial Performance. *Int. J. Adv. Res., Ideas Innov. Technol.* **2019,** *5* (2) , 613–617.

Reshmi, I. S.; Begum, N. N.; Md, H. M. Impact of CSR on Firm's Financial Performance: A Study on Some Selected Agribusiness Industries of Bangladesh. *Am. J. Econ. Fin. Manage.* **2018,** *4* (3), 74–85.

Richa Gautam, A. S. Corporate Social Responsibility Practices in India: A Study of Top 500 Companies. *Global Busi. Manage. Res. Int. J.* Jan **2010,** *2*, 41–56.

Selcuk, A. E. Corporate Social Responsibility and Financial Performance: The Moderating Role of Ownership Concentration in Turkey. *Sustainability* **2019,** *11* (3643), 1–10.

CHAPTER 3

Globalization and Corporate Social Responsibility

SUBAH SINGH YADAV[1*] and SATYAVEER SINGH[2]

[1]*Baroda Academy, Bank of Baroda, Jaipur, India*

[2]*Former MIS Expert, Asian Development Bank under India Technical Assistance Project 7625*

Corresponding author. E-mail: ssyadav397@gmail.com

ABSTRACT

The globalization of our economy is one of the objectives of our reforms. Some of the reforms' measures are aimed at putting our economy in line with the rest of the world and make it conducive for foreign investment. Globalization indicates the desire to integrate nation-states within the overall framework of the World Trade Organization (WTO). India is among the few economies proceeding to develop well. Amid the financial crisis, when the developed economies shrank collectively, the developing and emerging economies carried the complete burden of growth. CSR in the business world is a concept whereby companies not as it were considering their benefit and development, but too the interest of the society and environment by being dependable for the effect of their exercises on partners, workers, shareholders, providers, clients, and gracious social orders represented by NGOs. Most definitions portray CSR as a concept whereby companies coordinate social and environmental concerns in their business operations and their interaction with their shareholders on a volunteer basis. CSR has no boundaries and is not constrained by race, color, or religion. Sadly, concern for the community is often mistaken for socialism. On the contrary, every citizen is an asset in economic activity and has opportunities to succeed. There is sufficient ground to raise questions about the positive relationship between CSR, comprehensive development, and distributive justice. CSR initiatives do decrease in poverty to some extent in the prevailing practices, though it is not obligatory on the part of CSR activities to make poverty alleviation as a primary aim. Rather CSR targets labor, environment, and human rights, etc. as its focus areas. Of course, these are significant and vital issues but the absence of committed accountability to poverty, it cannot help directly to reduce poverty, may have some minimal indirect effect. The present societal marketing concept of companies is constantly evolving and has given rise to a new concept— CSR. Many of the leading corporations across the world had realized the importance of being associated with socially relevant causes as a means of protecting the goodwill and reputation, defending attacks and increasing business competitiveness.

3.1   INTRODUCTION

Globalization embarked on the Indian economy as a result of the implementation of economic reforms, when the then ruling party came into power in 1991 after a minor interruption of almost less than 2 years. Globalization envisages the integration of domestic economies across the world embracing trade and commerce relationships with other countries. India has changed its strategy for development since 1991. The changes in policies, when put together, constitute the reforms. The new policies complementary to each other have a common stance. These provide a market orientation to the economy. Important characteristics of reforms are globalization, liberalization, and privatization. Though Indian Economy during the 1980s touched higher growth trajectory, that is Growth rate of 5.7%, still it had to face some acute problems of increasing fiscal imbalance adversity of balance of payment, inflationary pressures, and lack of liquidity, drawing down of foreign currency resources to rock bottom level, political and social instability which caused lack of confidence in International Financial Markets. Moreover, the economic environment was concentrated around viable policies and regulations. Globalization poses complex policy challenges, it also offers vast opportunities. The process of economic reforms enabled India's integration in terms of agriculture, industry finance labor, and to some extent environment with the global economy. It helped in raising the bar of its growth rate and slashing down the magnitude of poverty. Even as we are a large economy at an aggregate level, we are still a poor country as measured by per capita income and several social indicators. The challenge before us is to make rapid strides in India's growth rate with the ultimate objective of inclusive growth. We need to meet that challenges squarely in this globalizing India. We are sure we will find a congenial way that makes our endeavor intellectually exciting and emotionally fulfilling.

Globalization as the name indicates means making the Indian economy responsive to the developments taking place at the global level and trying to play a greater role in the world economic environment. Therefore, globalization essentially speaks about a free flow of factors of production goods and services, labor, and capital across the globe without any governmental restrictions. The globalization of our economy is one of the objectives of our reforms. Some of the reform's measures are aimed at putting our economy in line with the rest of the world and make it conducive for foreign investment.

Globalization indicates the desire to integrate nation-states within the overall framework of the World Trade Organization (WTO). The term globalization has four parameters:

- Gradually reducing trade barriers to enable flow of goods uninterruptedly across national frontiers
- Providing an enabling regime wherein capital can flow freely among countries
- Establishing a policy and administrative environment for free-flow of technology
- Clearing the decks for free movement of labor among various countries of the world.

Amid the long-global stagnation, India is among the few economies proceeding to develop well. Whereas India posted growth rate, which is not comparable to its level of development from 2005 to 2008 when the country clocked each year at over 9% and, on normal, at 9.5% per annum, India still stands out in spite of small debilitating. As per the World Bank's projections, the world economy was to decelerate the rate in 2018 and develop at a pace slower than already expected. AS such growth rate in developing nations is specifically expected to decelerate. There are nations which, resisting this calm viewpoint, are anticipated to develop a little faster. India is one of them. India was anticipated to be the speediest developing economy in 2017 and 2018. It will be doable for India to lead the world development chart. Maintained, exceptionally fast comprehensive development is conceivable for India.

According to the World Bank's model, India was projected to be the fastest-growing large economy in 2015 and 2016. As per World Bank projection made in June 2015, global GDP was poised to grow at 2.8% in the fiscal compared to 2.6% in 2014. Advanced economies were expected to grow by 2.0% in 2015 up from 1.8 in 2014; while growth in developing countries was expected to decelerate to 4.4% in 2015 from 4.6 in 2014. It will be feasible for India to lead the global growth chart. Sustained very rapid inclusive growth is possible for India. It will also be good for the World since in today's interconnected global economy there are large and usually positive spillover effects. Recently, India has made a determined effort to cut down bureaucratic transaction costs, which have always been a stumbling block for small business and self-employed people. In respect of "Doing Business" ranking, there is still a great distance to go to India.

Uses and Abuses of Globalization

Advantages to the Economy

1) Reduction of tariffs and other trade barriers under GATT.
2) Voluminous increase in FDI.
3) Coming up speedily of institutions and administrative units to manage resources and mitigate risks across borders and over great distances.
4) Technology transfer from one economy to another across the world.
5) Exposure to all this ultimately increases of efficiency.

The Consumer is also benefited due to the availability of goods and services of international standards in a competitive environment.

1) The accelerated rate of growth because of industrial development and export growth.
2) Economic activities and trade leads to employment generation and poverty reduction.
3) Availability of innovation and specialization in products and services.
4) Capital is also available at competitive rates.
5) Infrastructure is also furthered to greater heights.

The World and India are at crossroads. The obligations of policy-makers, financial analysts, and civil society in common are colossal. Globalization could be a twofold edged sword – it offers gigantic openings but poses merciless challenges too. The global financial crisis of 2008/09 is a striking case of this situation. The crisis started in 2008 in America's a few prime-mortgage markets spread to the financial sector in common and caused the real sector to slow down around the world. Amid the financial crisis, when the developed economies shrank collectively, the developing and emerging economies carried the complete burden of growth. Right now whereas the progress of developed economies is slated to be stabilizing, there are refreshing concerns of growth slowdown in developing economies. Brazil and Russia are anticipated to see their GDP contract; India and China are likely to have vigorous developments.

Globalization seeks to make the Indian economy responsive to global free exchange between the Economies. There should be no limitation within the frame of licenses and control in taking up any mechanical action. Multinationals ought to be permitted to have free get to venture in Indian enterprises/ventures to empower the normal stream of capital and innovation. There should be no control on imports and exports. The tariff must to be based on a sound method of reasoning to empower free international trade. Globalization was received as a financial arrangement by many of the nations during the 1970s and 1980s. These nations have determined the benefits due to such introduction of their policies, the nations that have pulled in most extreme speculation amid last decade of 20th century – Taiwan, Singapore, Thailand, and China nowadays are distant more grounded and way better able to stand up to worldwide competition than the nations that have fizzled to liberalize or globalize.

3.2 RISKS OF GLOBALIZATION

Globalization exposes the economy to the following risk also:
1) The domestic industry will face tough international competition and there may be a fear of unemployment in the short run.
2) Under these circumstances, corporates that have resorted to research and quality control can stand out.
3) In the beginning stage of globalization, the domestic economy can face turmoil.

4) Due to free flow of capital exchange rate can be more fluctuating.
5) Developed countries have more concerns about their environment. Therefore, there is every possibility of shifting the industries affecting environment in developing countries.
6) Natural resources like forest and minerals of underdeveloped economies can deplete if not properly guarded.
7) On account of interdependencies of economies, the incidents happening around the world may have a direct impact on a country's economy.
8) The country may be impacted by the social, political, and cultural front.

3.3 PRIVATIZATION

The term privatization means distinctive implications. In a narrow sense, privatization infers the acceptance of private proprietorship in publicly owned enterprises. In a broader sense, it implies the acceptance of private management and control in the public sector enterprises. Privatization implies the transfer of possession and/or administration of an enterprise from the public sector to private hands. It, moreover, connotes the withdrawal of the State from an economic sector largely or completely. The privatization reaction is, in a genuine sense, a response to the around the world, the disappointment of government sector endeavors. State-owned undertakings accounted for 10–20% of the GDP in much of the less developed world. Essentially, all nations saw the development of the public sector during the 1960s and 1970s. In any case, the failure of public sector undertakings is a global wonder. As a response to the wasteful working of the state-owned enterprises, the wave of privatization has speeded all over the world.

The public sector was initially planned to be a potent mechanism of self-sustained development. However, it fizzled out to produce adequate internal resources for its development and has presently got to have serious misgivings for development in most of the countries. Since around 1980, there has been a trend over the world toward privatization. Privatization is also watched indeed over the Communist and socialist nations. Privatization permits competition, empowers the economy to respond to the requirements of the customer, advances productivity, and holds down costs.

Privatization also offers assistance to trim the measure of the authoritative apparatus leading to significant savings of funds to the exchequer. The government has taken concrete steps for empowering the private sector previously overwhelmed by the public sector. Disinvestment within the shape of exchange of a portion of the proprietorship of state-owned ventures is another shape of privatization embraced by the government. The government technique in this way is to hold the administration of the public sector in its hands whereas selling of part ownership.

The foremost genuine feedback against the public sector is the low rate of return, i.e., a large number of loss-making units. The public sector did not accomplish the productivity and efficiency of capital. The virtual nonappearance of competition did not give the opportunity of creating efficiency. The World Bank, IMF, and other monetary institutions pressurize the Governments to acknowledge privatization as the modern philosophy.

3.4   PROS AND CONS OF PRIVATIZATION

Privatization has the following advantages:

It improves the effectiveness of utilization of assets. The economy gets advantage by productive use of rare capital resources. Excessive restrictions driving to poor individual initiatives are dismantled. Technological up-gradation and change in management become the game-changer. Finally, the government is left out with more resources at its disposal and that can be gainfully used for growth and development purposes. However, privatization has the taking after antagonistic impacts also:

There is an apprehension of concentration of economic power and since wealth is gathered in few hands, the inequalities of income will widen the gap between the haves and haves not. This is typically opposite to the community development philosophy of the constitutional arrangement. Quite a few of the goods and services cannot be efficiently provided by the private sector. While the public sectors undertake such exercises eagerly. Privatization is likely to adversely affect social equity.

3.4.1   KNOWLEDGE-DRIVEN GLOBALIZATION?

In this era of information-driven globalization, it is conceivable for nations to overcome handicaps of geographical areas by using their comparative advantage in human resources. That blue-collar occupations move over geographic boundaries in the interest of cheap hands has long been portion of traditional wisdom. But what is modern is that progressively white-collar occupations, once considered secure from outside competition, are presently being offshored. The moving comparative advantage is most obvious within the service sector. Nor is it fair low-end services such as information preparing and call centers that are outsourced, but high end, skill-intensive services. In this way, it is that monetary analysts in Chennai give tax consultancy to clients in Chicago; engineers in Buenos Aires plans roads and bridges for Berlin; and radiologists in Manila give restorative diagnostics for patients in Manchester. On the other hand, it is low-end services such as clothing, janitor administrations, and taxi driving that stay location tied. This slant, running counter to the compulsions of geology, may have noteworthy suggestions for globalization. The hypothesis has been, and still is, is that develop economies will outsource low-end employments to developing and emerging economies, and will themselves move up the value chain to more profitable employments. The outsourcing of high-end occupations suggests that this story is not running concurring to script.

The number of occupations outsourced may be little, but the unimportant plausibility that they may be outsourced has disturbed an unwritten social contract. This can be since the exceptional plausibility of outsourcing, disintegrates the bargaining power of workers and compels them to keep their wage requests stifled. Just for an illustration, within the USA, over the two decades, the share of wages in national income has relentlessly gone down while the share of corporate benefits has expanded evidencing the declining bargaining strength of laborers. In this drift, if this trend is not arrested, workers might get restive and request for protectionist measures. What this implies is that free international trade has got the potential to raise worldwide welfare, but its advance may be hampered by political compulsions at the national level.

3.4.2   GLOBALIZATION AND CORPORATE SOCIAL RESPONSIBILITY

The concept of Corporate Social Responsibility (CSR) echoes a situation whereby companies coordinate social and environmental concerns in their commercial operations and their interaction with their stakeholders voluntarily. CSR has got to be a major center incorporate issues as well as in developmental practice. The shareholder's management approaches as well as the broadly acknowledged endeavor to legitimize CSR with an experimental contention that social execution contributes to financial performance are common expressions of the fundamental financial soundness in modern CSR research. Seen from this point of view, a "business case" for CSR is made, that is, the engagement of trade firms in social obligation is considered comparable to a venture in any other item qualities such as quality, benefit that contribute to the profit-making of the firm. The behavior of the business firm is coordinated toward profit-making and this is often defended as long as the firm complies with the rules of the definition set by the State.

3.4.2.1   *CORPORATE SOCIAL RESPONSIBILITY—AS A CONCEPT*

CSR is all about setting arrangements, destinations, and targets for the proceeding commitments by commerce and industry to act morally and contribute to financial advancement while improving the quality of life of the workforce and their families as well as of the local community and society at large. CSR in the business world is a concept whereby companies not as it were considering their benefit and development, but too the interest of the society and environment by being dependable for the effect of their exercises on partners, workers, shareholders, providers, clients, and gracious social orders represented by NGOs. Most definitions portray CSR as a concept whereby companies coordinate social and environmental concerns in their *business operations and their interaction with their shareholders on a volunteer basis.* Finally, CSR is reporting to all stakeholders about:

Commitment – Commitment to bring about social change.

Clarity – Clarity is all-important because social responsibility is a broad term and it needs to be debated and hammered out to meet each company's circumstances.

Congruence – Congruence is about ensuring that the company's attitude to its responsibilities toward society is consistent with how it runs the whole business, that is, its values.

3.4.2.2   CSR—WHAT DOES IT MEAN?

CSR is all about setting policies, objectives, and targets for excellence in three areas: Health and Safety, Environment and Social and Community welfare-oriented works.

Further CSR is concerned with:

> ➤ Improving employees' and contractors' safety through training, best practice, and team leadership
> ➤ Addressing emissions, energy efficiency, climate change, bio-diversity product life cycle innovations
> ➤ Activity engaging with employees, neighbors, legislators, and NGOs
> ➤ The monitoring and verifying performance and setting targets for continuous improvement

Components of CSR

> ➤ Corporate responsibility
> ➤ Responsible business
> ➤ Corporate citizenship
> ➤ Sustainable responsible business
> ➤ Corporate social performance

Integration of CSR and Sustainability with Business Strategy

The sustainable development process is essentially concerned with future, whereat emphasis is laid down on intervening measures having effects on future generations. It is a dynamic process having a prerequisite in building paradigms. The following are the major highlights of CSR:

- Sustainable development is defined as the advancement of economic development while maintaining the quality of the environmental and social system.
- Environmental resources provide a basis for social and economic development.
- In the financial sector, there is the visible trend to promote an environmentally and socially responsible lending and investment in the emerging markets.
- Banks are beginning to recognize that they have a social responsibility to fulfill as they emerge from the shadow of traditional banking.

- Responsible Banking is the new approach born out of the new market relations.
- Banking and finance's immediate environmental and social impacts are relatively low because most of the impacts are delivered through the activities of another businessman that rely on financial institutions – the business in a loan or investment portfolio.

Environmental and Social Impact of Business Activities

Such impacts result from substandard environmental and social practices which can be

- ➢ Overuse and Wastage of Natural Resources
- ➢ Damage caused by accidents and mishap
- ➢ Persistent damage caused by past polluting practices
- ➢ Environmental damage caused by continuing polluting activities
- ➢ Use of environmentally sensitive materials.

Accordingly, the CSR network, a UK based consultancy, released in 2004, the ten benefits in order of priority, of engaging in CSR are:

1. Increased profits
2. Access to capital
3. Reduced operating cost/increased operational efficiency
4. Enhanced broad image and reputation
5. Increase sales and customer loyalty
6. Increased productivity and quality
7. Enhanced capacity for acquisition and retention of employees
8. Potentially reduced regulatory oversight
9. Minimizing risk factor and enhanced risk management system
10. Moving closer to the competitors where markets are poised toward CSR

3.4.3 CSR AND SUSTAINABLE DEVELOPMENT (WITH PARTICULAR REFERENCE TO BANKS)

Sustainable development is continuous advancement of development while promoting/maintaining the quality of environmental and social systems so that we can do justice to future generations. For ensuring social and economic development, judicious exploitation of environmental resources may provide a strong base. In the financial sector, there is a visible trend to promote lending and investment based on environmental and social responses in the emerging markets. Banks are committed to their CSR responsibilities, which have initially emerged from conventional banking. Responsible Banking is the latest version sprouted out from the new market relations. Banking and finance's immediate environmental and social impacts are relatively low because most of the impacts are delivered through the activities of other businessman that rely on financial institutions, i.e., the business in a loan or investment portfolio.

Environmental and Social Impact of Business Activities:

Such impacts result from degradation relating to environmental and social practices which can be:

- Overuse and wastage of natural resource
- Damage caused by accidents and mishap
- Polluting practices have caused continuous damage
- Persistent polluting activities have damaged the environment
- Use of environmentally sensitive materials

3.4.3.1 INTEGRATION OF CSR AND SUSTAINABILITY WITH BUSINESS STRATEGY

CSR can play an essential part in making and empowering environment for the association between civil society and trade to endeavor for comprehensive development and feasible improvement and change in rural setting. CSR is a shape of corporate self-regulation with a social flavor coordinated into a commercial model. In a perfect world, CSR approach works as a built-in, self-regulatory component whereby businesses monitor and assures adherence to law, moral measures, and perfect standards with the extreme objective to altogether move forward the society. It operates in and on which it can have an impact under the aegis of CSR umbrella. Business ordinarily earmarks obligation for the effect of their functioning on Environment, Customers, staff, Communities, stakeholders, and all other parts of society. CSR is the well though consideration of public interest into corporate choice-making, and the honoring of triple foot line: pupil, planet, and benefit. It can sensitize populace additionally make them mindful of the benefits of CSR.

Integration of CSR and Sustainability with Business Strategy can be done through –

(a) Commitment to Sustainability – Banks must change their motto from ones that give priority to maximization of profit to a vision of social and environmental sustainability.

(b) Commitment to "Do NO Harm" – Banks may endeavor religiously not to commit harm by minimizing the environmentally and/or preventing socially detrimental impacts of their functioning and their operational activities.

(c) Commitment to responsibility – A bank should be responsible for the environmental and social impacts of their transitions.

(d) Commitments related to accountability – Banks must be account-able to their stakeholders particularly those that are affected by the activities and side effects of companies they finance.

(e) Commitment concerned to Transparency – Banks must hold the responsibility of being transparent to all stakeholders through robust, regular, and standardized disclosure. Added to this, also through being responsible for all concerned' needs for particular information regarding policies, procedures, and transactions of on banks.

3.4.3.2   CSR IN INDIA

(a) India has a gracious and long history of CSR. As regards CSR, the Tata group has been frontier and pioneer on this path. They were the first ones to implement CSR in India.

(b) As per the contention of Ratan Tata, they have never done CSR for any sort of propaganda or publicity stunt, but they have done it entirely for their internal satisfaction, and they feel to have achieved enough out of this.

(c) "Social responsibility is encapsulated as the key business process," is the essence of the Tata business excellence model which inex-tricably intertwines social responsibility into the framework of corporate management.

(d) CSR programmers at the Tata group of Companies extend a host of activities through its wide spectrum including family initiatives, tribal development, rural development, community development, social welfare, and water management.

(e) However, the catastrophe or irony of fate is that CSR Initiatives have been documented in a very little systematic manner in India.

The results of a study conducted by a Foundation for The Energy and Resource Institute (TERI) highlight the following facts:

(i) Not much ground has been covered under the fold of CSR activities, though serious and committed approach to CSR is taking off and increasing its reach

(ii) Collaboration work between companies and NGOs is increasing

(iii) Corporates are realizing that Good for society is good for business

(iv) Most interventions so far are philanthropic rather than strategic in nature.

Challenges of CSR:

There is sufficient ground to raise questions about the positive relationship between CSR, comprehensive development, and distributive justice. CSR initiatives do decrease in poverty to some extent in the prevailing practices, though it is not obligatory on the part of CSR activities to make poverty alleviation as a primary aim. Rather CSR targets labor, environment, and human rights, etc. as its focus areas. Of course, these are significant and vital issues but the absence of committed accountability to poverty, it cannot help directly to reduce poverty, may have some minimal indirect effect. Some inherent features limit CSR's ability to address poverty, which are:

1. CSR movements in its present form came into being due to the sharp reaction to criticism regarding environmental and social impacts on Transnational Corporations (TNCs).

2. The poor are those who do not have a stake in the business. Such an absence of centrality within the broad framework of the definition of CSR also reduces its relevance in addressing poverty.

3. As far as poverty reduction is concerned, CSR in its current practice is not expected to have a major impact in developing countries.

4. There are many reasons to have doubts about whether changing the face of CSR can it more amendable to achieving this objective?

5. It is significant for CSR techniques to wind up key to business methodology and part of the long-range planning process.
6. Stakeholders are putting questions more on CSR activities of the organizations today. They are daring the companies' choices making toward this path. It has necessitated consolidating stakeholders' opinions. In India, the CSR chiefs face several difficulties in overseeing CSR exercises.
7. The most concerning issue is the absence of spending assignments pursued by the absence of help from representatives and the absence of necessary knowledge.
8. Lack of demonstrable skill is another issue faced by this segment.
9. Small organizations do not look into CSR exercises and those which attempt them neglect to disclose it to the general public. In the process, they miss out on individuals and their trust in them.
10. There is a lack of interest in the local community in participating and contributing to CSR activities of companies. This is largely attributable to the fact that there exists little or no knowledge about CSR within the local communities as no serious efforts have been made to spread awareness about CSR and instill confidence in the about such initiatives.
11. Many organizations believe that corporate social duty is a fringe issue for their business and customer satisfaction is significant for them.
12. They envision that customer satisfaction is presently just about price and service yet they neglect to call attention to significant changes that are occurring worldwide that could blow the business out of water.
13. There is an absence of enthusiasm for the nearby network in taking an interest and adding to CSR exercises of organizations. This is to a great extent owing to the way that there exists almost no learning about CSR inside the nearby networks as no genuine endeavors have been made to spread mindfulness about CSR and ingrain trust in the local communities about such activities.
14. Lack of communication between the organization and the network at the grassroots.
15. Understanding is absent among local organizations concerning CSR ventures. This absence of consensus frequently brings about

duplication of exercises by corporate houses in regions of their intervention.

16. There is a need for capacity building of the local non-governmental organizations as there is a serious dearth of trained and efficient organizations that can effectively contribute to the ongoing CSR activities initiated by companies. This seriously compromises scaling up of CSR initiatives and, subsequently, limits the scope of such activities.

3.5   CONCLUDING REMARKS

CSR is marching forward as an increasingly significant activity to the business at the national and international level. As globalization spreads its footprints and big corporates become providers around the globe, these corporates have increasingly recognized the sheer advantages of providing CSR programs in their respective areas of working. CSR activities are, these days, being undertaken across the globe. With its pointed concentration on international trade based on comparative advantages, multinational enterprises, and global supply chains-economic globalization is increasingly raising CSR concerns. These concerns are mainly related to human resource management practices, environmental protection, health and safety, and among other things. CSR is also quite useful in locating business impacts on labor condition, local communities and economies, and initiating appropriate measures to ensure business helps to maintain and enhance the public good. This is of vital importance for export-orientated ferns in emerging economies.

Corporate sustainability is an evolving process and not an end. The government has done a good job by initiating the Companies' bill. But on the issue of inclusion, in the fold of spending under CSR activities, it is not clear and it has been left to the companies to decide. Worldwide, the concept of CSR has been accepted as an element for success and survival of business along with fulfilling social objectives. However, the challenge for the companies is to determine a strong and innovative CSR strategy that should deliver high-performance in-ethical, social and environmental sectors to meet all the stakeholders' avowed objectives.

3.6   CONCLUSION

CSR has no boundaries and is not constrained by race, color, or religion. Sadly, concern for the community is often mistaken for socialism. On the contrary, every citizen is an asset in economic activity and has opportunities to succeed. This invisible culture can shape brighter future for nations. If employees do not see the point of CSR initiatives or understand the message, initiatives are unlikely to be effective. Organizations must realize that government alone will not be able to get success in its endeavor to uplift the down trodden of society. The present societal marketing concept of companies is constantly evolving and has given rise to a new concept – CSR. Many of the leading corporations across the world had realized the importance of being associated with socially relevant causes as a means of protecting the goodwill and reputation, defending attacks and increasing business competitiveness. It stems from the desire to do well and get self-satisfaction in return as well as societal obligation of business. The Indian corporate sectors are planning to introduce CSR in the small and medium enterprises (SME) sector to increase its reach in remote areas. Also some companies have already started using the CSR as a strategy, which aims at mutual development of company and the community simultaneously.

KEYWORDS

- **globalization**
- **liberalization**
- **reforms**
- **technology transfer**
- **social corporate responsibility**
- **leading corporations**
- **business competitiveness**

REFERENCES

1. Agle, B. R.; Mitchell, R. K.;, Sonnenfeld, J. A. Who Matters to CEOs? An Investigation of Stakeholder Attributes and Salience, Corporate Performance, and CEO Values. *Acad. Manag. J.* **1999,** *42*, 507–525.

2. Avi-Yonah, R. S. National Regulation of Multinational Enterprises: An Essay on Comity, Extraterritoriality, and Harmonization. *Columbia J. Transnat. Law* **2003**, *42*, 5–34.

3. Barber, B. Can Democracy Survive Globalization? *Govern. Opp.* **2000**, *3*, 275–301.

4. Baumhart, R. C. How Ethical are Businessmen? *Harv. Bus. Rev.* **1961**, *39* (4), 6–12, 16, 19, 156–176.

5. Beck, U. *What is Globalization?*; Polity Press, Cambridge,2000.

6. Bowen, H. R. *Social Responsibilities of the Businessman*; New York, 1953.

7. Chakrabarty, B. *Corporate Social Responsibility in India*; Routledge: New York, 2011.

8. Chandler, A. D.; Mazlish, B., Eds. *Leviathans. Multinational Corporations and the New Global History*; Cambridge University Press: Cambridge, 2005.

9. Cochran, P. L.; Wood, R. A. Corporate Social Responsibility and Financial Performance. *Acad. Manag. J.* **1984**, *27*, 42–56.

10. Friedman, M. *Capitalism and Freedom*; University of Chicago Press: Chicago, 1962.

11. Friedman, M. The Social Responsibility of Business is to Increase its Profit. *The New York Times Magazine*, Sept 13, 1970. Reprint in Donaldson, T.; Werhane, P. H., Eds. *Ethical Issues in Business: A Philosophical Approach*; Prentice Hall: Englewood Cliffs, NJ; pp 217–223.

12. Frooman, J. Globalization, Production and Poverty. United Nations University. World Institute for Development Economics Research. Research Paper No 2005/40, 1999.

13. Hoekman, B.; Kostecki, M. *The Political Economy of the World Trading System. From GATT to WTO*; Oxford University Press, Oxford, 1995.

14. India, G. O. The Companies Act, Aug 29, 2013. Retrieved Mar 2016 from Ministry of Corporate Affairs.

15. Jamali, D.; Mirshak, R. Business-conflict Linkages: Revisiting MNCs, CSR, and Conflict. *J. Bus. Ethics* **2010**, *93* (3), 443.

16. Kahn, J. Standoff Brings Calls to Boycott Chinese Goods. *New York Times*, Apr 11, 2001, p. A-1.

17. Jensen, M. C. Value Maximization, Stakeholder Theory, and the Corporate Objective Function. *Bus. Ethics Quart.* **2002**, *12*, 235–256.

18. Kobrin, S. J. Sovereignty@bay: Globalization, Multinational Enterprise, and the International Political System. In *The Oxford Handbook of International Business*; Rugman, A. M., Brewer, T. L., Eds.; Oxford University Press: New York, 2001, pp 181–205.

19. Levitt, T. The Dangers of Social Responsibility. In *Managerial Marketing Policies and Decisions*; Meloan, T., Smith, S., Wheatly, J., Eds.; Houghton Mifflin: Boston, MA, 1970; pp 461–475.

20. Mishra, S. I.; Damodar, S. Does Corporate Social Responsibility Influence Firm Performance of Indian Companies. *J. Bus. Ethics* **2010**, *95* (4), 571–601

21. Outlook, I. C. A Snapshot of CSR Spend in India in FY 2014–15, Oct 2015 Retrieved from ngo.box.org.

22. Parker, B. *Globalization and Business Practice. Managing Across Borders*; Sage: London, 1998.

23. Reserve Bank of India RBI Bulletin. Shahid Bhagat Singh Marg, Mumbai, 2011–2014.
24. Vogel, D. J. Is There a Market for Virtue? The Business Case for Corporate Social Responsibility. *CA Manag. Rev.* **2005,** *47*, 19–45.
25. Waters, M. *Globalization*; Routledge: New York, 1995.

CHAPTER 4

The Extent of CSR and Sustainability in the Ghanaian Mining Sector

KWASI DARTEY-BAAH[1*], KWESI AMPONSAH-TAWIAH[1], and YAW A. DEBRAH[2]

[1]Department of Organisation and Human Resource Management, University of Ghana Business School, Accra, Ghana

[2]Swansea University, University of Wales, Cardiff, United Kingdom

[*]Corresponding author. E-mail: kdartey-baah@ug.edu.gh

ABSTRACT

The concept of corporate social responsibility (CSR) remains foreign in many developing countries, even though its role in the success of businesses cannot be overemphasized. Using the case of a major mining firm in Ghana and a qualitative approach, the study sought to explore the understanding and extent of CSR and sustainability and also identify the challenges companies face in undertaking CSR dubbed projects. The findings show that CSR is almost an obligation in the mining sector as a result of the nature of the activities of mining companies. This study recommends that issues of health and safety as a vital part of CSR (internal) should be duly considered as well as ensure that the CSR activities undertaken by mining companies are geared toward making the communities self-sustaining and less dependent on them.

4.1 INTRODUCTION

The relevance of corporate social responsibility (CSR) in the survival and success of organizations today cannot be overemphasized. Indeed, organizations that intend on successfully pursuing their objectives need to appreciate the implications for being socially responsible. Amponsah-Tawiah and Dartey-Baah (2011) iterate that some social issues may have an indirect bearing on an organization's operations and these issues, if ignored, can be detrimental to the success of that organization since the fulfillment of legal requirements alone does not necessarily lead to organizational success.

The concept of CSR that originated in the USA as philanthropic (Coronado and Fallon, 2010), has attracted a lot of attention from national policy makers in both developed and developing economies, international organizations, the general public and researchers (Arli and Lasmono, 2010 as cited in Nyuur et al., 2014). This attention has resulted in many definitions by governments, companies, business associations, business consultants, non-governmental organizations, shareholders, employees, consumers and communities of the concept as well as a number of terminologies being used interchangeably with CSR (Ofori et al., 2014). In addition, Amponsah-Tawiah and Dartey-Baah (2011) highlighted some of the popular terminologies as business ethics, corporate citizenship, sustainability or sustainable development, corporate environmental management, business and society, business and governance, business and globalization, as well as stakeholder management. Many researchers believe that CSR is a practical and profitable endeavor and organizations stand to benefit a great deal, and in diverse ways, from engaging in the practice of good and strategic CSR (Sen et al., 2006; Beckmann, 2007; Du et al., 2010; Arli and Lasmono, 2010).

Evidently, CSR has been linked to, and most often interchanged with the concept of sustainability. Sustainability became popular in the late 1980s and early 1990s after it was defined by the World Commission on Environment and Development (WCED) in the Brundtland Report in 1987 as "development that meets the needs of the present generation without compromising the ability of future generations to meet their own needs" (p. 43). In fact, many businesses in recent times, especially in the extractive industry, have pursued CSR in the lens and frame of sustainable development (Dashwood, 2012).

The mining industry is one that is generally thought of as "dirty" and destructive by nature of the activities of the mining companies. Ventura and Saenz (2015) maintained that "historically, the mining industry has taken a 'devil may care' attitude to the impacts of its activities by operating without the so-called 'social license,' hence causing major devastation, and then closing operations after having depleted mineral deposits of all their economic value" (p. 605). By extension, developing countries tend to suffer the most from the activities of mining companies; Abugre (2014) alludes to the fact that most African countries that are endowed with natural resources are characterized by gross exploitation, disregard, and violation of national and international laws concerning environment standards by the foreign companies. Abugre further maintains that this is largely due to the ineffective enforcement of laws in these developing countries.

Dashwood (2012) iterates that most major mining companies adopt CSR policies as a strategic response to address reputational issues surrounding public concern over the environmentally damaging practices associated with mining; while Amponsah-Tawiah and Dartey-Baah (2011) reiterate that there cannot be any meaningful discussion in the area of social and environmental responsibility without regard to the mining industry.

The concept and practice of CSR remains foreign in many developing countries (Amponsah-Tawiah and Mensah, 2015) and thus, a dearth in literature still remains, with regard to CSR in Africa. Nonetheless, some countries in Africa have made some notable contributions to the concept of CSR and its practice: South Africa (Visser, 2005) and Kenya (Mwaura, 2004) being the most notable with countries such as Tanzania (Egels, 2005), Nigeria (Amaeshi et al., 2006) also making significant progress. In Ghana, CSR, particularly in the mining industry, began as a defensive mechanism to dull down the effects of the various grievances put forward by mining communities against the activities of mining companies, but now, it is a strategic and proactive measure being vigorously pursued by most of the mining companies (Amponsah-Tawiah and Dartey-Baah, 2011). Moreover, organizations in Ghana, especially in the mining, service and manufacturing industries, are currently being called upon to aid the government in undertaking social development projects (Amponsah-Tawiah and Mensah, 2015). It, therefore, becomes imperative to assess the extent of CSR and sustainability in Ghanaian mining industry. This study focuses on Anglogold Ashanti Ghana, a South African multinational mining company with a subsidiary in Ghana, and assesses the company's understanding and practice of CSR and the promotion of sustainability.

4.2   LITERATURE REVIEW

4.2.1   CORPORATE SOCIAL RESPONSIBILITY

According to Abugre (2014), current literature has seen increasing pressures of stakeholder on management to adopt ethical and philanthropic practices and societal responsibility (Carroll, 1991; Berger et al., 2007); and this has formed the concept of CSR. Amponsah-Tawiah and Dartey-Baah (2011) maintain that CSR is a highly contested topic, throwing more light on the roles, responsibilities of companies as well as the relationship with stake-holders. Similarly, Ventura and Saenz (2015) iterate that there has been a shift, in recent times, from the traditional motive of profit maximization in business toward a more ethical and responsive focuses of business to the local communities and the environment. However, Amponsah-Tawiah and Dartey-Baah (2011) observe that despite the growing attention on CSR, the concept lacks agreement in literature with regard to definitions, rules, structures, or procedures.

Carroll (1979) explains CSR as the social responsibility of business that encompasses the economic, legal, ethical, and discretionary expecta-tions that society has of organizations at a given point in time. In this definition, Carroll introduced four key components of the concept where the economic CSR refers to the responsibility of firms to produce goods that society needs and to sell them at a profit in order to ensure perpe-tuity of business, the legal part deals with the obligation of firms to obey the laws, rules, and regulations regarding their business and within the context in which they operate, the ethical side challenges organizations to exhibit internationally acceptable standards and norms in the conduct of their business, and lastly, the discretionary component challenges firms to go beyond the legal requirements to undertake voluntary activities that would benefit society based on social norms. The discretionary part of CSR is sometimes referred to as philanthropy. Additionally, the World Business Council for Sustainable Development (WBCSD, 1999) defined CSR as "…the continuing commitment by business to behave ethically and contribute to economic development while improving the quality of life of the workforce and their families as well as of the local community and society at large" (p. 65). By inference, this definition emphasizes CSR as not a one-off event, but as a continuous or a never ending process. Further, the definition connotes commitment, of resources, to process of developing their various stakeholders of such as their human resources, the local communities, as well as the entire society.

After a review of the varied definitions of the concept of CSR, Amponsah-Tawiah and Dartey-Baah (2011) defined CSR as "the strategic decision of an organisation to voluntary act upon the social factors that have the potential of militating against the fulfillment of corporate goals" (p. 108). This definition provides some insights into the concept of CSR. First, it stresses CSR as a strategic decision, meaning that CSR is the long-term plan of a business based on the internal and industrial analysis. Second, it is a voluntary act, meaning that the concept entails deliberate and conscious efforts from organizations that go beyond legal require-ments. Lastly, this definitions also falls on social factors that are critical in the success of organizations. In its entirety, this definition explains CSR as not just charitable gestures from firms toward society or maintaining the quality of society and the environment, but largely as social activities that firms must undertake in order to ensure their very survival and perpetuity.

Similar to the definition by Carroll (1979), Lantos (2001) proposed a model of CSR based on three variables; ethics, altruism, and strategy. Lantos maintains that in undertaking CSR, firms must be ethical; to do what is right and socially acceptable, firms must be altruistic; to be selfless and go to the extent of forfeiting a portion of business profit in undertaking activities that benefit the society, and lastly, firms must be strategic; to integrate these social activities into the long-term business goals of the organization to ensure fulfillment of corporate goals. In reviewing the above definitions, it is quite evident that earlier definitions of the concept (Carrol, 1979; WBCSD, 1999) focus more on ethics, philanthropy, and voluntarism in improving quality social life for the various stakeholders of firms while later definitions (Lantos, 2001; Amponsah-Tawiah and Dartey-Baah, 2011) highlight the strategic "twist" to the definition of concept whereby emphasis is laid on the need to undertake CSR strategically, as a part of overall long-term corporate goals, for the sake of ensuring organizations' success.

While advocates of CSR stress the importance of firms being socially responsible, other scholars deem the whole concept and the practice of it as unnecessary in its entirety for firms to pursue. Proponents of this latter view (Friedman, 1970; Halfon, 1998; Jensen, 2001; Henderson, 2005) have argued that the sole responsibility of business is to maximize profit for shareholders. They further argue that CSR lowers economic efficiency and profit of companies, imposes unequal costs among competitors, imposes hidden costs passed on to stakeholders, and places responsibility on business rather than individuals. Moreover, these proponents even view the practice of CSR as unethical, maintaining that firms' use of share-holders' money to be socially responsive is wrong, tantamount to theft, and a violation of shareholders' rights (Friedman, 1970; Halfon, 1998 as cited in Ofori et al., 2014).

Nonetheless, many researchers believe, and there is evidence to suggest that CSR is a practical and profitable endeavor and organiza-tions stand to benefit a great deal, and in diverse ways, from engaging in the practice of good and strategic CSR (Carroll, 1979; Sen et al., 2006; Beckmann, 2007; Crane et al., 2008; Du et al., 2010; Arli and Lasmono, 2010). These advocates argue for the recognition of the interaction between businesses and society, and the need for organizations to ensure the welfare of both their businesses and the society at large. Lindgreen and Swaen (2010) outline some benefits that companies can reap in engaging in CSR: cost and risk reduction, improved corporate reputation and competitive advantage, and creating a win-win situation through synergistic value creation.

4.2.2   BRIEF OVERVIEW OF CSR IN AFRICA

Amponsah-Tawiah and Mensah (2015) posit that CSR is historically foreign to the developing world, adding that the spread of the concept and its practice is not as encouraging as expected, when the violations of laws and abuse of natural resources in these developing countries are taken into consideration. Abugre (2014) reiterates this assertion that most African countries that are endowed with natural resources are characterized by gross exploitation, disregard, and violation of national and international laws concerning environment standards by the foreign companies; largely due to the ineffective enforcement of laws in these developing countries. Tobey and Perera (2012) also maintain that because of the strong presence of multinational corporations (MNCs) in Africa, the continent provides ideal opportunities for these MNCs to practice CSR, due to the economic and social hardships that plague most of the African countries. Amponsah-Tawiah and Dartey-Baah (2011) state that "CSR has not been part of the corporate agenda of many companies in the developing world" (p. 108).

That notwithstanding, some countries in Africa have made some notable contributions to the concept of CSR and its practice: South Africa (Visser, 2005) and Kenya (Mwaura, 2004) being the most notable, with countries such as Tanzania (Egels, 2005), Nigeria (Amaeshi et al., 2006) also making significant progress. Nyuur et al. (2014) posit that CSR as a development issue, especially in Sub-Saharan Africa (SSA), is still at the budding stage; while Ofori et al. (2014) add that most of the literature on CSR in Africa show that CSR is mainly philanthropic in nature, with greater focus on social and community development. Perhaps, this buttresses the point made by Tobey and Perera (2012) that Africa provides an ideal situation for CSR due to the social and economic hardships. Hence, companies are geared toward aiding in improving the economic and social lives of the people. Abugre (2014), however, maintains that information on CSR practices in Africa is greatly insufficient; hence, a need for greater amount of research in Africa to broaden the scope and create sufficient awareness and practice of the concept across the continent (Amponsah-Tawiah and Dartey-Baah, 2011).

Amponsah-Tawiah and Dartey-Baah (2011) stated that, in Ghana, it is almost impossible for local companies to undertake social development programs due to factors such as low per capita income, weak currency, capital flight, low productivity, and low savings. Thus, in Ghana, MNCs have been called upon to aid the government in undertaking social development projects and programs, and consequently, major mining, manufacturing, telecommunications, and banking companies have spear-headed CSR in the country, and have vigorously undertaken essential social development programs (Amponsah-Tawiah and Mensah, 2015). These MNCs have contributed greatly in the areas of health, education, agriculture, power supply, job creation; and in the forms of donations, constructions, and program sponsorships, among others. In 2006, the Ghana Business Code (GHBC) was introduced by the Association of Ghana Industries (AGI), Ghana Employers Association (GEA) and the Ghana National Chamber of Commerce and Industry (GNCCI), to provide a framework to guide operations of business in an ethical and acceptable manner, to facilitate the practice of CSR in the country with a focus on the triple bottom line-people, profit, and planet (Amponsah-Tawiah and Dartey-Baah, 2011).

4.2.3   SUSTAINABILITY

According to Emas (2015), the overall goal of sustainability or sustainable development is the long-term stability of the economy and environment, which is the only achievable through the integration and acknowledgement of economic, environmental, and social concerns throughout the decision-making process. Harris (2000) also argues that the increasingly wide acceptance of the concept of sustainability was as a result of the growing awareness of challenges associated with traditional development such as the uneven distribution of the benefits of development, with income inequalities remaining persistent and sometimes increasing over-time, and the negative impacts of development on the environment and on existing social structures including pollution and deforestation. The concept of sustainability, like CSR, is a heavily contested one, not lending itself to a single definition (Soderbaum, 2011). However, a widely recognized definition of the concept was formulated by the World Commission on Environment and Development in 1987 in the Brundtland Report as: "a development which meets the needs of the present without compromising the ability of future generations to meet their own needs" (WCED, 1987, p. 43). Dashwood (2012) asserts that governments in advanced industrialized economies and a growing number of emergent and developing economies had come to accept the norm of sustainable development by the early 1990s. Harris (2003) observes that increased discussion and patronage of the concept have produced three (3) essential components of sustainability, such as economic sustainability (associated with continued production of goods and services as well as improved national economic factors), environmental sustainability (concerned with maintaining a stable resource base and avoidance of natural resource depletion), and social sustainability (concerned with continued provision of adequate social services for people). These three elements, as noted by Harris (2003), make the nature of sustainable development strongly normative and thus, difficult to analyze; thus, it is only justifiable to develop a theory to explain sustainable development as interdisciplinary in nature. Notwithstanding this challenge, a great deal of sense can still be made out of the concept.

As indicated earlier, sustainability has been used interchangeably with CSR over the years. There seems to be a high level of coherence and compatibility between the two concepts because of the focus on improving economic, environmental, and social conditions. It can be further deduced that these two concepts complement each other, in that, while sustainability gives an ideal, normative (Harris, 2003) insight into holistic development, CSR provides a practical way (Carroll, 1979; Sen et al., 2006) of addressing development issues. Wilkinson et al. (2004) note that currently, many organizations have adopted CSR as a means of managing, organizing, structuring, and reporting their environmental and social impacts (as cited in Wilkinson, 2013). Thus, organizations, in undertaking their CSR activities, provide information about their sustainability targets, especially in the construction and mining industries (Wilkinson, 2013). Dashwood (2012) argues that CSR is not only philanthropic, but also denotes an obligation companies have toward the three pillars of sustainable development; economic, social and environmental dimensions. This view is strongly shared by states and NGOs that the sustainable development agenda will be incomplete without the emphasis on protecting the environment. Dashwood (2012) further iterates that organizations assume the roles of change agents, giving varying responses in terms of timing and degree of commitment to CSR, which are expressed as sustainable development.

4.2.4   THEORETICAL UNDERPINNINGS

A number of theories and approaches to CSR have been produced as a result of the extensive discourse on the concept over the years. The theories were classified by Garriga and Mele (2004) into four broad categories, such as instrumental, political, integrative, and ethical theories. Garriga and Mele further identified approaches under each of these theories. Nyuur et al. (2014) noted that the most commonly used approaches in literature are the legitimacy approach under the political theory and the stakeholder approach under both the integrative and ethical theories. These two approaches together with the triple bottom line approach also under the ethical theory are briefly reviewed for purposes of this study.

The legitimacy approach holds the notion that an organization is in some form of social contract with the society in which it operates. On this approach, researchers (Suchman, 1995; Kunetsov et al., 2009) argue that the society in which an organization operates give legitimacy to the activities of that organization through the society's perceptions that the firm's activities are desirable, proper, or appropriate within a socially constructed system of norms, values, beliefs, and definitions. Hence, this approach maintains that organizations ensure that in order to be granted the "social right" to operate or legitimacy, they continually operate within the accepted norms, bounds, and value systems of their respective societies. Nyuur et al. (2014) observed that the legitimacy view is supported by findings that society tends to reward organizations that are considered to be socially responsible in various ways. Indeed empirical studies and reviews (Sen et al., 2006; Du et al., 2010; Arli and Lasmono, 2010) suggest that society rewards organizations who are perceived to be socially responsible in the areas of customer loyalty, willingness to pay premium prices for the company's products, or services, possibility of other stakeholders investing and or seeking employment in the organization, among others. The stakeholder approach holds the view that every organization has various stakeholders, for instance, shareholders, employees, customers, suppliers, local communities, government and among others; and these organizations have the responsibility of satisfying the needs of every stakeholder, even though these needs may be divergent and sometimes conflicting (Friedman, 2006). This approach connotes that the success of an organization depends on that organization's ability to build a relationship based on trust and mutual benefit with the various stakeholders (Kunetsov et al., 2009). Nyuur et al. (2014) indicated that the basic similarity between the legitimacy and stakeholder theory is that of a relationship based on trust. They further maintain that both approaches highlight the importance of a trustworthy interaction between business and society to maximize economic and social values for both parties.

The triple bottom line approach holds that for an organization to be seen as socially responsible, its activities must be directed geared toward profit, people, and planet known as the 3Ps (Elkington, 1997). This approach argues that as organizations are seeking to maximize profit, they should operate in a manner that does not destroy the physical environment, and also support social development and ensure quality life for the societies in which they operate. This approach underlies the concept of sustainability or sustainable development and its three pillars of economic (profit), environmental (planet), and social (people) development. Ofori et al. (2014) maintain that the triple bottom line is a strategic move for profitability and growth for firms in undertaking CSR from the single bottom line of economic development.

Amponsah-Tawiah and Dartey-Baah (2011) maintain that CSR in the Ghanaian mining industry began as a defensive mechanism to offset the negative effects of the numerous complaints from the local communities on their profitability. In other words, these mining companies were perceived largely as unresponsive to the negative effects of their activities to the environment and to the society, and as such they lacked the social right or legitimacy to operate. Furthermore, the mining companies were seen to be focused on satisfying their shareholders' interests of increased profits, to the neglect of the needs of other stakeholders such as the local communities and the general society. Thus, CSR in Ghana and in the mining industry in particular was geared toward gaining the legitimacy from the society and to be perceived as being responsive and concerned with the welfare of the society in which they operate (legitimacy approach). Additionally, these companies consequently sought, through the practice of good CSR, to satisfy the needs of not just the shareholders but the local communities, the government, the general society as well as other stakeholders (stakeholder approach). To add to this, the concept of sustainability and its three pillars has added a new strategic dimension to the practice of CSR (the triple bottom line), where mining companies have integrated economic, social, and environmental issues of development into their overall corporate goals, which tends to increase the overall profitability and growth of firms.

4.2.5   CSR AND SUSTAINABILITY IN THE MINING INDUSTRY

Dashwood (2012) notes that mining organizations were confronted with serious reputational crisis in the mid-1990s. This was a consequent of concerns raised by the general public about the environment and increasing awareness of the environmental destruction as a result of mining activities; leading to strong opposition in the developed countries such as USA, Canada, and Australia, to the commencement of new mining projects. Similarly, Hamann (2003) iterated that incidents of serious environmental degradation in the mining industry in the mid-1990s contributed to this bad reputation of mining companies. Dashwood (2012) observes that these mining companies consequently began to seek new mining opportunities in the developing countries and the former Soviet Union. Global environmental NGOs brought to the attention of these companies, the implications of the environmental and social practices of mining. Thus, in a strategic response to address issues of reputation in the mining industry, mining companies answered the calls by NGOs and adopted the practice of CSR (Dashwood, 2012).

Evidently, a change was realized in mining companies' responses to issues of environmental and social welfare in their operations in the early 2000s (Dashwood, 2007). Furthermore, upon pressures from the NGOs and the awareness they created on the damage caused by mining, these mining companies were forced to adhere to norms and principles of sustainable development (Dashwood, 2012). Hilson (2001) asserted that from the late 1990s, mining companies generally took a proactive stance toward environmental issues, but to a lesser extent, socio-economic and community matters. Hilson (2001 as cited in Ventura and Saenz, 2015) highlighted some sustainability initiatives of mining companies as: improved environmental planning, improved stakeholder and community consultation, implementation of mining environmental management tools and strategies, formation of partnerships with relevant mining bodies, improved waste management at mine sites, improved mine training, implementation of cleaner mine technology, improved relationships with mining regulatory bodies.

4.2.5.1   CSR AND SUSTAINABILITY IN THE GHANAIAN MINING INDUSTRY

Similar to the story of CSR in the global mining industry, Amponsah-Tawiah and Dartey-Baah (2011) also indicated that CSR in the mining industry in Ghana began as a defensive mechanism to respond to the numerous complaints of the local communities and civil societies about the negative environmental and social impacts of mining activities. Hilson and Potter (2003) reported that between 1990 and 1998 more than 30,000 people were displaced in Ghana's Tarkwa District, together with contamination of rivers and destruction of farms and forest lands. However, CSR in the Ghanaian mining industry today is that of a proactive strategy of engagement; where some of the mining companies are involved in a range of community development works such as the funding and supporting of community assistance programs through the establishment of community relations department (Amponsah-Tawiah and Dartey-Baah, 2011). This community development approach to CSR has been adopted by all mining companies in Ghana, although the nature of CSR programs vary among the companies, depending on the type of product mined, size of company, background of company as well as the length of operation (Amponsah-Tawiah and Dartey-Baah, 2011).

Jenkins and Obara (2006) state that there is a clear distinction between CSR that creates dependency on companies and the type of CSR that ensures sustainable development of the community such that these local communities are empowered over time to spearhead their own develop-ment. Amponsah-Tawiah and Dartey-Baah (2011) observed that many mining companies in Ghana use sustainable livelihood programs, as part of their CSR, to equip the local communities with certain skills in areas as grass cutter and snail farming, cane and basket weaving, soap and pomade making, among others, in the hope of reducing the dependence of these communities on the companies and ensuring self-sustenance of the local communities. Thus, CSR in the Ghanaian mining industry is an activity that mining companies must undertake for their own sake. As a strategic and proactive endeavor, it serves as a means for companies to gain the social legitimacy to operate through the satisfaction of the diverse interests of the stakeholders and a practical means for pursuing economic, environmental, and social development. Therefore, in order to be known to be practicing CSR, most mining companies in Ghana issue periodic reports on their environmental and social practices and performances together with the economic performance (Amponsah-Tawiah and Dartey-Baah, 2011).

In a study which sought to examine the understanding of CSR issues by the stakeholders in the mining industry in Ghana and the apprecia-tion of occupational health and safety; Amponsah-Tawiah and Mensah (2015) found that all the stakeholders in the mining industry associated CSR to community relations and development. Thus, occupational health and safety was not duly recognized as a dimension of CSR. Amponsah-Tawiah and Mensah (2015) maintain that CSR is of two dimensions: internal and external. While the external deals with stakeholders outside the organization, the internal dimension focuses on internal stakeholder, mainly the employees, with regard to the occupational health and safety. Nonetheless, the authors documented that there was some level of appreciation of issues of occupational health and safety. The study by Jenkins and Obara (2006) sought to examine two multinational mining companies in Ghana and the approaches used in community develop-ment. The findings show that the two mining companies used various community development strategies in areas of stakeholder engagement, farming and small-scale business in order to create a self-sustaining community and reduce local community dependence on these mining companies. The authors, however, indicated that there were weaknesses in their CSR strategies and this posed challenges in their bid to make the communities sustainable.

4.2.6 RESEARCH QUESTIONS

- What is the understanding of CSR and Sustainability in the mining industry and Anglogold Ashanti, Ghana, in particular?
- What is the extent of CSR and sustainability at Anglogold Ashanti in Ghana?
- What are the shortcomings and challenges that confront Anglogold Ashanti in undertaking CSR and sustainability?

4.2.7 METHODOLOGY

4.2.7.1 DESIGN

The qualitative method was adopted for this study in order to gain in-depth understanding and the extent of CSR and sustainability issues in the mining industry, with Anglogold Ashanti as a case study. Also, because of the insufficient information in literature on CSR and sustainability in the Ghanaian mining sector, the qualitative approach was thought to be the best for this study.

4.2.7.2 SAMPLING AND DATA COLLECTION

Consequently, data for this study were collected through an interview based on an interview guide. Based on the purpose of the study and out of convenience, the Sustainability manager at Anglogold Ashanti, Ghana, was interviewed on-site. This personnel was considered to be key for the study as he handled all issues of CSR, sustainability and community development of Anglogold Ashanti, Ghana, in the local communities.

4.2.7.3 DATA ANALYSIS

Responses from the interviewee were recorded during the interview after permission was sought from the interviewee. Afterwards, recorded responses were transcribed and analyzed using content analysis (Miles and Huberman, 1994), where the responses given by the interviewee to the questions asked were examined critically to draw out conclusive information to aid in the discussion of this study.

4.2.7.4 ETHICAL CONSIDERATIONS

The interviewee was duly informed of the purpose of the interview and the study as solely academic. Anonymity and confidentiality of information were assured before the start of the interview while permission was also sought from the interviewee to record the responses given to the questions. Aside these, all other research ethics were duly considered throughout the conduct of this study.

4.2.7.5 BRIEF PROFILE OF ANGLOGOLD ASHANTI

AngloGold Ashanti currently has two wholly owned and managed operations in Ghana; Obuasi and Iduapriem. The operations are located in the Ashanti and Western Regions of Ghana, and were acquired following a merger between the former AngloGold Limited of South Africa and Ashanti Goldfields Company Limited of Ghana. The new entity, Anglo-Gold Ashanti Limited, was formed in April 2004. The Iduapriem mine, wholly owned by AngloGold Ashanti since September 2007, comprises the Iduapriem and Teberebie properties in a 110 km^2 concession. Iduapriem is located in the Western Region of Ghana, some 70 km north of the coastal city of Takoradi and 10 km southwest of the Tarkwa mine. Obuasi is located in the Ashanti Region of Ghana approximately 60 km south of Kumasi. Mining operations are primarily underground to a depth of 1.5 km. Some surface mining in the form of open pit and tailings reclamation occurs. Obuasi, currently, treats sulphide ores from underground at the south plant, following the decommissioning of the tailings treatment plant in October 2010. The south plant also treats sulphide tailings and has a capacity of 360,000 tonnes per month (Anglogold Ashanti in Ghana, 2014).

4.3   FINDINGS

4.3.1   WHAT IS THE UNDERSTANDING OF CSR AND SUSTAINABILITY IN THE MINING INDUSTRY AND ANGLOGOLD ASHANTI, GHANA, IN PARTICULAR?

4.3.1.1   CORPORATE SOCIAL RESPONSIBILITY

The study sought first to determine the understanding of the concepts of CSR and Sustainability at Anglogold Ashanti. When the interviewee was asked how CSR is understood in the organization, he asserted that in Ghana, when you mention CSR, people think of it as a company giving gifts to people, that is, being charitable and/or philanthropic; however, he mentioned at Anglogold Ashanti, CSR is almost like an obligation. He stated that;

"For any multinational it is an obligation to undertake corporate social stuff; you said it is a responsibility, which means that it has to be done. One of our values as a company is to make the communities we operate in better off for our presence in those communities and so because of that we can't say that because corporate social responsibility is not like a legal requirement so you won't fulfil it."

He also indicated that the extractive industry in particular is somewhat compelled by the mining agencies to undertake CSR and this has influenced the understanding of CSR as an obligation or something that the organization must undertake. He added that

"In the mining companies, it is almost like an obligation, because the Minerals Commission, the Chamber of Mines and all those entities expect that you will fulfil certain social obligations to the community. So in the mining company, we don't joke with our CSR."

He further iterated that CSR is a means of gaining not just the legal license but also the equally important social license. According to him

"[...] you know we operate with two things; legal license and the social license. With the legal license all you need to do is to fulfil some legal requirements as in...environmental protection agency permit, minerals commission permit, government of Ghana ministry of finance permit, those are the legal licenses."

He went further to assert that mining companies need the social license or legitimacy from the communities to operate because of the nature of their activities, citing instances where some companies have lost billions because they lacked this social license to operate. Adding that

"A social license is the goodwill that will make sure that you operate freely, the communities are happy with your presence. If they are not comfortable with your presence in the community then you cannot operate freely because they are not happy with you... So that is what makes CSR very key to organizations in the extractive industries."

In addition, he indicated that at Anglogold Ashanti, the concept of CSR is largely termed as *Community Investment;* stating that

"[...] we won't say CSR but we call it community investment because we believe we have to invest in the communities we operate in [...] we don't see it as a favour we see it as a responsibility to our communities, that is it."

4.3.1.2   SUSTAINABILITY

With regard to sustainability, he iterated that the understanding of sustainability at Anglogold Ashanti is primarily embedded in the values of the company. He asserted that the overall corporate goals and every activity that the company engages in is geared toward the continued operation of the company and also make the communities in which the companies operate in sustainable. He mentioned that

"[...] we say the people are the job and the job is the people. All you are trying to do is to make everything you are doing a sustainable entity." In furtherance of this, he stated that *"[...] one of our core value as an organization is to treat each other with dignity and respect so we treat every employee, every external person with dignity and*

respect, so if you are saying that the people are the business and the business is the people, your values say then treat each other with dignity and respect."

He outlined the broad areas or systems that make up sustainability at Anglogold Ashanti, such as the Human Resource, Safety, Health and Environment (SHE), Community and Security. He said

"[...] in our sustainability space HR is key because if you get the people aspect wrong, you get everything wrong."

Thus, according to him, by employing the people in and outside the local communities, the company is partly ensuring that members of these local communities can fend for themselves in a sustainable manner. Also, employing qualified people ensures that the company operates in a profitable way that sustains the company. Going further, he indicated that the company has systems in place one of it being known as SHE so as to guide the company in understanding and dealing with sustainability issues. He made the following statements in support of this system:

"We have what we call safety health and environmental aspect of our operations on Anglogold we call "SHE". Safety of our people is key, the health of our people is also key, the environment in which we operate, we need to respect the environment it is one of our values as well"

"The safety is what we deal with when we come to the actual work we do. We know the mining area, we deal with heavy equipment... so it's a high risk area so you have to be very alert when it comes to safety other than that you will always end up with fatalities. People shouldn't go to work and come back as dead bodies."

"Your employees should be healthy if they are not healthy they won't deliver so that is key and the environment that you are operating in should be clean, it should be a healthy and human-friendly environment that is also one bit of sustainability."

He went further to talk about security of the people both in and outside the organization as part of the sustainability systems in place at Anglogold as well as the welfare and comfort of the communities within which the company operates. According to him

"[...] you should be able to provide a secured environment for your people to operate in. Also, the communities you are operating in, the people should be comfortable with your presence, so these are the areas that underpin our sustainability phase."

4.3.1.3   CSR AND SUSTAINABILITY

With respect to the relationship between CSR and Sustainability, he maintained that CSR is a component of sustainability, thus, sustainability is the broad term under which CSR falls, stating that "*Sustainability is the broad discipline, CSR is just a minute aspect of the sustainability discipline.*" Acknowledging the definition of sustainability "*as ability to operate efficiently now whiles you still make room for generations yet unborn,*" he reaffirmed

"That is why in our sustainability discipline we take care of our employees, their health, their safety, their security, we will take care of the environment because we don't have to destroy the environment, we take care of the community because there are people who live in those community."

Additionally, he noted that

"[...] but the CSR activities, they are just a minute aspect of the entire sustainability space because the CSR activities don't come to employees, they go to the external world so if you take the community and the environment, they will benefit from the community initiatives… so that is the inter-linkage between CSR and sustainability, you can't divorce the two."

4.3.2   WHAT IS THE EXTENT OF CSR AND SUSTAINABILITY AT ANGLOGOLD ASHANTI IN GHANA?

Second, the study sought to assess the extent of CSR and sustainability at Anglogold Ashanti. In lieu of this, the interviewee was asked if Anglogold Ashanti had policies and strategies to guide the undertaking of CSR. To this, the interviewee answered in the affirmative, further stressing that he was even in charge of designing the CSR policy. He also added that the company has a community policy to guide its activities. He stated that

> *"The Minerals Commission requires that every mine develops policies, we have a community policy and a corporate social responsibility policy...it is part of your permit processes for the mine."*

He added that the CSR policy is shaped by guidelines from the Minerals Commission and this guides the company's CSR strategies, stating

> *"[...] based on the guideline from the Minerals Commission you would develop your policy and it is your corporate social responsibility policy that is going to shape your corporate social responsibility strategy, plan and the activities."*

Asked to elaborate on some of the CSR strategies, the interviewee mentioned that the main strategy that the company uses in undertaking CSR and sustainability is the Engagement and Collaboration with the Municipal Assemblies and the local communities. He iterated that

> *"Our number one strategy is engagement with the communities and municipal assemblies. When people are well engaged and informed, they tend to appreciate a lot of things."*

Through this, the company is able to interact with the community to know which CSR activities to conduct, how to undertake, when to undertake them as well as the degree of priority to attach to them. He also added that the company has a Grievance Mechanism to allow the community and all stakeholders to voice out complaints and wishes to the company which also shapes the nature of CSR that the company does, stating that

> *"You need to give people an avenue to vent out their concerns and frustrations...so people can walk into our offices, they can write letters, they can go through the municipal assembly." Furthermore, he mentioned that Anglogold Ashanti does Needs Assessment to have adequate knowledge about the pressing needs of the people in the communities so that the company can undertake meaningful and adequate CSR. He said that "We conduct needs assessment through the municipal assemblies so as to know where to channel our*

resources to areas that are needed the most because the municipal assemblies have the municipal development plan."

To further answer the question of the extent of CSR and sustainability at Anglogold, the interviewee stated that the company undertakes CSR in many forms including sponsorships, donations, initiatives, constructions, under socioeconomic and environmental development in the areas of water and sanitation, education, agriculture, development in health, and even culture and heritage. He further cited the following examples to buttress his claim:

"Anglogold Ashanti has a school opened to the public, every member of the community can access the school for their kids. This is a school with facilities such as constant supply of water and electricity... Although the students pay fees, the company's overall contributions per month to the school's operations amount to over GHC 100,000."

"We have a hospital that is the second largest hospital in Ashanti region where bills are subsidized up to GHC 160,000 every month... They access the hospital, the National Health Insurance Scheme operates there, and every health delivery facility you want to access is there ... the company recently bought an ultra-modern scan machine that can give you 3D picture of a baby in your womb."

We have a community trust fund that operates, and every year since 2012, the trust fund churns out projects in the region of GHC 500,000."

"Currently, Anglogold Ashanti funds the supply of electricity to two communities in the Ashanti region amounting to GHC 300,000 every month...We have also sponsored the construction of roads for some communities."

"We have sponsored several individuals in the areas of farming and small-scale enterprises."

Moreover, he added that the company contributes to upholding culture and tradition and the protection of the physical environment, citing that *"if you go and undertake any project in any area and there is a shrine there, it is our responsibility to relocate the shrine there...you have to be sensitive to culture."*

"[...] at times the communities will tell you to perform certain purification rites. We pay for the purification rites to be performed some of which run into thousands of Ghana cedis. When they finish the purification, we have to relocate these shrines, called sacred grooves, to a desired location for the community."

4.3.3   WHAT ARE THE SHORTCOMINGS AND CHALLENGES THAT CONFRONT ANGLOGOLD ASHANTI IN UNDERTAKING CSR AND SUSTAINABILITY?

With regard to shortcomings, the interviewee mentioned that the main shortcoming of Anglogold Ashanti in CSR and sustainability is their failure to adequately publicize their CSR activities. He stressed that

"[...] in Anglogold, our main shortcoming is that we don't shout enough. Organisations in other sectors do something amounting to GHC 20,000 and it is all over the news, everybody is talking about it. That GHC 20,000 project is likely to be our sustainability budget for a week."

Concerning the challenges that confront the company, the interviewer iterated the issue of mistrust between the company and the communities because of the legacy left by the previous owners of the mine. He stated categorically that

"Anglogold Ashanti took over the mine in 2004. You have about 90 years' legacy that you have to resolve and previously that mine was practically owned by the government. If the government is the owner and regulator of the mine, who was checking them to be compliant, environmentally and socially...so these legacies were built up and there is a lot of mistrust between the community and the mine."

This he stressed poses a challenge to the company in undertaking CSR because the people expect a lot from the mine based on dealings with the previous owners.

Another challenge he mentioned was that of external factors particularly with fluctuations in prices of gold in the international market, adding that

"[...] we don't have any control over the gold price, if the gold price is high, or we make a lot of profits, obviously our CSR budget will go up but if the gold price is down, our CSR budget will come down."

Lastly, he talked about the issue of over-dependence of the local communities and municipal assemblies on the mine for their livelihood. He stated that *"There is a paternalistic relationship and dependence on the mine that has been there over years. They are used to handouts from the mine...so the locals expect the mine to cater for them."* He added that not only the local communities, but also the municipal assemblies depend on the mine, stating that *"We have a municipal authority that relies on the mine for almost everything, making it appear as if we are now the government therefore it is our responsibility to provide ... because when they go to government it will delay."*

4.4   DISCUSSION

The findings show that CSR in the mining industry in general, and at Anglogold Ashanti in particular, is understood as more of an obligation rather than a favor that the company does, and this is termed as Community Investment at Anglogold Ashanti. This is so because it is required by agencies such as the Minerals Commission and the Chamber of Mines who formulate and enforce regulations in the industry. In addition, the findings show that CSR is obligatory for mining companies because of the need to acquire the social license or the legitimacy, together with the legal license, to operate due to the destructive nature of mining activities. These findings seem to agree with the assertion made by Amponsah-Tawiah and Dartey-Baah (2011) that some social issues may have an indirect bearing on an organization's operations and these issues, if ignored, can be detrimental to the success of that organization since the fulfillment of legal requirements alone does not necessarily lead to organizational success. In line with the legitimacy theory (Suchman, 1995; Kunetsov et al., 2009) which argues that the society in which an organization operates give legitimacy to the activities of that organization through the society's perceptions that the firm's activities are desirable, proper, or appropriate within a socially constructed system of norms, values, beliefs, and definitions. Hence, CSR has become a "must" for these mining companies in order to gain that legitimacy or social license to survive and succeed.

Furthermore, the findings show that the understanding of the concept of sustainability at Anglogold Ashanti is embedded in the core values of the company, that is, respect and dignity for the people and the communities in which the company operates. Additionally, issues of sustainability are captured under systems such as the Human Resource, Safety and Health of the workers, protection of the Environment (SHE), Security of the workers and the people as well as the welfare of the Community. These tenets are somewhat similar to the three pillars of sustainability (Harris, 2003), and the triple bottom line approach (Elkington, 1997). By employing the human resource, the company empowers them economically (profit), ensuring their health, safety and security as well the welfare of the community adds to social sustainability (people), while protecting the environmental ensures environmental sustainability (planet). The findings also show that the company acknowledges the similarity and linkage between CSR and sustainability, in that, CSR is a tenet of sustainability. Wilkinson et al. (2004 as cited in Wilkinson, 2013) note that currently, many organizations have adopted CSR as a means of managing, organizing, structuring and reporting their environmental and social impacts. As sustainability is seen to be highly normative (Harris, 2003), CSR provides a practical way (Sen et al., 2006) of addressing development issues. This seems to be the case at Anglogold, as their sustainability is embedded in their corporate values (normative) and the CSR is an aspect of the sustainability that seeks to develop the communities in which they operate, as an obligation. However, another finding was that CSR was seen as mainly external of the company, thus, issues of occupational health and safety fell under the broad concept of sustainability in the company but not under CSR. Amponsah-Tawiah and Mensah (2015) maintain that CSR is of two dimensions, the external dimension that has to do with the external environment, and the internal dimension that has to do with the employees in the organization. Contrarily, CSR at Anglogold Ashanti failed to acknowledge health and safety of employees as a vital part of CSR in particular.

Again, the findings reveal that the company has a mining policy and a CSR policy as part of the requirements for a permit from the Minerals Commission. These policies guide the CSR strategies. In addition, the company had put some strategies in place to guide CSR such as Engagement with the local community and municipal assemblies, a Grievance Mechanism, and Needs Assessment. This reaffirms the iteration of

Amponsah-Tawiah and Dartey-Baah (2011) that through the establishment of community relations departments, CSR in the Ghanaian mining industry has become proactive and strategic, where some of the mining companies are involved in a range of community development works such as the funding and supporting of community assistance programs. To strengthen the above, the study reveals that Anglogold Ashanti undertakes CSR in many forms including sponsorships, donations, initiatives, and constructions, under socioeconomic and environmental development in the areas of water and sanitation, education, agriculture, development in health, small-scale enterprises and even culture and heritage. Similarly, Jenkins and Obara (2006) showed that the two companies in Ghana used various community development strategies in areas of stakeholder engagement, farming and small-scale business in order to create a self-sustaining community and reduce local community dependence on these mining companies. Analysis of the specific examples given show that CSR at Anglogold goes beyond the immediate local communities to other parts of the country that are not directly affected by mining activities. For instance, Kumasi is not directly affected by activities on the mine; however, the company has built the second largest hospital in the city.

As regards to the shortcomings of the company, it was revealed the insufficient and inadequate publicity of CSR activities was the company's main shortcoming in undertaking CSR. In addition, the study revealed that some of the major challenges that confront the company in undertaking CSR and sustainability are: mistrust between the company and the people as a result of the legacy left by previous owners, fluctuations in the price of gold on the international market, and overdependence of the local communities and municipal assemblies on the mines. The issue of mistrust poses a great challenge to CSR in the company, as Kunetsov et al. (2009) indicated that the stakeholder approach connotes that the success of an organization depends on that organization's ability to build a relationship based on trust and mutual benefit with the various stakeholders. Nyuur et al. (2014) also indicated that the basic similarity between the legitimacy and stakeholder theory is that of a relationship based on trust. Hence, without trust, the company cannot engage successfully with stakeholders to operate, and subsequently, undertake adequate CSR. With respect to the overdependence, it seems to confirm what Jenkins and Obara (2006) wrote that a very fine line exists between CSR that creates dependency and CSR that sustainably develops a community or region, and thus mining companies are confronted with the challenge of developing CSR programs to ensure goodwill for the company while addressing the long-term developmental needs of communities in a sustainable manner without creating a culture of dependency.

4.5   CONCLUSION

In a nutshell, CSR and sustainability in the mining sector have moved from the defensive, reactionary position to a more strategic and proactive one, where the survival and success of mining companies are dependent on the social license or legitimacy to operate based on the perceptions formed by society about the manner of conduct of the companies. It is, therefore, imperative that mining organizations always go the extra mile in undertaking adequate CSR and giving much publicity to their CSR activities so as to gain this social license. Additionally, there is also the need to consider duly, issues of health and safety as a vital part of CSR-internal (Amponsah-Tawiah and Mensah, 2015), as well as ensuring that the CSR activities they undertake are geared toward making the communities self-sustaining and less dependent on them.

4.6   LIMITATIONS AND RECOMMENDATIONS FOR FUTURE STUDIES

One major limitation of this study is that it focused on one company in the entire mining industry in Ghana, thus, posing a challenge to the generalizability of the findings. Also, the interview was granted out of convenience on the first visit to the company due to the busy schedule of the interviewee, and thus, some of the responses may not have been as detailed as expected. Nonetheless, the findings of this study are credible and reliable despite these limitations.

However, future studies should look at multiple case studies in the mining industry so as to compare and contrast findings. Additionally, future studies could employ other approaches such as the quantitative approach in data collection and analysis to further strengthen the findings of this study.

KEYWORDS

- **corporate social responsibility**
- **sustainability**
- **mining sector**
- **MNEs**
- **Ghana**

REFERENCES

Abugre, J. B. Managerial Role in Organizational CSR: Empirical Lessons from Ghana. *Corporate Governance* **2014,** *14* (1), 104–119.

Amaeshi, K. M.; Adi, B. C.; Ogbechie, C.; Olufemi, O. A. Corporate Social Responsibility in Nigeria: Western Mimicry or Indigenous Influences? *J. Corp. Citizenship* **2006,** *24,* 83–99.

Amponsah-Tawiah, K.; Dartey-Baah, K. Corporate Social Responsibility in Ghana. *Int. J. Busi. Soc. Sci.* **2011,** *2* (17), 107–112.

Amponsah-Tawiah, K.; Mensah, J. Exploring the Link between Corporate Social Responsibility and Health and Safety in the Mines. *J. Global Respon.* **2015,** *6* (1), 65–79.

Anglogold Ashanti in Ghana. 2014. Retrieved 29 April 2016, from http://www.anglogoldashanti.com/en/AboutUs/Regionsandoperations/Ghana/Pages/default.aspx

Arli, D. I.; Lasmono, H. K. Consumers' Perception of Corporate Social Responsibility in a Developing Country. *Int. J. Consumer Studies* **2010,** *34* (1), 46–51.

Beckmann, S. Consumers and Corporate Social Responsibility. *Aust. Market. J.* 2007, *15* (1), 27–36.

Carroll, A. B. A Three Dimensional Conceptual Model of Corporate Performance. *Acad. Manage. Rev.* **1979,** *4* (4), 497–505.

Carroll, A. B. The Pyramid of Corporate Social Responsibility: Toward the Moral Management of Organisational Stakeholders. *Bus. Horiz.* **1991,** *34* (4), 39–48.

Coronado, G.; Fallon, W. Giving with One Hand. *Int. J. Soc. Soc. Policy* **2010,** *30* (11/12), 666–682.

Dashwood, H. S. Canadian Mining Companies and Corporate Social Responsibility: Weighing the Impact of Global Norms. *Can. J. Polit.. Sci.* **2007,** *40* (1), 129–156.

Dashwood, H. S. CSR Norms and Organizational Learning in the Mining Sector. *Corp. Govern.: Int. J. Busi. Soc.* **2012,** *12* (1), 118–138.

Du, S.; Bhattacharya, C. B.; Sen, S. Maximising Business Returns to Corporate Social Responsibility (CSR): The Role of CSR Communication. *Int. J. Manage. Rev.* **2010,** *12* (1), 8–19.

Elkington, J. *Cannibals with Forks: The Triple Bottom Line of 21st Century Business*; Capstone Publishing: Oxford, 1997.

Halfon, R. Corporate Irresponsibility: Is Business Appeasing Anti-business Activists? Series: Research Reports, No. 26, Social Affairs Unit, London, 1998.

Hamann, R. Mining Companies' Role in Sustainable Development: The "why" and "how" of Corporate Social Responsibility from a Business Perspective. *Dev. SA* **2003,** *20* (2), 237–254.

Hilson, G. *Mining and Sustainable Development: The African Case, Environmental Policy & Management Group*; Imperial College Centre for Environmental Technology (ICCET), Royal School of Mines: London, 2001.

Hilson, G.; Potter, C. Why Is Illegal Gold Mining Activity so Ubiquitous throughout Rural Ghana? *Afr. Dev. Rev.* **2003,** *15* (2), 237–270.

Kunetsov, A.; Kuznetsova, O.; Warren, R. CSR and the Legitimacy of Business in the Transition Economies: The Case of Russia. *Scand. J. Manag.* **2009,** *25* (1), 37–45.

Lantos, G. P. The Boundaries of Strategic Corporate Social Responsibility. *J. Cons. Market.* **2001,** *18* (7), 595–630.

Miles, M. B.; Huberman, A. M. *Qualitative Data Analysis: An Expanded Sourcebook*, 2nd ed.; Sage Publications: Thousand Oaks, CA, 1994.

Mwaura, K. Corporate Citizenship: The Changing Legal Perspective in Kenya. Paper presented at the Interdisciplinary CSR Research Conference, Nottingham, 2004.

Nyuur, R. B.; Ofori, D. F.; Debrah, Y. Corporate Social Responsibility in Sub-Saharan Africa: Hindering and Supporting Factors. *Afr. J. Econ. Manag. Studies* **2014,** *5* (1), 93–113.

Ofori, D. F.; Nyuur R. B.; S-Darko, M. D. Corporate Social Responsibility and Financial Performance: Fact or Fiction? A Look at Ghanaian Banks. *Acta Commercii* **2014,** *14* (1), 1–11.

Sen, S.; Bhattacharya, C. B.; Korschun, D. The Role of Corporate Social Responsibility in Strengthening Multiple Stakeholder Relationships: A Field Experiment. *J. Acad. Market. Sci.* **2006,** *34* (2), 158–166.

Soderbaum, P. Sustainability Economics as a Contested Concept. *Ecol. Econ.* **2011,** *70* (6), 1019–1020.

Tobey, D. H. Sr.; Perera, B. Y. Corporate Social Responsibility Initiatives: A Stakeholder Model for Aligning Competing Values in West Africa. *Afr. J. Econ. Manag. Studies* **2012,** *3* (1), 95–115.

Ventura, J. C.; Saenz, S. Beyond Corporate Social Responsibility. Towards a Model for Managing Sustainable Mining Operations. Qualitative Research Based upon Best Practices. *Soc. Responsib J.* **2015,** *11* (3), 605–621.

Visser, W. Corporate Citizenship in South Africa: A Review of Progress Since Democracy. *J. Corp. Citizenship* **2005,** *18*, 29–38.

Wilkinson, S. J. Conceptual Understanding of Sustainability in the Australian Property Sector. *Prop. Manag.* **2013,** *31* (3), 260–272.

Wilkinson, S. J.; Pinder, J.; Franks, A. Conceptual Understanding of Corporate Social Responsibility in the UK Construction and Property Sectors. Session T6 Paper 380, CIB, Toronto, 2004.

World Commission on Environment and Development (WCED). *Our Common Future*; Oxford University Press: Oxford, 1987.

CHAPTER 5

Environmental Accounting—A New Dimension of Sustainable Development

SANDIP BASAK* and SAHITA MITRA

Department of Commerce, Heramba Chandra College, Kolkata, India

Corresponding author. E-mail: sandip.cma@gmail.com

ABSTRACT

Industrialization is considered as the stepping stone of the development of any country, where the unplanned industrialization and discharge of waste by industries in unsystematic way are the reasons behind the environmental pollution. It is the prime responsibility of each and every corporate house to take some measures to protect the environment for the purpose of maintaining the sustainable development in the society. For the sustainable development of the society, a healthy environment is indispensable. When every corner of the world is suffering from the harmful impact of the global warming, the corporates must consider environmental expenditure and liabilities as a serious issue and provide some stringent ways to solve the matter. Therefore, nowadays environmental matters are being given top most priority by most of the countries around the world including India. Reporting of environmental matters is taken as significant dimension of corporate accounting and reporting practices. So, this study tries to analyze the mechanism of environmental accounting from the angle of the corporate houses through the entire world.

5.1 INTRODUCTION

Rapid industrialization is one of the important criteria for development of each and every nation. But unplanned industrialization calls for environmental pollution which can be a serious problem in front of the government in terms of high amount of social cost toward providing for a safe and secured health to the people of the respective nation. On the other hand, it is the prime urge of every person of every nation to have the advantage of sustainable development over the years. Sustainable development refers to the economic development which is conducted without depleting the natural resources and without polluting the environment. Here lies the necessity of environmental accounting. It tries to achieve the sustainable development, maintain a healthy relationship with the community and pursue an efficient environmental conservation activity. These accounting procedures allow a corporate to measure the cost of environmental conservation during the regular course of business.

5.2   PROBLEM ANALYSIS

It is the basic need of the people of every country to get the benefits of sustainable development and to live in an environment which is completely hygienic in nature. Better to say, people would always prefer such an environment which can minimize the cost of health-related issues to zero. In this globalized world, corporate houses have been using the resources from the environment rapidly and thereby considered as the main destroyers of the environment by their result of operations. So, corporates must have some duties to compensate the entire society and to do so they have to consider all the environmental costs and liabilities simultaneously. But it is a big challenge to every corporate as well as the government to identify the way by which the recordings and measurements of all those environmental expenditures and liabilities will be done.

5.3   LITERATURE REVIEW

Actually, sustainability of a business is dependent on how well an enterprise contributes toward the development and protection of the society and environment within which its operation takes place and how far it remains transparent to its stakeholders whose interest are associated with the firm's credibility. On the other hand, credibility of any organization is closely associated with the environmental performance of the respective organization. Some experts' opinions are mentioned in the following:

- Amer et al. (2018) in their study showed that the good practice of environmental accounting by the corporates is essential for sustainability development but most of the organizations often ignore large environmental costs.
- Anil et al. (2017) in their study stated that the main purpose of green accounting is to help businesses in managing their traditional goal along with environmental goal.
- Savita et al. (2014) in their study described that business houses in India should make a solid environmental policy, take appropriate measure for pollution control, comply with the statutory requirements, and reveal adequate details of environmental aspects in the annual reports.
- Moneva et al. (2010) in their study opined that the enterprises which obtained higher rate of environmental performance would disclose better financial performance levels in the future.
- Alok et al. (2008) in their study disclosed that some steps should be taken globally and nationally to formulate the accounting and valuation techniques as well as the reporting guidelines to incorporate environment related issues in the corporate accounting and reporting system.

On the basis of abovementioned opinions of the authors, it can be stated that environmental issues are really a serious matter of concern and hence every corporate ought to report all the information relating to the measures taken by the said corporate for the purpose of protection of the environment.

5.4   OBJECTIVES OF THE STUDY

The objectives of this study are as follows:

- ➤ To describe the mechanism of environmental accounting system.
- ➤ To show the relevant issues associated with environmental accounting.
- ➤ To disclose the reasons behind adaptation of environmental accounting by the corporates.

5.5   ENVIRONMENTAL ACCOUNTING—AN OVERVIEW

Environmental accounting is an important tool for understanding the role played by the corporate houses in the economy toward the environmental safety and welfare of the society. It takes into account all the environmental costs in the form of depletion of natural resources or pollution in the environment. It also considers the contributions of the corporate houses to protect the environment from different harmful activities caused by them as a result of their operations.

- ✓ **Concept of Environmental Accounting:** Environmental accounting refers to the practice of incorporating principles of environmental management along with the conservation into reporting practices and thereby allowing the stakeholders to know about the company's current status on the basis of the measures taken by the management to protect the environment.
- ✓ **Elements of Environmental Accounting:** As per environmental accounting guidelines issued by Ministry of the Environment (Japan), this accounting system incorporates three factors which are:
  - **Environmental Conservation Cost:** Environmental accounting provides a structure for systematically identifying, measuring, and recording of environmental conservation cost arisen as a result of operations of the corporate. Actually, environmental cost is the investment and costs measured in monetary value. Categories of such costs are reflected in the following table:

TABLE 5.1   Categorical Distribution of Environmental Conservation Cost.

Category	Content
1. Business area cost	This cost is incurred to control environmental impacts resulted from key business operations within the business area.
2. upstream/down-stream cost	This cost is incurred to control environmental impacts resulted from key business operations upstream or downstream.
3. Administration cost	Streaming from administrative activities
4. R&D cost	Streaming from R&D activities
5. Social activity cost	Streaming from social activities
6. Environmental remediation cost	Cost associated with environmental degradation
7. Other cost	Related to environmental conservation measures

Source: Environmental Accounting Guidelines, March 2002, Ministry of the Environment.

- **Environmental Conservation Benefit:** It refers to such kind of benefit which can be obtained from the prevention, reduction, and avoidance of environmental impact, removal of such impact, restoration following the occurrence of a disaster and other activities. This benefit is measured in physical units. Actually environmental conservation benefit is the difference between the environmental impact volume during the base period and the environmental impact volume during the period under audit.
- **Economic Benefit Associated with Environmental Conservation Activities:** It refers to such type of benefits which is concerned with the contribution to the profit resultant of environmental conservation activities a company or other organization carries out as measured in terms of the monetary value. Basically, it is the difference between expense in the base period and expense in the current period.

✓ **Forms of Environmental Accounting:**
  (1) **Environmental Management Accounting (EMA):** Management accounting with a specific focus on data related to material, environmental cost information, etc. This can be further classified in the following ways:
    (a) Segment Environmental Accounting
    (b) Eco Balance Environmental Accounting
    (c) Corporate Environmental Accounting
  (2) **Environmental Financial Accounting (EFA):** Financial accounting with a specific emphasis on reporting environmental liability costs and other relevant costs.
  (3) **Environmental National Accounting (ENA):** It is a national level accounting with a specific focus on natural resources stocks, other related costs, etc.

✓ **Nature of Environmental Accounting**
  (1) **Relevance:** Environmental accounting should provide relevant, material, and significant information relating to the company's environmental conservation costs and benefits derived from related activities which are significant for the decision-making of stakeholders.
  (2) **Reliability:** Inaccurate or biased data should not be used in environmental accounting and it helps in building the trust and reliability

of stakeholders. Data regarding environmental accounting should be represented accurately, faithfully.

(3) Understandability: To understand the disclosure of required data, it is necessary to eliminate the possibility of any mistaken judgment about the company's environmental conservation activities.

(4) Comparability: Environmental accounting provides the basis for the comparison of performance of the corporate houses. Information so provided must be comparable with different companies lying under the same sector.

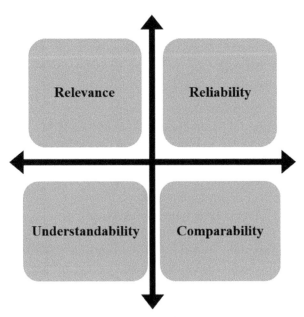

FIGURE 5.1   Natures of environmental accounting.
Source: Presentation by the researchers.

5.6   ENVIRONMENTAL ACCOUNTING MECHANISM

Conceptual model:

The objective of this model is to illustrate the different activities which can be adopted by the enterprises in facilitating the process of environmental accounting and reporting. The model is described as under:

1. The first stage is to identify the environmental reporting parameters. The selection of the environmental reporting parameter is depends upon the organization according to their respective objective. These parameters can be environmental policy, health safety and environment, energy conservation, sustainability reporting, waste management, water management, renewable energy sources, environmental information system, environmental disclosure practices, environmental targets, environmental reporting indicators, environmental cost and benefits, environmental liabilities and environmental assets, etc.

2. In the second stage of the environmental accounting process, the organization is required to clearly define the meaning of each parameter and on the basis of which it can measure the environmental performance.

3. In the third stage, organization tries to specify the environmental targets to be achieved by the organization. So, the company needs to frame the short term as well as the long-term environmental policy of the organization.

4. In this stage, organizations need to develop the environmental performance indicators such as environmental policy framework, health and safety standards to be followed, energy conservation practices to be followed, waste management programmed to be undertaken, water management policies, etc.

5. In this stage, the company tries to estimate the actual environmental performance in terms of the predetermined standard performance indicators. Measurement can be either qualitative or quantitative in nature. For example, waste management programs are to be measured quantitatively while environmental policy framework needs to be qualitatively measured.

6. In the last stage, the company needs to report the environmental performance results. Organizations usually present the integrate report, that is, simultaneous presentation of environmental performance and financial performance. This draws the clear view regarding the environmental impact on the financial performance of that establishment.

The abovementioned stages are shown in Figure 5.2 depicted below.

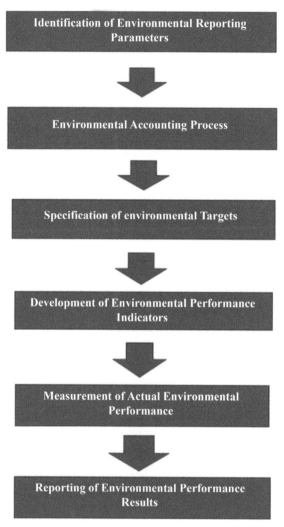

FIGURE 5.2   Conceptual model.
Source: Presentation by the researchers.

From Figure 5.2, in a comprehensive manner, it can be stated that the environmental accounting mechanism must be started with the identification of environmental reporting parameters by the corporate house and ended with reporting of environmental performance results of the said corporate.

5.7   THE REASONS BEHIND ADAPTATION OF ENVIRONMENTAL ACCOUNTING BY THE CORPORATES

Company incurs different type of cost while providing the goods and services to their customers. Environmental cost is one of them. Environmental performance is one of the important parameters for the success of the business. Environmental costs and performance need management attention for the following reasons:

✓ Due to investment in "greener" process or technology to redesign of processes/products many environmental costs can be significantly reduced or eliminated. Many environmental costs (e.g., wasted raw materials) may provide no added value to a process, system, or product.

✓ Environmental costs may be obscured in overhead accounts or else overlooked.

✓ So many companies have realized that environmental costs can be offset by generating revenues through sale of waste, by-products, or transferable pollution allowances, etc.

✓ Appropriate management of environmental costs may promote the environmental performance and play a significant role in the success of the business.

✓ Analyzing and understanding the environmental costs can facilitate more accurate costing and pricing of products and help corporates in designing more environmentally preferable processes, products, and services in the future.

✓ The company can have the competitive advantage than other companies in case of processes, products, and services that can be demonstrated to be environmentally preferable.

✓ Accounting for environmental costs can contribute toward the overall development of environmental management system.

5.8   FINDINGS

On the basis of abovementioned analysis, following points have been identified.

> There are no specific standards framed by the government or any organization authorized by the government of any country in the arena of environmental accounting system.

> There is no appropriate and specific measurement process of environmental conservation benefit.

> Ascertainment of actual environmental performance is not an easy task for the corporates.

> Proper guidelines must be required to identify different environmental performance indicators.

> Management of each and every corporate house, whether it is public or private, listed or unlisted, ought to take environmental accounting as a prime responsibility for the sake of entire society in which its operation takes place.

5.9 CONCLUSIONS

Globally, environmental accounting and reporting practices are in the incipient stage. In India as well as in the other countries, environmental accounting is not practiced widely. There is no clarity regarding rules, regulation, and policy framework for environmental accounting and reporting for national, state, and even at company reporting level. There is a lack of intention of global authority to frame a policy for environmental accounting. It is recommended that different government/nodal agencies should come forward to imply the policy of the environmental accounting. The companies (i.e., MNCs and National Level companies) should take initiative to comply with the rules and regulations framed by the authorities for the environmental accounting regardless of the nature of business, size of business, the capital structure, and turnover of the business. On the other hand, there is a lack of awareness regarding the environmental issues among the different stakeholders of the society. So, the government and the NGOs should come forward to organize campaigns on the environmental issues.

This study suffers from time bound and unavailability of some data regarding environmental accounting practices of the corporate houses across the world.

KEYWORDS

- **sustainable development**
- **environmental accounting**
- **environmental expenditure**
- **environmental liabilities**
- **industrialization**

REFERENCES

Kumar, A. N; Pranitha, S. T; Kumar, K. N. A Study on Green Accounting and its Practices in India. *IOSR J. Bus. Manag. (IOSR-JBM)* **2017,** *1,* 30–34.

Moneva, J. M.; Ortas, E. Corporate Environmental and Financial Performance: A Multivariate Approach. *Ind. Manag. Data Syst.* **2010,** *110*(2), 193–210. DOI: 10.1108/02635571011020304.

Pramanik K. A.; Shil, C. N.; Das, B. Corporate Environmental Reporting: An Emerging Issue in the Corporate World. *Int. J. Bus. Manag.* **2008,** *3*(12), 146–154.

Ranga, S.; Garg, R. Legal Framework for Environmental Accounting in India. *Int. J. Manag. Soc. Sci. Res. (IJMSSR)* **2014,** *3*(6), 2319–4421.

Shakkour, A.; Alaodat, H.; Alqisi, E.; Alghazawi, A. The Role of Environmental Accounting in Sustainable Development – Empirical Study. *J. Appl. Finance Bank.* **2018,** *8*(1), 71–87.

WEB-LINKS

https://www.sciencedirect.com/topics/earth-and-planetary-sciences/environmental-accounting

https://www.researchgate.net/publication/323376894_Environmental_Accounting_Reroting_Practices_in_India-Issues_and_Challenges/link/5a90f7d745851535bcd5ab28/download

https://www.accountingedu.org/environmental-accounting.html

https://www.env.go.jp/en/policy/ssee/eag05.pdf

https://www.topaccountingdegrees.org/faq/what-is-environmental-accounting/

https://www.denso.com/jp/ja/csr/pdf/EN_Environmental_Accounts_Guideline.pdf

https://en.wikipedia.org/wiki/Environmental_accounting

https://www.nap.edu/read/4982/chapter/17

https://mde.maryland.gov/programs/Businessinfocenter/GreeningYourBusinessFacility/Pages/eca.aspx

http://thecommercepedia.blogspot.com/2015/03/environmental-accounting-and-reporting.html

https://www.academia.edu/38630981/Environmental_Accounting_and_Reporting

CHAPTER 6

Corporate Social Responsibility in Academic Spin-offs

FERNANDO ALMEIDA

Faculty of Engineering of Oporto University, INESC TEC, Porto, Portugal

ABSTRACT

Corporate social responsibility (CSR) assumes a key role in today's society. Companies, regardless of their size, must be proactive in dealing with ethical and social issues, namely offering environmental protection, employee protection, sustainability of policies implemented and increased employee motivation and productivity. This study, through four case studies using semi-structured interviews, seeks to explore the role and relevance of social responsibility practices implemented at academic spin-offs, and also identifying the main benefits, challenges, and difficulties in their implementation. The findings indicate a significant and diverse number of CSR practices organized and implemented through close collaboration and partnership with other stakeholders particularly with the support of parent universities, science parks, and other organizations.

6.1 INTRODUCTION

The role of universities has changed over the past decades. In addition to the traditional roles of training human capital and increasing knowledge, there are new roles with high social and economic impact. The third mission of university argues that the university must be entrepreneurial and open to the community, promoting the development of its territory through links with other relevant actors, for example through the creation of spin-offs or start-ups, partnership projects, consortium projects or protocols. These actions can transform accumulated academic and scientific knowledge into catalyzing innovations for social and economic growth.

Academic spin-offs have their own specificities. These types of companies are created by students, researchers, and/or professors with the aim of commercially exploiting the knowledge, technology or research results developed by them in their research activity at the university. Academic spin-offs have a major impact, especially on local economic development, as they create jobs and develop innovative products that meet the needs of specific and differentiated customers and generate high economic value.

In order to ensure the sustainability of academic spin-offs, it is essential to have ethical conducts that value the human being and society. Therefore, it is mandatory the existence of sustainable practices that promote the balanced growth of academic spin-offs. Social responsibility should also be one of these companies' main concerns. Consequently, business practices in academic spin-offs should develop processes with the purpose of including social and environmental concerns in their activities and strategies; in order to create a set of values that involve all stakeholders. It is, therefore, recognized that socially responsible academic spin-offs not only increase employee satisfaction and customer loyalty, but also have a greater capacity for competitiveness and innovation.

Social responsibility in academic spin-offs has to be shared between the established start-up and the university from which it originates. Both entities play a key role in promoting sustainable development practices. Social responsibility has multiple dimensions. In this sense, this study seeks to explore the role of academic spin-offs in each of these dimensions, respectively:

- Environmental dimension—explores the environmental concerns that academic spin-offs have in their business operations.
- Social dimension—analyzes the social concerns of academic spin-offs to contribute to a better society.
- Economic dimension—analyzes the role of spin-offs in contributing to regional economic development.
- Stakeholder dimension—explores the interaction of academic spin-offs with universities, employees, suppliers, customers, and the community.
- Volunteer dimension—explores the ethical values that academic spin-offs promote and support volunteering initiatives.

This study employs a qualitative methodology by conducting four case studies with academic spin-offs. To this end, semi-structured interviews will be used to explore the role and relevance of corporate social responsibility (CSR) practices in academic spin-offs and how these practices can be organized and leveraged through the relationship with universities.

The manuscript is organized as follows: Initially, a literature review on the concept and dimensions of CSR is performed. Still in this phase, it is explored the role of CSR at universities. After that, the methodology and associated methods adopted in the realization of this study are presented. Consequently, the main findings are identified and discussed. Finally, the conclusions of this work are drawn.

6.2   LITERATURE REVIEW

6.2.1   THE CONCEPT AND DIMENSIONS OF CORPORATE SOCIAL RESPONSIBILITY

Organizational culture plays a key role in the performance obtained by a company. It is the foundation of the organization contributing to its success in the medium- and long-term. Several authors emphasize the importance of organizational culture. Robbins and Judge (2014) advocate that organizational culture is constituted by habits, values, attitudes, and expectations. As well Robbins and Judge (2014) add the fundamental role that the sharing of organizational culture by members of the organization plays in business productivity and job satisfaction. Anderson et al. (2008) consider that company culture represents their personality. Therefore, when an organization is created, the values of its founders are transmitted to future generations so that they can identify with the organizational culture and feel as active members of it, thus becoming an added value for the organization.

New management paradigms defended by Ehrhart (2013) and Schein (2016) mention that organizational culture is a fundamental component of organizations. In this sense, the principles of looking for financial performance should be conjugated simultaneously with the principles of social performance. In this sense, organizational performance is achieved by associating and developing financial resources with the social concerns of the community (Sparrow and Cooper, 2014; Stephan et al., 2016;

Martins et al., 2017). This line of thinking defends that organizations in their strategy and culture must implement socially responsible practices.

CSR tends to be a prerequisite in the activities performed by organizations. It serves as a conductor, transversal, and inspiring thread of the various areas of action of an organization. Chandler (2016) considers that social responsibility is inherent to the organization itself being a part of its strategy, culture, ethics, and values. Taghian et al. (2015) add that social responsibility must involve stakeholders, namely their current and future concerns, making organizations socially responsible and sustainable. Currently, social responsibility is no longer merely a voluntary option or a privilege of large companies. Therefore, it is up to all organizations, regardless of their nature, size, and sector of activity, to seek a balance between their needs and the economic, environmental, and social issues they have to meet.

CSR covers many areas and dimensions. One of the best-known models is presented by Dahlsrud (2008), which emphasizes the following components:

- Environmental dimension— organizations should promote business practices that benefit the environment. Practices that promote the use of recycled materials, renewable energy sources, among others, should be encouraged.
- Social dimension—organizations should adopt practices that benefit the whole society and its sustainable way of life.
- Economic dimension—the economic dimension should be considered when establishing CSR practices. From one perspective, it is necessary to have practices that can promote economic development, but at the same time are affordable for the company.
- Stakeholder dimension—the business decisions should be assessed in terms of their impact on employees, suppliers, customers, and other relevant stakeholders.
- Volunteer dimension—volunteer actions and initiatives must be carried out by companies in accordance with their ethical principles.

CSR comprises internal and external dimensions (Hawn and Ioannou, 2016). The internal dimension of CSR involves socially responsible practices consented to the organization's employees and mainly involves issues of human capital development, health, and safety at work, communication, and change management. On the other hand, the external dimension includes elements that interact with the organization, namely shareholders, partners, suppliers, customers, and the entire surrounding community. According to Hameed et al. (2016), both internal and external dimensions influence employee's organizational identification and contribute to increasing the perceived external prestige and perceived internal respect.

The motivations for organizations promote socially responsible practices are based on the fundamental principles and pillars of their mission, vision, and values. These practices provide organizations with value creation, increased employee engagement, increased productivity, increased customer and supplier satisfaction, and a better brand reputation and image of the organization (Galbreath, 2010; Kadlubek, 2015).

6.2.2 THE ROLE OF CORPORATE SOCIAL RESPONSIBILITY AT UNIVERSITIES

The university is a privileged space for academic and professional training and the production of knowledge. It must also play a key role in promoting the values of citizenship that incentive the sustainable development of society and the economy. In this sense, Hope (2012) argues that the mission of universities should go beyond the limits of their traditional purpose and prepare students for the full exercise of citizenship. Smith et al. (2017) complement this vision by arguing that university education should be focused on solving problems and responding to the demands of the community that promotes quality of life.

The University Social Responsibility (USR) should be perceived by institutions as a social, political, and educational priority. Giuffré and Ratto (2014) advocate that USR must be based on a holistic vision that articulates the various parts of the institution in a project of social promotion of ethical principles and sustainable social development. Equally important as highlighted by Freitas et al. (2014) is the commitment of university organizations to create partnerships between the public, private, and third sector. In this way, the necessary efforts can be divided and shared between various institutions and achieve a much greater social impact. In this sense, university institutions are increasingly integrating social responsibility into their mission statements as a form of commitment to society and the governments that finance public higher education institutions (Rahman et al., 2019).

USR is seen as the capacity that a university offers in spreading and putting into practice a set of principles and values through the four essential processes of the university that include its management, teaching, research, and extension (Wigmore-Álvarez and Ruiz-Lozano, 2012). Therefore, each university institution is socially committed to the country and region in which it operates. In line with this situation, Vallaeys (2008) argues that the social functions of universities should be delineated by some essences, namely: (1) ensure the social responsibility of science; (2) promote the formation of democratic citizenship; and (3) contribute to development through the training of students as agents of development.

The university must keep pace with the major transformations in society. Universities are gradually taking on a strategic role in developing innovation systems and increasing cooperation between universities and industry (Ankrah and Al-Tabbaa, 2015; Mascarenhas et al., 2018). This is due to the growing recognition of the importance of university research in the emergence of new innovations and also due to structural economic changes that place budgetary constraints on universities through public funding (Çengel, 2017; Schiuma and Carlucci, 2018). In this sense, universities are obliged to look for new sources of resources for research.

Academic entrepreneurship presents itself as the third mission of universities that adds a new component to their traditional teaching and research functions. In this new function, concepts such as knowledge transfer, technology transfer, service contracts, licensing and creation of academic spin-offs are included. For academic spin-offs, the university serves as a source of competitive advantage by providing qualified work, specialized facilities, and a source of knowledge (Rasmussen and Wright, 2015). Additionally, many of them are located within science parks, which facilitate the access to knowledge, increase synergies between the various companies and reduce labor costs (Berbegal-Mirabent et al., 2015).

Social responsibility is also a relevant function to be developed by academic spin-offs. According to Pattnaik and Pandey (2014), these companies have a high potential for generating financial returns, but their effect on CSR is still little explored. The only relevant study developed in this area is presented by Penttilä (2018) who analyzed whether CSR practices generate spin-off returns. The findings of this study indicated that high-CSR spin-offs earn 2.5–3.0% more than low-CSR counterparts. However, this study did not intend to explore the practices developed by these spin-offs in the multiple dimensions that constitute the CSR.

6.3 METHODOLOGY

6.3.1 DESIGN

The study adopts a qualitative methodology based on four case studies performed with Portuguese academic spin-offs. Within the scope of this study, three research lines were defined: (RQ1) explore the CSR practices implemented by academic spin-offs in multiples dimensions; (RQ2) challenges and difficulties in executing those CSR practices; and (RQ3) connection between the academic spin-off and the parent university in implementing those CSR practices.

The case study is a research method that aims to understand complex social phenomena while preserving the holistic features of real-life events. Yin (2017) points out that case studies prove to be especially indicated as strategy when: (1) there are exploratory questions that seek to understand the form or causes of a given phenomenon; (2) the researcher has little control over the events; and (3) the phenomena are contemporary and should be observed in the context in which they occur. Additionally, Queirós et al. (2017) mention that case studies are relevant in the identification and analysis of multiple variables under analysis. In the context of this study, it can be seen that case studies turn possible to understand an emerging phenomenon about which the existing information in the literature is very scarce especially when applied to the specific domain of academic spin-offs. The case studies were conducted using semi-structured interviews, which allowed us to collect the opinions of the various interviewees on each of the previously formulated research questions. The semi-structured interview is characterized by a compromise between the previously established script of questions and some spontaneity and improvisation. Jamshed (2014) argues that this approach offers a high degree of flexibility, allows a greater focus on the key topic of the interview, and offers conditions for the emergence of spontaneous responses.

A case study protocol composed of seven elements (i.e., background, design, data collection, analysis, plan validity, study limitations, and schedule) was defined to ensure the case study reliability. This approach is highlighted as crucial by Golafshani (2003) who advocates the use of reliability, validity, and triangulation to reflect the multiple ways of establishing truth in a case study research method. Furthermore, all semi-structured interviews have been transcribed. This approach allowed us to identify and highlight key quotes in each response, which in a later analysis allowed the identification of patterns within the data.

Figure 6.1 shows the various phases of the methodology. The methodology was broken down into three phases. In the preliminary phase, a theoretical framework of the subject is carried out and the relevant research lines for this study are defined. Next, the methodological aspects of the study are defined, namely the structure of the case studies and the academic spin-offs that participated in this study were selected. In the fieldwork stage, the case study was conducted with each selected entity and, after that, each interview is transcribed and registered. Finally in the analysis stage, an individual and joint analysis of each case study are conducted in order to compare it with the other findings obtained from the other conducted interviews. Still at this stage, the obtained results are compared with the previously published studies and the main conclusions are drawn.

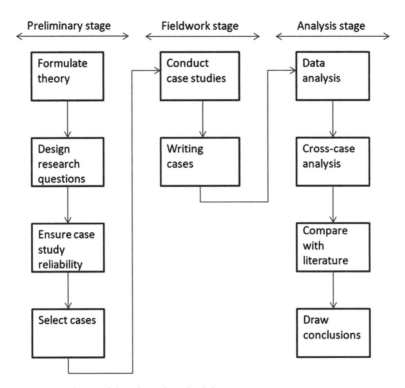

FIGURE 6.1 Phases of the adopted methodology.

Table 6.1 presents the background and context of the case studies. Each of them corresponds to one different academic spin-off. The spin-offs were selected according to their geographical area and sector of activity. Four different sectors of activity were considered, respectively: (1) marketing, (2) retail, (3) information technology, and (4) health.

TABLE 6.1   Overview of Case Studies.

Case study	Description
CS1	Digital marketing service provider that creates, develops, and implements Web Marketing solutions.
CS2	Company that develops and integrates innovative technology in retail solutions.
CS3	Company that provides computer programming and technology consultancy services in the field of artificial intelligence and Internet of things (IoT).
CS4	Company that develops mobile applications and services (apps) to the e-health sector.

6.3.2   INTERVIEW STRUCTURE

Table 6.2 presents the structure of the case study protocol. Two dimensions were considered: diagnostic and evaluative. The diagnostic dimension intends to analyze the process of defining a CSR policy, namely identify who initiated this process in each academic spin-off, which practices were implemented and what is the role of the parent university in this process. Finally, the evaluative dimension aims to assess the means established to measure the success of a CSR policy and explore the main benefits and challenges of implementing a CRS policy.

TABLE 6.2   Case Study Protocol.

No.	Question
Diagnostic dimension	
Q1	Has a CSR policy been established?
Q2	Who led this process?
Q3	What practices have been implemented?

TABLE 6.2   *(Continued)*

No.	Question
Q4	What is the role of the parent university in this process?
Evaluative dimension	
Q5	How is the success of CSR policy measured?
Q6	What are the main benefits of the CSR for the company and university?
Q7	What are the main challenges and difficulties in implementing the CSR policy?

6.4   ANALYSIS AND DISCUSSION OF RESULTS

6.4.1   DIAGNOSTIC DIMENSION

Q1. Has a CSR Policy Been Established?

All interviewed spin-offs indicated that they have a CSR policy. The implementation of the CSR policy is carried out formally through the definition of company values. The organizational values represent the beliefs and attitudes that give personality to the company and allow defining the ethics for the behavior of employees inside and outside the organization. The application of ethical values is seen as essential by those companies to achieve positive results in the long-term.

CS2 mentions that much more important than formally defining the values and ethical principles of the organization, it becomes fundamental to practice these values through daily actions and attitudes. The values are presented as a fundamental part of the organizational identity since they represent the ethics that govern the way of acting of employees and the organization as a whole. CS1 mentions that these ethical values increase in importance as the company grows and in which emerges the risk of practices' segmentation by departmental silos.

One point that has also been explored is how the organization's values should be established. To this end, the organization should ask about a number of issues such as: (1) What are the ethical and moral convictions that the founders of the company consider fundamental?, (2) What values and processes should the organization and its employees adopt in their relationships?, (3) What are the main points of interface between the organization and its external environment?, (4) What social and environmental concerns does the organization have?, and (5) Do the organization's ethical principles contribute to a more ethical and sustainable business?

Q2. Who Led This Process?

In all case studies, it was unanimous that this process was led by the founders of the academic spin-offs. Contrary to what is typically mentioned in the literature in which Yuan et al. (2017) and Henderson (2018) emphasize the role of the CEO in defining a CSR policy; in academic spin-offs, this role is shared by all the founders. It is often the case that the founders of the spin-off play the role of Chief Executive Officer (CEO), but this is not always the case for all academic spin-offs, since the founders can often take on other roles in the company such as Chief Technical Officer (CTO), Chief Financial Officer (CFO), marketing manager, and among others. In other cases especially in the initial phase of the foundation of an academic spin-off, these processes are typically hybrid and the same person has to play multiple roles.

The definition of the CSR policy is typically made prior to the formal establishment of the start-up. When building the business plan, the organizational values that govern the company are already specified and these elements are fundamental to guideline the behavior of the employees of the organization.

Q3. What Practices Have Been Implemented?

A very significant and diverse number of practices have been identified. Externally, there was a full consensus that business should be conducted with honesty, integrity, and transparency. Also mentioned by all academic spin-offs was the involvement in community activities. The General Data Protection Regulation (GDPR) is another element that has contributed to greater transparency of CSR practices. Thus, companies in the context of their activities are obliged to provide information on data processing and privacy policy. This new legislation protects individuals with regard to the processing of personal data and the free movement of such data. According to Sweet (2016), the GDRP has contributed to increasing citizens' privacy, trust, and loyalty. From an internal point of view, all the case studies mentioned the importance of offering a work–life balance, which can be achieved through the definition of flexible working practices. Additionally, the offer of training for employees was also highlighted as relevant.

The creation of sustainable products and the efficient use of energy were emphasized by CS3. One of the many possibilities that the use of IoT enables is energy efficiency in industry, which aims at reducing costs, increasing competitiveness, and sustainability. CS3 also mentioned that the use of sensors generates information in real-time, which allows monitoring and controlling the emission rates of pollutant gases. Another point mentioned by CS3 is the share of real-time information with partners when something in a solution goes wrong. This contributes to increasing the level of trust of partners and customers in the company.

After sales, service was emphasized by CS4 as a relevant CSR practice. At this level, the company offers 24-h day assistance, forums, and online chats to support customers' doubts. This approach allows them to react to customers' complain immediately. CS4 also adopts a product testing approach before placing a product on the market. This increases the degree of user involvement with the company (Haukipuro et al., 2016).

In turn, CS1 and CS2 hold conferences with the community. These conferences were held in partnership with other companies namely with other academic spin-offs. There are also initiatives aimed at disseminating the activities of these companies to final-year students in higher education and secondary education. For example, there are ideas competition initiatives that are supported by these companies. There is also an incentive from these companies for their employees to participate in entrepreneurship and innovation activities.

Q4. What Is the Role of the Parent University in this Process?

Despite the unequivocal growth potential offered by academic spin-offs, the financial capacity of these companies is very limited in their incubation phase and in their first years of activity. In this sense, and as most CSR practices that involve the community require significant financial resources, the establishment of partnerships for the implementation of these initiatives becomes essential. Two entities emerge as assuming a central role: science parks and parent university.

Science parks turn possible to share resources and facilities with other installed start-ups. This allows the organization of initiatives in conjunction with other companies installed in the same science park. Furthermore, the administration of the science parks helps in the process of attracting sponsorship for the realization of these initiatives.

The parent university also plays an important role in the development of CSR practices. This role can be more formal or informal. It has been found that in universities that have Technology Transfer Office (TTO) this role is more formal. However, its existence does not restrict or decrease the role of universities in this process. When there is no TTO, then the coordinator/director of each course in the educational institution assumes a more relevant role in supporting this process.

6.4.2   DIAGNOSTIC DIMENSION

Q5. How Is the Success of CSR Policy Measured?

Despite the importance of conducting CSR practices, none of the companies considered in the case studies quantitatively assesses the success of these initiatives. This assessment is carried out informally by each involved company typically highlighting the positive and negative aspects of these events. Two of the case studies that adopt the SCRUM methodology in the development process mentioned the existence of retrospective sessions to assess the success of CSR practices. The difficulty in quantifying the financial benefits of a CSR policy is addressed in the literature. Cramer and Bergmans (2003) propose that the added value offered by CSR can be estimated considering the sum of cost reductions that can be quantified directly and the future profits that can be qualitatively evaluated.

Q6. What are the Main Benefits of the CSR for the Company and University?

All the interviewed companies considered that the CSR practices should not intend to have an immediate objective of obtaining benefits for the companies. Nevertheless, a number of benefits were recognized that mainly emerge in a medium and long-term context.

One of the aspects that were unanimously recognized is the enhancing visibility and reputation, especially through the increase in media coverage. This situation, and the organization of these initiatives itself, contributes to increasing the motivation of employees, which encourages both professional and personal development. Furthermore, these actions promote creativity. According to McVicker (2016), thinking outside the box is a competence that companies should increasingly encourage among their employees. Finally, the increased visibility of the company helps to attract new candidates to the company.

Another aspect emphasized by CS3 is the increased efficiency of the organization that CSRs practices make possible. The search for new and more sustainable production methods contribute to increasing the differentiation of the products and services offered by companies compared to the competition. This increases sales and customer loyalty. Therefore as stated by Nave and Ferreira (2019), CSR plays a double role of organization: (1) by increasing the added-value and (2) by defining their development strategies.

The establishment of partnerships in the organization of CSR initiatives enables these collaborations to be extended to other areas of the organization. CS1 mentioned that through it new internationalization partnerships were established, while CS3 mentioned the establishment of partnerships in the searching for more sustainable and ecological production methods. It was also mentioned the potential that CSR initiatives offer in the attractiveness of new investors. This situation is also reported by Lee et al. (2017) who identified a positive effect of CSR performance on foreign ownership.

Finally, it was unanimously considered that an improved social environment promotes business activity which will, consequently, be beneficial to the organization itself. The increase in the economic and social conditions of the population where the company operates contributes to business development (Khan and Quaddus, 2015; Stephan et al., 2016).

Q7. What are the Main Challenges and Difficulties in Implementing the CSR Policy?

Despite the growing interest in the implementation of CSR practices evidenced by academic spin-offs, several challenges and difficulties persist. One of the difficulties common to all interviewed companies is the difficulty in allocating financial and human resources on CSR practices. Shen et al. (2015) confirm this vision and state that financial restrictions and the lack of training and stakeholder awareness represent the main barriers to the implementation of CSR practices in the textile industry. These results suggest that those identified pieces of evidences are equally valid for other sectors of activity. In the case of academic spin-offs, these financial and human difficulties are increased due to the financing restrictions inherent to start-up activities and the reduced number of employees.

Despite this and as pointed out by CS1 and CS3, the existence of young and highly qualified human resources increases the level of awareness of these employees due to ethical and social issues. Many of them, outside their working environment, are involved in solidarity activities such as the food bank against hunger and solidarity sports initiatives.

Another encountered difficulty is the need for CSR initiatives to ensure proper internal and external support. Sometimes due to commitments established in business projects, it becomes difficult to allocate human resources to participate in CSR initiatives. Turning project delivery pressures compatible with CSR activities emerge as a challenge. The nonexistence of clear CSR guidelines creates additional difficulties for the organization of CSR initiatives. Nasrullah and Rahim (2014) advocates that the absence of clear CSR guidelines in companies makes these initiatives difficult to manage and replicate.

CS2 also mentions difficulties in managing employee involvement in these initiatives. Sometimes there is a lack of consensus and some brainstorming sessions become necessary to clarify the main points that are intended to address with each initiative. Another situation reported by CS2 is the need for CSR activities to be faced by companies as an innovation practice. In fact, as established by Rexhepi et al. (2013) and Shen et al. (2016), there is a relationship between innovation and CSR, so that higher innovation firms receive more financial benefits from their CSR activities.

6.5 CONCLUSIONS

The establishment of a CSR policy is relevant for academic spin-offs. All the interviewed companies have established and implemented a CSR policy that is put into practice through the definition of company values and several initiatives that are carried out in partnership with parent universities, science parks, and other organizations. The establishment of partnerships in the realization of CSR initiatives becomes even more relevant for academic spin-offs that have a reduced number of employees and significant financial restrictions mainly in the first years of activity.

A very significant and diverse number of CSR practices were identified. One of the fundamental pillars for the implementation of these practices is the code of conduct that employees should follow, supported by honesty, integrity, and transparency. The GDPR has also contributed to increasing the transparency of the relationship between academic spin-offs and external stakeholders. Other practices were also identified such as employee training, the existence of flexible working practices, adoption of after-sales services, the holding of conferences with the community, and the creation of sustainable products and efficient use of energy.

Typically academic spin-offs do not have formal mechanisms for assessing the success of CSR initiatives. This assessment is typically recorded in an informal manner, but it was possible to identify several benefits brought to the academic spin-offs, such as increased external visibility and reputation, promotion of creativity, the establishment of partnerships and the promotion of an economic and social environment more favorable to the establishment of new businesses. On the other hand, the main challenges and difficulties include the lack of human and financial resources to allocate to these initiatives ensure the participation of stakeholders, nonexistence of clear CSR guidelines and difficulties in managing employee's engagement.

As a future work, it would be relevant to perform a longitudinal study to monitor the impact of CSR practices on the development of academic spin-offs. The aim is to explore how the various practices of CSR practices have contributed to the financial return of these companies to increase their visibility and reputation, to increase the number of partnerships, or to increase their human capital. Finally, it would also be relevant to carry out an empirical work to comparatively analyze the impact of CSR practices on academic spin-offs and corporate spin-offs, distinguishing the importance of the role of parent universities and parent companies in this process.

KEYWORDS

- **corporate social responsibility**
- **academic spin-offs**
- **start-ups**
- **business ethics**
- **competitiveness**
- **business management**

REFERENCES

Anderson, C.; Spataro, S. E.; Flynn, F. J. Personality and Organizational Culture as Determinants of Influence. *J. Appl. Psychol.* **2008**, *93* (3), 702–710.

Ankrah, S.; Al-Tabbaa, O. Universities-industry Collaboration: A Systematic Review. *Scandinavian J. Manag.* **2015**, *31* (3), 387–408.

Berbegal-Mirabent, J.; Ribeiro-Soriano, D. E.; García, J. L. S. Can a Magic Recipe Foster University Spin-off creation? *J. Bus. Res.* **2015**, *68* (11), 2272–2278.

Çengel, Y. Universities as Cornerstones in Science, Technology and Innovation Ecosystems. *Int. J. Res., Innov. Commercial.* **2017**, *1* (1), 23–40.

Chandler, D. *Strategic Corporate Social Responsibility: Sustainable Value Creation*; SAGE Publications: Thousand Oaks, CA, 2016.

Cramer, J.; Bergmans, F. *Learning About Corporate Social Responsibility: The Dutch Experience*; IOS Press: Amsterdam, The Netherlands, 2003.

Dahlsrud, A. How Corporate Social Responsibility Is Defined: An Analysis of 37 Definitions. *Corp. Soc. Respon. Environ. Manag.* **2008**, *15* (1), 1–13.

Ehrhart, M. *Organizational Climate and Culture*; Routledge: London, 2013.

Freitas, S.; Mayer, I.; Arnab, S.; Marshall, I. Industrial and Academic Collaboration: Hybrid Models for Research and Innovation Diffusion. *J. Higher Educ. Policy Manag.* **2014**, *36* (1), 2–14.

Galbreath, J. How Does Corporate Social Responsibility Benefit Firms? Evidence from Australia. *Eur. Bus. Rev.* **2010**, *22* (4), 411–431.

Giuffré, L.; Ratto, S. A New Paradigm in Higher Education: University Social Responsibility (USR). *J. Educ. Human Dev.* **2014**, *3* (1), 231–238.

Golafshani, N. Understanding Reliability and Validity in Qualitative Research. *Qual. Rep.* **2003**, *8* (4), 597–606.

Hameed, I.; Riaz, Z.; Arain, G.; Farooq, O. How Do Internal and External CSR Affect Employees' Organizational Identification? A Perspective from the Group Engagement Model. *Front. Psychol.* **2016**, *7*, 1–13.

Haukipuro, L.; Väinämö, S.; Torvinen, H. End-user Involvement Enhancing Innovativeness in Public Procurement. Evidence from a Healthcare Procurement. *J. Innov. Manag.* **2016**, *4* (4), 98–121.

Hawn, O.; Ioannou, I. Mind the Gap: The Interplay between External and Internal Actions in the Case of Corporate Social Responsibility. *Strategic Manag. J.* **2016,** *37* (13), 2569–2588.

Henderson, R. More and More CEOs are Taking Their Social Responsibility Seriously. *Harv. Bus. Rev.* **2018**. Retrieved 17 February 2019 from https://hbr.org/2018/02/more-and-more-ceos-are-taking-their-social-responsibility-seriously

Hope, M. Becoming Citizens through School Experience: A Case Study of Democracy in Practice. *Int. J. Progress. Educ.* **2012**, *8* (3), 94–108.

Jamshed, S. Qualitative Research Method-interviewing and Observation. *J. Basic Clin. Pharm.* **2014**, *5* (4), 87–88.

Kadlubek, M. The Essence of Corporate Social Responsibility and the Performance of Selected Company. *Procedia Soc. Behav. Sci.* **2015**, *213*, 509–515.

Khan, E.; Quaddus, M. Examining the Influence of Business Environment on Socio-economic Performance of Informal Microenterprises: Content Analysis and Partial Least Square Approach. *Int. J. Soc. Soc. Policy* **2015**, *35* (3/4), 273–288.

Lee, J.; Kim, S.; Kwon, I. Corporate Social Responsibility as a Strategic Means to Attract Foreign Investment: Evidence from Korea. *Sustainability* **2017**, *9*, 1–11.

Martins, A.; Martins, I.; Pereira, O. Challenges Enhancing Social and Organizational Performance. In *Handbook of Research on Human Resources Strategies for the New Millennial Workforce*; Ordoñez de Pablos, P., Tennyson, R., Eds.; IGI Global: Hershey, PA, 2017; pp 28–46.

Mascarenhas, C.; Ferreira, J.; Marques, C. University–industry Cooperation: A Systematic Literature Review and Research Agenda. *Sci. Public Policy* **2018**, *45* (5), 708–718.

McVicker, D. What Happens To Your Life When You Start Thinking Outside-The-Box, 2016. Retrieved 17 February 2019; from https://www.collective-evolution.com/2016/03/27/what-happens-to-your-life-when-you-start-thinking-outside-the-box/

Nasrullah, N. M.; Rahim, M. M. Understanding of CSR and Its Standards. In *CSR in Private Enterprises in Developing Countries*; CSR, Sustainability, Ethics & Governance: Springer, Cham, 2014.

Nave, A.; Ferreira, J. Corporate Social Responsibility Strategies: Past Research and Future Challenges. *Corp. Soc. Respons. Environ. Manage.*, in Press **2019**, 1–17.

Pattnaik, P. N.; Pandey, S. C. University Spinoffs: What, Why, and How? *Technol. Innov. Manage. Rev.* **2014**, *4* (12), 44–50.

Penttilä, S. Does Being Good Pay Off? Corporate Social Responsibility and Spin-off Returns. Aalto University, 2018. Retrieved 15 February 2019; from https://aaltodoc.aalto.fi/handle/123456789/32521

Queirós, A.; Faria, D.; Almeida, F. Strengths and Limitations of Qualitative and Quantitative Research Methods. *Eur. J. Educ. Studies* **2017**, *3* (9), 369–387.

Rahman, A.; Castka, P.; Love, T. Corporate Social Responsibility in Higher Education. *Corp. Soc. Respon. Environ. Manage.*, In Press **2019**, 1–13.

Rasmussen, E.; Wright, M. How Can Universities Facilitate Academic Spin-offs? An Entrepreneurial Competency Perspective. *J. Technol. Transfer* **2015**, *40* (5), 782–799.

Rexhepi, G.; Kurtishi, S.; Bexheti, G. Corporate Social Responsibility (CSR) and Innovation–The Drivers of Business Growth? *Procedia Soc. Behav. Sci.* **2013**, *75*, 532–541.

Robbins, S.; Judge, T. *Organizational Behavior*; Pearson PLC: London, 2014.

Schein, E. *Organizational Culture and Leadership*; Wiley: New Jersey, 2016.

Schiuma, G.; Carlucci, D. Managing Strategic Partnerships with Universities in Innovation Ecosystems: A Research Agenda. *J. Open Innov.: Technol. MarketComplexity* **2018**, *4* (25), 1–13.

Shen, L.; Govindan, K.;Shankar, M. Evaluation of Barriers of Corporate Social Responsibility Using an Analytical Hierarchy Process under a Fuzzy Environment—A Textile Case. *Sustainability* **2015**, *7*, 3493–3514.

Shen, R.; Tang, Y.; Zhang, Y. Does Firm Innovation Affect Corporate Social Responsibility? Harvard Business School, 2016, Working Paper 16-096. Retrieved 18 February 2019; from https://www.hbs.edu/faculty/Publication%20Files/16-096_392dc4f5-d30a-4be9-9bb2-d8f774cf08a6.pdf

Smith, J.; Pelco, L.; Rooke, A. The Emerging Role of Universities in Collective Impact Initiatives for Community Benefit. *Metropol. Univ.* **2017**, *28* (4), 9–30.

Sparrow, P.; Cooper, C. Organizational Effectiveness, People and Performance: New Challenges, New Research Agendas. *J. Org. Effect.: People Perform.* **2014**, *1* (1), 2–13.

Stephan, U.; Patterson, M.; Kelly, C.; Mair, J. Organizations Driving Positive Social Change: A Review and an Integrative Framework of Change Processes. *J. Manag.* **2016**, *42* (5), 1250–1281.

Sweet, E. The New EU General Data Protection Regulation—Benefits and First Steps to Meeting Compliance. *ISACA J.* 2016. Retrieved 17 February 2019; from https://www.isaca.org/Journal/Pages/default.aspx

Taghian, M.; D'Souza, C.; Polonsky, M. A Stakeholder Approach to Corporate Social Responsibility, Reputation and Business Performance. *Soc. Respon. J.* **2015**, *11* (2), 340–363.

Vallaeys, F. Responsabilidad social universitaria: una nueva filosofía de gestión ética e inteligente para las universidades. *Revista Educación Superior y Sociedad* **2008**, *13* (2), 193–220.

Wigmore-Álvarez, A.; Ruiz-Lozano, M. University Social Responsibility (USR) in the Global Context: An Overview of Literature. *Busi. Prof. Ethics J.* **2012**, *31* (3–4), 475–498.

Yin, R. *Case Study Research and Applications: Design and Methods*; SAGE Publications: Thousand Oaks, CA, 2017.

Yuan, Y.; Tian, G.; Lu, L.; Yu, Y. CEO Ability and Corporate Social Responsibility. *J. Bus. Ethics* **2017**, 1–21.

CHAPTER 7

Role of Integrated Marketing Communication for Promoting Indian Women's Health and Wellbeing: With Reference of CSR Perspective

SHARMILA KAYAL[1] and RUMA SAHA[2*]

[1]Adamas University, Barasat 700126, Kolkata, India

[2]Manipal University Jaipur, Rajasthan, India

*Corresponding author. E-mail: ruma.saha.kolkata@gmail.com

ABSTRACT

The domain of integrated marketing communication is inevitable in the era of industrialization especially in sphere of corporate social responsibility (CSR). In this paradox, the role of public service advertisements is indispensible. A public service advertisement are the informative and tries to make people aware about many social and wellbeing phenomenon; which proved as an articulate and persuasive strategic approach. In the era of industrialization, the different industry and corporates comprises with the social commitment of peripheral development activities and its promise enhances the various clusters indulge with self-help group (SSG's and SSH's), the small scale industry, the non-government organization for better healthcare. In this context, the CSR activity generally focuses on women's health care and wellbeing through different promotional event because they are indirectly targeted group for peripheral upliftment for their philanthropically nuances. This present aims to explore the various public service advertisements as a part of integrated marketing communication for the purpose of executing the activities of CSR. The content analysis method will be applied with fifteen distinct themes with fifteen main categories of PSA's regarding women's healthcare and wellbeing. Thematic approach shall be prevailed to explore the phenomenon of integrated marketing communication. This present research highlights the how the various leading industry/corporations adopted the social concern of women's health and wellbeing as PSA's and it caters to the need of CSR activities with its holistic approach to the society in true sense.

7.1   INTRODUCTION

7.1.1   *WHAT IS INTEGRATED MARKETING COMMUNICATION?*

Integrated marketing communication (IMC) refers to combining all the methods used in brand promotion to promote or advertise a product to their target audience. All aspects of marketing communication works together for the purpose of increasing sales figure at cost effective ways Management Study Guide (MSG).

Components of IMC:

1. Foundations
2. Corporate culture
3. Brand focus
4. Consumer experience
5. Communication tools
6. Promotional tools
7. Integration tools

IMC encourages all aspects of marketing mix to work together to promote products and services within target audience who are the prospective end-users. This creates brand consciousness as a result whenever the targeted audiences go for shopping and remember the brand name MSG.

7.1.1.1   *WHAT IS CSR?*

Corporate social responsibility is the full-form of CSR. It is an approach that is used to encourage sustainable development by delivering duties related to society, environment, economy at large which in a way also benefits its' stake holder. In other word, it can be said that it is a movement which aimed at encouraging corporations or enterprises to be aware of their business effect on the rest of the society that includes their stake-holders too (Lexicon).

7.1.1.2   HOW IS IT RELATED TO INTEGRATED MARKETING COMMUNICATION?

CSR is considered as parameter in the current competitive atmosphere the reason behind it is partly as it fulfils stakeholders' expectation. Corporate philanthropy was popular since 1980s eventually it became strategic philanthropy. Two purposes were served through this. First, there is an attempt to build up the important relationships, second to build positive image which will add to the goodwill of the company. During 1990s through this philanthropic activity, company was gaining tangible value in the form of brand image (Coy, 2011).

7.1.1.3   PUBLIC SERVICE ADVERTISEMENT AS MARKETING COMMUNICATION

Public service Advertisement is also a part of marketing communication which is circulated without any cost and is for welfare of public. It is designed for the purpose of communicating and communicated via media for societal improvement as well as overall wellbeing of community. Public service advertisement has evolved during World War I; its objective is beyond money making rather resolve societal problems in disguise. PSA in a way change the behavioral aspects of the community rather than focusing on just sales profit. This type of advertisement uses an approach which is more action oriented and encourages people to think about the social issues and be aware (Zkjadoon, 2016).

7.2   REVIEW OF THE RELATED LITERATURE

7.2.1   CSR AND PUBLIC HEALTH

In the research paper "A call to action on women's health: putting corporate CSR standards for workplace health on the global health agenda" by David Wofford et al. (2016), they focused on how corporation fails to address important health issues related to woman health like reproductive health of woman workers. The research has found that CSR policy has largely neglected the area of health needs of woman workers. The researchers argued that global health community needs to re-think the role of companies in public health especially women (Wofford, 2016).

In a recent research article on "CSR in global health: an exploratory study of multinational pharmaceutical firms" by Hayley Droppert and Sara Bennett in 2015, it is said that the increasing pressure of civil society on pharmacy companies has forced them to reform its CSR policy. The methodology applied in this research is exploratory study with in-department review of CSR policy of pharmacy companies as well as interview conducted for representatives of six big pharmacy companies selected on the basis of highest earning in last year. Findings of the research shows that primary factor which motivate CSR policy and engagement are reputational benefit, better raking of sustainable indices, employee satisfaction, long-term economic return, improved population health etc. (Droppert and Bennett, 2015).

7.2.1.1   CORPORATE SOCIAL RESPONSIBILITY

In the recent book on "The CSR Agenda" by Crane et al. in 2008, a critical analysis and discussion is done on the matter of how corporate world is practicing CSR policy and which obliging factor guides it in their formulation (Crane et al., 2008).

In the research article on "CSR in the 21st Century: A View from the World's Most Successful Firms" by Snider et al. in 2003, it is investigated how firms are communicating to their stakeholders about their CSR policy. The research methodology was qualitative in nature. An analysis was done of Forbe magazine websites especially ethical and moral sections of fifty US top ranking companies and fifty non-US top ranking companies on the basis of stakeholder theory. The result gave thematic outcome with the focus on how managers of multi-national firms are taking this social responsibility and what are its implications on them. The researchers also focused on business ethics in this regards (Snider et al., 2003).

In a recent research on "CSR" by Tai and Chuang (2014), it showed that enterprise is not only a profit making tool, but also has the responsibility to prove good citizenry. In order to prove good citizenry, the enterprise has some social responsibility to fulfill. Researchers address CSR implications in active and passive ways in which MNCs or MNEs can get affected by sustainable development. The research involved both qualitative analysis and quantitative survey to analyze the promotion of social responsibility by the enterprises into workplace. The result aimed at determining the real analysis of CSR implementation and implication within enterprise (Tai and Chuang, 2014).

Research is done on "How CSR pays off" by Burke and Logsdon in 1996. The researcher tried to investigate social responsibility programs that create specific benefits for the firm. The researcher has developed five strategy dimensions to identify the value created for the company by CSR program. In the conclusion, researchers gave guidelines for managers to incorporate these dimensions in analyzing their social responsibility (Burke and Logsdon, 1996).

The research article on "Beyond women workers: gendering CSR" by Ruth Pearson (2007) explores the holistic approach of CSR which address its impact on different gender. The researcher has analyzed this with the help of the concept of social reproduction. The analysis has examined the issues related to gender biasness and how the term "social" is used to encourage the workers in production. The findings of this research suggests inclusion of gender dimension into the all round notion of CSR (Pearson, 2007).

7.2.2   INTEGRATED MARKETING COMMUNICATION AND PSA

In the research article on "Company Advertising with a Social Dimension: The Role of Noneconomic Criteria" by Minette E. Drumwright (1996), it is examined what objectives does the manager of the company advertising with social dimension have and try understand the reason behind their success story. The researchers have developed models to explain this process. The research tries to analyze and discuss mechanism underlying social campaign's effectiveness with company oriented objective for campaign. They also discussed ethical considerations and managerial implication of these campaigns (Drumwright, 1996).

Recent research on "Marketing communications and corporate social responsibility (CSR): marriage of convenience or shotgun wedding?" by Jahdi and Acikdilli (2009) examines the roles of various vehicles of

IMC with respect to CSR policies to their stakeholders. Researchers also examined the impact of this type of communication on brand image of the company. The findings of the research shows that marketing communication tools plays important role in conveying CSR message and also enhancing company's image in society to their stakeholders (Jahdi and Acikdilli, 2009).

7.2.2.1   PSA AND WOMAN HEALTH

Research is done on "An analysis of 6 decades of hygiene-related advertising: 1940–2000" by Aiello and Larson in 2001. They focused on all hygiene related advertisement and examine potential changes in social framework which lead to regulatory changes due to recent trends in advertising. Their period of study was restricted to 1940–2000. They have studied mostly the magazine advertisements. The methodology involved content analysis of the advertisements. Specific advertisements were grouped into few categories like personal hygiene, dishwashing, house cleaning, and laundry. These categories were further examined for the claim of aesthetics, time-saving, health-effects, and microbial effects. Findings of the research show that in the entire study, time period 10.4% of the total advertisements is devoted to PSA. Apart from this, decade of 1960s showed remarkable decline in hygiene related advertisement when compared to 1940s and 1950s. There is a significant growth in the PSA from 1980s onward. The result of the study also reflects a cyclical attention for PSA especially with the category of personal hygiene and house cleaning during the period in study (Aiello and Larson, 2001).

Research has taken place on "Alcohol Advertising and Violence against Women: A Media Advocacy Case Study" by Woodruff in 1996. The research article focused on prevention of violence against woman by addressing social factors like sexist advertising image in alcohol beverage. The research aimed at studying this Dangerous Promises Campaign based on issue like sexist advertising image contribute to incite violence against woman. The goal of this campaign is to convince the alcohol companies to remove sexist alcohol advertisement. The study focuses on media advocacy as prime cause of success of this campaign. This research examines the outcomes and strategies of Dangerous Promises Campaign till date and study the extent of media advocacy gaining attention while doing policy making (Woodruff, 1996).

Another research by Waller on "Consumer offence towards the advertising of some gender related products" in 2007 shows how controversial advertising campaign cause offensive to people. The paper focuses on the importance of proper way of message delivery through these advertisements else it might sound unpleasant and offensive which in turn creates negative publicity or emotions. The researcher has survey among 265 university student to find whether they consider gender-related product advertisement offensive or vulgar due to their execution techniques. The result shows that there were number of execution techniques of advertisement for gender-based products which are considered offensive. Moreover, statistical comparison is also done on the basis of age and gender (Waller, 2007).

Research is also done on "The portrayal of the menstruating woman in menstrual product advertisements" by L. B. Courts in 1993. The researcher has conducted a comparative conceptual analysis of menstrual product advertisement to show media constructed realities of contemporary woman. The research aimed at understanding how the media portrayed woman defines menstruation and their status as menstruating woman. The outcome of the research shows that the media portrayed woman involves in complex menstruation management system and avoid being discovered of their menstruating status by others. The portrayed women as a result feminize menstrual products to avoid tainted state of feminity as an antidote (Courts, 1993).

7.3 RESEARCH GAP

> ➢ There is a lot of research in advertising and IMC as well as in CSR but there is a gap in literature in the area of public service announcement as CSR initiative.
> ➢ Moreover public service advertisement is a type of communication which is meant for public awareness without any profit motive so it also serves as CSR objective of societal responsibility to its stakeholders. There is a gap in this area of research.
> ➢ Furthermore, not adequate research is done with the geographic location of India where CSR policies of the companies and its relation with PSA is yet to be studied.

➢ Moreover, there is gap in research work on how public service advertisement on women health and well-being in Indian scenario is fulfilling objectives of CSR policy of Companies.

7.4 CONCEPTUAL FRAMEWORK

Public Service Advertisements and Corporate Social responsibilities in Women's health development and well-being goals are major contemporary issues. Innovation in this regard as PSA's represents an important tool for achieving CSR while sustainable development remains a challenge for business and in corporate sectors which emphasizes the direction that innovation activities can take place in a justified manner. The objective of this involvement is to specify innovation as well as the social responsibility outlines and to propose a conceptual framework of their complementarity in an enterprise perception. This approach enables for the present study to mirror on the role of innovation in liable entrepreneurship by exemplifying a structure which brings together these concepts in an integrated approach.

7.5 OPERATIONAL DEFINITION

❖ **Integrated Marketing Communication:** The early inception of IMC has been established into one of the most persuasive, dominant managerial structures; and its prominence has developed around the world domain (Avery and Orasmae, 2017). It is a planning in a very structured way in determining the effective and most consistent message for its suitable target audiences (Percy, 2008).

❖ **Public Service Advertisements:** The public service advertising generally endures with verbal and visual procedures. It can be best understood or applicable in the arena of public service advertising which well amalgamated with text and its visual contributing contents of an icon that have mainly in a system of non-language to support the language and the semiotics method as a typical analytic technique for analyzing the public service advertising mechanism proportionately to be used and responded in its contexts (Tinarbuko, 2008). A public service advertisement is enormously used by several in expectations of "selling" good health behaviors (Dorfman and Wallack, 1993). The advertisements generally on the other hand established the agenda for health issues, deliberating status on policy-oriented strategies for addressing health problems, and the main purpose of counter-ads is to encounter the dominant view that public health glitches mirror personal health habits (Dorfman and Wallack, 1993).

❖ **Corporate Social Responsibility:** CSR has emerged as an inescapable precedence for business/corporate leaders in universal arena. The various corporations if has to analyze their potential prospects for social responsibility using the identical frameworks that could monitor their core business or industrial affluent choices, they would rather ascertain that CSR can be much more than a cost effective, a continual constraint, or a charitable deed or it can be a basis of opportunity, innovation, and competitive advantage of gain (Porter and Kramer, 2006).

❖ **Women's Health and Wellbeing:** The report of the World Health Organizations aligned with the sustainable development goals in vision of The Global Strategy for Women's, children's and Adolescent's health (2016–20130) is to *"by 2030, a world in which every women, child and adolescent in every setting realizes their rights to physical, mental health and wellbeing, has social and economic opportunities and is able to participate fully in shaping prosperous and sustainable societies"* (UN Report, 2015).

❖ **Indian Scenario/Perspective:** India is one of the few countries in the world where women and men have closely about the equal life expectancy at birth. The fact that the typical female improvement in life expectancy is not evidently seen in India which advocates that there are systematic and grass root problems associated with women's health. Indian women have high mortality rates, particularly during childhood and in their reproductive years (Velkoff and Adlakha, 1998).

7.6   THEORETICAL FRAMEWORK

The CSR working group and its direct/indirect peripheral activities, the participation or active involvement of Community, Governance and operations, Workplace commitment and Environmental sustain-ability are the key factors which is generally associated with the CSR activity in different industry or organizations (both government and non government sector).. In this present study, it can be stated that these above-mentioned attributes are the independent variable in order to locus operands to the targeted group. Here, it mainly relies on the PSA to reach the potential consumers through IMC. PSA in this regard helps to fixation their mind (target group) in repeated through mass media in order to improve their cognition for brand communication as well as to take part in CSR activities.

7.6.1   THE MODEL OF "BRAND COMMUNICATION PLAN"

According to a study on "Brand Communication Plan" by Moriarty et al. (2016) discussed about the principle on finding or establishing the right audience to disseminate the right message to be adopted right medium or vehicles of communication to reach the target group. Following is the model which is relevant for this present study in order to understand how the PSA inculcating the CSR activities by fulfilling the criterion of IMC.

It is very clear that in CSR, how PSA helps in fragmenting the message through proper IMC. The vision of corporate or any industry is need not to do profit, rather if proper focus should be given to people not as the consumers or customers than they inculcate the established feelings which is much more important in respect of brand recognition or the brand value by establishing the good, positive image, and reputation. It should be personal not as mechanical because in a personal note only it will be very much effective to uphold the relation which should not be only profit basis but to touch their emotions by providing philanthropically attribution to its peripheral or a society as a whole.

7.6.2   DIFFUSION OF INNOVATION THEORY

The Diffusion of Innovation Theory by Everett Rogers (1962) also adopted in media especially to understand the PSA perspective. This theory is relevant to understand the target group and their level of acceptance to the various public service advertisements which is disseminated the various information regarding women's health and wellbeing.

First, it is the Innovator(s), then the early adopters, the early majority, then the late majority, and finally the Laggards. Each of these clusters plays a significant role in the process and the potential audiences tend to correlate with things like education, health and wellbeing, financial stability, and social class. There are always outliers, those who do not seem like in apt into the category they are placed in but catch themselves there anyway. On the other hand, it is quite possible that the Innovators came from any social strata and there may be absence of any formal education at all but they have an innate sense that something needs to be done and they find themselves doing it (Aeon, 2018). Early Adopters tend to be educated and have financial stability as one would guess, come from the higher levels of society.

7.7   RESEARCH QUESTIONS

Following are the basic research questions which are been to formulate and to analyze the taken components minutely for a prerogative emancipation of the components.

RQ 1. What is the main content of PSA's in relation to CSR?

RQ 2. Is it really practical to be implemented the success/failure through advertisements?

RQ 3. How IMC implies in to PSA?

RQ 4. Who are the main target group/audiences in relation to PSA in CSR?

RQ 5. How it's been assimilated the women's health and wellbeing?

RQ 6. Is the content of PSA for CSR activities are highly fragmented?

RQ 7. What is the element lies in PSA for this special group of women?

RQ 8. How the various leading industry/corporations adopted the social concern of women's health and wellbeing?

7.8   OBJECTIVE OF THE STUDY

Based on the research questions, the broad objectives of this study are:-

> ➢ To understand various public service advertisements as a part of IMC for the purpose of executing the activities of CSR.
> ➢ To explore the phenomenon of IMC.
> ➢ To know how the various leading industry/corporations adopted the social concern of women's health and wellbeing as PSA's and it caters to the need of CSR activities.

7.9   METHODOLOGY

Qualitative methodology is done for this present research. This present aims to explore the various public service advertisements as a part of IMC for the purpose of executing the activities of CSR.

7.10   DEFINING THE UNIVERSE

Thematic approach is prevailed to explore the phenomenon of IMC. This present research highlights the how the various leading industry/corporations adopted the social concern of women's health and wellbeing as PSA's and it caters to the need of CSR activities with its holistic approach to the society in true sense.

Following are the parameter and the contents were taken for this study to critically analyze the core concepts in order to understand the phenomenon.

a)   The website of Ministry of Health & Family Welfare

b)   The website of Ministry of Women and Child Development

c)   The website of Ministry of Rural Development

d)   The website of Ministry of micro, small, and medium Enterprises

e)   The website of Ministry of Skill Development &Entrepreneurship

f)   The website of Ministry of Drinking Water & Sanitation

g)   The website of National Health Mission.

The YouTube content and the PSA which were available and made in this regard are been divided into fifteen distinct theme and fifteen main categories is put forth and analyzed in respect to content analysis.

7.11   UNIT OF ANALYSIS

The content analysis method has been applied with fifteen distinct themes with fifteen main categories of PSA's regarding women's healthcare and wellbeing.

TABLE 7.1   Themes Taken for the Study.

1) Women's physical health	2) Gender equality
3) Social determinants of health	4) Women's health education
5) Combating gender stereotypes	6) Sanitation
7) Involuntary or unwanted sterilization	8) Hygiene
9) Women's mental health	10) Sexual reproductive rights
11) Stigmatizing women	12) Sexual and reproductive health
13) Discriminating against women	14) Impact of socio-economic inequalities
15) Gender-biased sex selection	16) Breast feeding

TABLE 7.2   Main Categories Taken for Study.

1) Depressive disorder of women	2) Dengue
3) Major cause of death of women in India	4) HIV/AIDS
5) Family planning	6) Iodine intake
7) Polio	8) Swine flu
9) Smoking/drinking alcohol	10) Institutional delivery
11) Mental health during pregnancy	12) Pre-natal care
13) Pregnancy (physical health)	14) Delivery (ante-natal & post-natal care)
15) Institutional delivery	16) Female feticide

7.12   FINDINGS

In order to explore how health messages are communicated to motivate behavior change in the concept of women's health and wellbeing, a content analysis was performed on all 13 print advertisements and six television public service announcements released in the various media and are enlisted by Government websites of 2014–2018 time period, which marked the 4 year interval gap of the theme related to women's health and wellbeing campaign. Content analysis is a method of research for "making reliable and valid implications from data to their context, with the drive of providing knowledge, new insights, a demonstration of facts and a practical guide to action" (Krippendorff, 1980). By carrying out a content analysis, the researcher is able to analyze messages and prepare the conclusions from data. To ensure precise results, the researcher develops a coding sheet in which categories are created for what exactly the researcher aspect for in the selected content. By creating categories and coding the content, certain characteristics of the message are been analyzed and interpreted for underlying themes and patterns (Krippendorff, 1980). Afore research was conducted to explore how health messages are communicated to motivate behavior change in the concept of women's health and wellbeing campaign, the researcher developed a coding sheet modeled after Atkin's re-search of effective PSA strategies, which were drawn from the diffusion of innovations theory and brand communication plan and CSR conceptual model; henceforth the research about successful health communication strategies (2018). Each PSA was analyzed with the same coding sheet to keep findings consistent. The coding sheet consists of sixteen categories: which is been enlisted in previous (Table 7.2).

PSAs were regarded a total of sixteen times by the researcher, each time to detect any element for each category. The researcher accessed these PSAs through the government's website and through the mass media, which is available on the campaign website. First, the researcher identified what message(s) about depressive disorder of women were being communicated to publics. The PSAs were then viewed to explore the possible method messages were communicated based on effective PSA strategies to facilitate behavior change; PSAs were studied based on the presence of messages of awareness, instruction, and persuasion (2018). Messages of awareness were considered to exist if the PSA defined the health topic, viewers were educated about what, how, when, and where to fix the health problem, and if viewers were prompted to explore the subject of family planning, iodine intake and polio reduction to a fuller extent. Messages of instruction were considered to exist if the action to prevent the taboo-related women's health and wellbeing was defined, positive effects of the action were clarified, encouragement and direction were provided to enhance self-efficacy, and if the ad referred back to the mass campaign website for further direction. Messages of persuasion were considered to exist if the source and the messenger were credible, gave "how to" information, demonstrated the desired behavior, and gave verbal reinforcement to publics. PSAs were also coded for their content. The researcher has also analyzed the different PSAs to see if they defined a target audience, were applicable in real-life situations and if the overall message how far was understandable and is been summarized in a systematic manner. These factors were further verified to determine the possible effectiveness or ineffectiveness in yielding behavior change among publics. Technical and artistic factors were also considered when analyzing PSAs to determine how the message was communicated through use of wit, music, humor, continuity of symbols, and social essence theme. Finally, the messages or information was checked to identify who was delivering the message—a celebrity, ordinary person, minority, or through animation or by popular cartoon character. The researcher again also documented qualitative comments for each PSA and was able to conjecture that the amount of the taken subject did not anticipate in any means. By coding PSAs for the existence of the above factors, the author was able to draw37—different content wise research in Communications campaign PSAs to motivate behavior change among publics.

7.13   ANALYSIS

> **Women's Physical Health:**

TABLE 7.3   PSA on HIV Test.

NACO India	Public service ad on HIV/AIDS	
93,392 views	Published on 30 Nov 2015	Promoting HIV testing among pregnant women
Main theme of this PSA-"KICK"		

The first attribute which has been taken for this study on the importance of HIV test in pregnancy. It is an initiative which is beautifully demonstrated the concept by portraying the foetus which is giving signal to its mother to undergo this test but the message compel the public to live in practical world and strictly test the HIV for both the lives.

TABLE 7.4   PSA on IUCD.

MOHFW	Public service ad on intra-uterine contraceptive devices	
31,799 views	Published on 16 Jul 2012	Promoting HIV testing among pregnant women
Main theme of this PSA-"KICK"		

This is an initiative of the technical support to the Government of India for developing a PSA for intra-uterine contraceptive devices (IUDs / IUCDs): The usage of IUD as family planning method in India has remained stagnant at around 2–3% since 1992 (Report, GOI, 2012). As a part of the national policy, the Ministry of Health and Family Welfare (MOHFW) has been endorsing long-term methods of contraception such as IUDs for spacing between children. Population Services International (PSI) approached MOHFW, and shared desk research and PSI's research which has presented both neonatal and maternal health outcomes improve when there is a gap of 3 years between births; and developed a communications strategy to communicate this to lower income women of reproductive age.

After receiving sanction from MOHFW, PSI established two creative concepts and tested them with the target audience in semi-rural Jharkhand and Rajasthan. After integrating changes, PSI developed a 60 s for PSA and posters in Hindi. The campaign has been extremely appreciated by the Ministry of Health and Family Welfare and PSI translates the commercial into 11 Indian languages.

➢ **Gender equality:**

TABLE 7.5   PSA on Gender Equality.

TATA (http://bit.ly/women_safety for more information)	Public service ad on gender equality	
1,217,252 views	Published on 1 Aug 2017	• Tata Tea—"Inequality gets learnt. Equality needs Teaching"
The campaign of *"Alarambajne se pehlejaago re"*- Tata Tea		• Alarm Bajne Se Pehle#JaagoRe

This PSA focuses on how often have the people say, *"Ladki se haar-gaya?"* When the society, the parents raise their children with such biases, generally it creates gender-based societies. A biased society objectifies genders and promotes gender-based violence, especially against women. The message underlies that this is not how we raise our kids. This message very nicely illustrated that is common across India, which displays how often individual knowingly or unknowingly impart the children to be gender-biased. This is exemplary gender sensitivity message to be adopted at homes to tackle this issue.

> **Social determinants of health:**

TABLE 7.6   PSA on Social Determinants of Health-1.

Jindal South West (JSW) Foundation	Public service ad on social determinants of health	
2,284 views	Published on 30 Jul 2012	• Stroke risk factors and stroke symptoms
		• Endorsed by the Indian Stroke Association and World Stroke Organization in 2007
Indian Stroke Association: public service announcement (Hindi with English subtitles)		• By Bollywood veteran actor Mr. Anupam Kher

This above-mentioned table demonstrates the PSA on social determinants of health which depict the scenario of avoiding the heart stroke risk factors and its avoidable factors. The consequences of this also integrated in this PSA.

TABLE 7.7   PSA on Social Determinants of Health-2.

The ecological commission of the *"Holy Malankara (Indian) Orthodox Syrian Church"*	Public service ad on social determinants of health	
5,898 views	Published on 1 Jun 2017	"Every Drop Counts"—Save Water—Campaign	Ecological Commission—MOSC
Campaign aimed at increasing awareness of the need to value water and to use it wisely. (Hindi with English subtitles)		

The Ecological Commission of the *"Holy Malankara (Indian) Orthodox Syrian Church"* has propelled a campaign aimed at increasing the awareness of the need to value water and to use it astutely. India is rapidly becoming a water stressed country, and the water resources are under terrific pressure from a growing population, ongoing development, pollution, wetland destruction, alien invasive plants, and the effects of global warming is also the factors associated with it. To construct eco-spirituality centers at various places owned by the Church for hopeful meditation and for organizing eco-camps and also to educate the faithful regarding the perils of environmental degradation and much more. It is a humble representation of a social awareness PSA.

➢ Women's health education

TABLE 7.8   PSA on Combating Gender Stereotypes.

UNICEF	Combating gender stereotypes	
4,822 views	Published on 19 Jul 2017	• "Education Curriculum"
		• #JaagoRe
Tata Tea Jaago Re—Let's build a safer society for women (Hindi with English subtitles)		

The Indian society lingers to be riddled with gender-based crimes, because the society fails to pre-act. To shape a safer society for women one must exercise gender sensitivity at home itself, and to make sure that the children are well alerted toward all genders. Education curriculum must begin gender sensitization right from the grassroots level of education. In this regard, Tata Tea is petitioning the HRD Ministry to make gender sensitization programs compulsory in schools.

➢ Sanitation

Women in many parts of India risk their dignity and even their lives for the most basic rights on an everyday basis. They are often confronted with gender bias, lack of education, access to sanitation, good health, etc. With this campaign, the main aim to inspire, inform, and empower the mass to fight and volunteer for every women's right.

TABLE 7.9   PSA on Sanitation.

Astral pipes	Sanitation (every women's right)	
1,130,618 views	Published on 21 May 2017	• #EveryWomansRight • An initiative by Astral pipes
Tata Tea Jaago Re—Let's build a safer society for women (Hindi with English subtitles)		

➢ **Hygiene**

TABLE 7.10   PSA on Sanitation and Clean Environment.

World Bank	Sanitation and clean environment	
10,709 views	Published on 20 Sep 2012	• What will it take to keep children healthy in Indian Society? • hashtag#ittakes • #whatwillittake • #ittakes
Campaign of total sanitation and clean environment (Hindi with English subtitles)		

The campaign did the survey and asked the women in India that what will it take to improve their lives and the sample area chosen from Dhangaurand of Delhi reveals that all it takes and require is good sanitation and a clean environment.

TABLE 7.11   PSA on Sanitation and Cleanliness.

Lifebuoy (HUL)	Sanitation (maternal & child health)	
19,369,851 views	Published on 18 Feb 2013	• Lifebuoy • Help a Child Reach • Gondappa
Campaign of maternal and Child health and cleanliness (Hindi with English subtitles)		

Infant Mortality under the age of five is prevalent in India and it affects to maternal death as well.

TABLE 7.12   PSA on Sanitation and Cleanliness.

LIQVD Asia	Sanitation (awareness on hand washing)	
22,591 views	Published on 22 Feb 2013	• Creative communication • Lifebuoy hand washing campaign
Campaign of hand washing (Hindi with English subtitles)		

Lifebuoy (HUL) took up the occasion at the Maha Kumbh Mela, Prayagraj in association with Ogilvy Action to spread the significance of washing hands as a preventive measure to avoid diarrhea and other hygiene-related diseases. The Lifebuoy Hand washing campaign was executed with a creative communication medium by imprinting a message on about 2.5 mn Roti's to the venerator who was assembled in mass gathering at Prayagraj of Uttar Pradesh.

➤ **Women's mental health**

Gender is a critical determinant of mental health and mental illness. According to the World Health Organization, 1 in 4 women are likely to have major depression at some point in their lives (WHO report, 2016). "Women FOR women" has the power to teach, endow and inspire individuals who might be struggling with their mental health conditions to seek the help need.

TABLE 7.13   PSA on Women's Mental Health.

The live love laugh foundation	Women's mental health	
22,591 views	Published on 8 Mar 2019	• Creative strategy • Mental Health Awareness Campaign
Campaign of mental health awareness (Hindi with English subtitles)		

➤ **Sexual reproductive rights**

Generally, the society teaches boys to be "tough boys" and not to cry, but instead the society should teach them not to make women in their lives cry.

"Start with the Boys", a PSA directed by Vinil Mathew and produced by Alex Kuruvilla, Managing Director, Conde Nast India, marks a powerful point about domestic violence.

TABLE 7.14   PSA on Sexual Reproductive Rights.

Vogue India	Sexual reproductive rights	
1,952,606 views	Published on 21 Oct 2014	• #StartWithTheBoys
		• Film by Vinil Mathew starring Madhuri Dixit for #VogueEmpower
Campaign of start with the boys (Hindi with English subtitles)		

> ➢ **Stigmatizing women**

The Samsung India has taken an initiative in caring for the dreams of girls in India. Samsung Technical School in ITI Jaipur changes life of Ms. *Seema Nagar*, a girl from a small village in Rajasthan. There are 20 Samsung Technical Schools across India. 10 of them are a joint collaboration between Samsung India and the Ministry of Micro, Small & Medium Enterprises (MSME). 10 other schools are in ITIs in partnership with the State Governments of Delhi, Bihar, Kerala, Rajasthan, and Bengal. It made an impactful campaign as CSR activities and made this beautiful PSA.

TABLE 7.15   PSA on Stigmatizing Women-1.

Samsung India	Stigmatizing women	
81,215,854 views	Published on 29 May 2017	• Samsung technical school—A CSR initiative—We care for the girl child
		• #SapneHueBade
Campaign of start with the boys (Hindi with English subtitles)		

Another massive attempt on Voting rights, equal pay, and safe space; these are some of the major talking points surrounding the role of women in India, in recent times. But preconceived notion is anyone stopped to think how, even in this day and age, women could be just as guilty of an entrenched gender-bias as men? Green ply, in association with "Archana Women's Center"—a Kerala-based organization that works toward the empowering women—drives home this idea with a simple experiment and made this PSA as their CSR activities.

TABLE 7.16   PSA on Stigmatizing Women-2.

Greenply plywood	Stigmatizing women-2	
1,096,501 views	Published on 5 Mar 2019	Green ply—A CSR Initiative— #StopSayingWomenCant
Campaign of stop saying women can't (Hindi with English subtitles)		

➢ Sexual and reproductive health

The health ministry of India recently suggested that sex education be banned in the country. This is a satirical message to look at India's attitude toward sex through a "government approved" sex education lecture. This PSA is a work of fiction that bears no resemblance to any human being living, dead, or abstaining from sex and illustrates the right benefit of implementing the sexual and reproductive health education from the basic education in school/college curriculum.

TABLE 7.17   PSA on Sex Education in India.

East India comedy	Sex education in India		
7,546,845 views	Published on 14 Jul 2014	•	EIC: Sex education in India
Campaign of "government approved" sex education lecture (Hindi with English subtitles)			

➢ Discriminating against women

For generations, Vicks has been trusted to touch lives and provide care for families around the world. They made very effective PSA on everyone deserves the essence of good touch of care. Everyone deserves to feel what it means to be cared for and to care for someone. To experience the difference, it makes in one's life, to have someone that will unconditionally love us and care for us. In the hope that every individual, at their own turn, can do the same and transform someone's life with the touch of care when needed.

TABLE 7.18   PSA on Discriminating Against Women.

Vicks India	Discriminating against women	
10,001,392 views	Published on 29 Mar 2017	• Vicks—Generations of Care • #touch of care
Campaign of "touch of care" (Hindi with English subtitles)		

➤ Impact of socio-economic inequalities

TABLE 7.19   PSA on Socio Economic Inequalities.

Skylark India	Socio economic inequalities	
6,692 views	Published on 25 Mar 2014	• Power of "Right to Information" • #Indianeedsasuperhero
Campaign of "Power of RTI" (Hindi with English subtitles)		

This PSA enables that India needs a superhero and the power of "Right to Information" from Skylark Productions on Vimeo.

➤ Gender-biased sex selection

TABLE 7.20   PSA on Gender-Biased Sex Selection.

PIB India	Gender-biased sex selection	
489 views	Published on 14 Feb 2017	• Let's make this world a better place by preventing Gender-biased Sex selection • Courtesy: Ministry of Women & Child Development Govt of India • Women and driver
Campaign of "preventing gender biased sex selection" (Hindi with English subtitles)		

> **Breastfeeding**

TABLE 7.21   PSA on Breastfeeding.

PIB India	Importance of breastfeeding		
245,851 views	• Published on 5 Aug 2018	•	"POSHAN"Abhiyan
	• Published on 24 May 2015	•	Exclusive Breastfeeding
Campaign of "effectiveness of breast feeding" (Hindi with English subtitles)			

Malnutrition remains a main threat to the survival, growth, and development of children. Today, nearly every second child in India is a victim of malnutrition. It means they are physically and mentally weak due to which they are targets to many ailments, deformities, disabilities, and allergies affecting normal growth mentally and physically. This PSA is available in 18 Languages: Hindi, English, Assamese, Bengali, Garo, Gujarati, Kannada, Khasi, Konkani, Malayalam, Manipuri, Marathi, Mizo, Oriya, Punjabi, Tamil, Telugu, and Urdu which are produced by: Ministry of Women and Child Development, Government of India with active support from UNICEF, and other development partners.

TABLE 7.22   PSA on Breastfeeding for 6 Months.

BBC media action	Importance of breastfeeding for 6 months	
14,648 views	Published on 6 Aug 2016	• Importance of exclusive breastfeeding for 6 months
Campaign of "effectiveness of breast feeding for six months" (Hindi with English subtitles)		

An inquisitive brother wants to play with her little sister, but she keeps crying. This television PSA of BBC Media Action that aims to convey the importance of exclusive breastfeeding and no matter what, the only answer to baby's hunger and thirst is mother's milk is the central theme of this PSA campaign.

> ## Gender sensitization

TABLE 7.23   PSA on Gender Sensitization.

TEDX	Gender sensitization	
14,835 views	Published on 30 Nov 2018	• Gender sensitization promotion
Campaign of "DISHA" (Hindi with English subtitles)		

This is an interview of PSA which enacts with a transgender rights activist, *Disha* talks about her story, and how gender sensitization is essential in today's world. *Disha Pinky Shaikh*, a transgender rights activist and a poet from Ahmednagar, Maharashtra, started her journey to educate and sensitize people on the gender issues. She started using social media with public service message as a platform to express her views and also her poetry. The cause has definitely impacted many young minds. This talk was given at a TEDx by its CSR activities event using the TED conference format but independently organized by a local community.

The following graph demonstrates the taken theme and it's prevalent as public service advertisements.

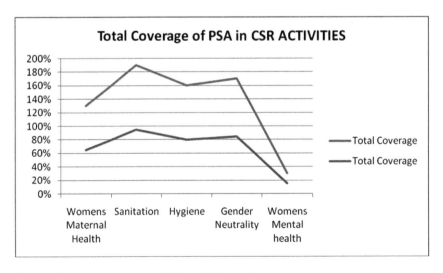

GRAPH 7.1   Total coverage of PSA in CSR activities.

7.14   DISCUSSIONS

CSR generally focuses for generalizing justifications like sustainability, moral obligations, license to operate, and reputation. Gender is a critical determinant of mental health and mental illness. According to the World Health Organization, one in four women is likely to have major depression at some point in their lives (WHO Report, 2016). "Women FOR women" has the power to educate, empower, and encourage individuals who might be struggling with their mental health conditions to seek the help they need. "WOMEN EMPOWERMENT" is the need of the hour. This has triggered a sense of solidarity to stand up and to fight against and to work best to eradicate such atrocities and gender inequality; and in this regard, the PSA is been made by postman pictures which Published on 6 Jan 2014 on the theme of women empowerment. This PSA was funded by Whistling Woods International Film School as an initiative to honor the completion of 100 years of Indian Cinema and was awarded with the required funding in order to convert his concept into a public service film. The Government is emphasizing to build toilets inside home but the truth is that in most of the villages in India, there is no sewerage system. It is the responsibility of the industry/corporations to make people aware through PSA as their CSR activities.

7.15   LIMITATIONS

Qualitative analysis which has been adopted for this present study reveals only the strength of the message but not includes the impact of the message or the effect on target audience. The study lacks with adequate literature on this domain especially on the field of IMC and CSR perspective of PSA on Women's health and wellbeing. There is also lack of adequate data from government site related to Research which has been done in women health with PSA of IMC usage category.

7.16   CONCLUSIONS

The affirmative decisions and portrayal of media regarding healthcare public service advertisements are often times heavily scrutinized by the public. Given the current public service accountability to the target group embedded with IMC, service providers may feel intense pressure to produce higher results with fewer resources. This could inadvertently assess their ethical fortitude and their social consciousness. In order to determine what CSR orientation and viewpoint future healthcare providers through PSA may hold. The results of the study indicate that future healthcare providers as CSR activities through PSA may hold patient care in high regard as opposed to profit maximization. However, the results of the study also show that future healthcare providers as CSR activities through PSA within the industry/corporate may continue to need effective IMC strategies, ethics, regulations, and legal sanctions to guide their actions and behavior in portraying women's health and wellbeing content to reach the particular target group or society as a whole.

7.17 DIRECTIONS FOR FURTHER RESEARCH

This study is only limited to various themes related to the kind of public service advertising technique and its hidden cues or meanings for women's health and wellbeing for IMC with Corporate Social Advertising activities. Further research could be taking an in depth analysis of several different theme perspective with variety of print ads (or any other medium) relating to that item and studying the various applications to it. This study can also be used as an extension to study if the taken parameters would have got larger amount of time frame and if being exposed to the effect studies present in different popular industry with corporate ad as CSR initiative.

KEYWORDS

- **public service advertisements**
- **integrating marketing communication**
- **corporate social responsibility**
- **women**
- **health and wellbeing**

BIBLIOGRAPHY

(n.d.). Retrieved 7 Feb 2019, from 1. https://www.researchgate.net/publication/256034218_A_Conceptual_Framework_of_Corporate_Social_Responsibility_and_Innovation

(n.d.). Retrieved Feb/Mar 2019, from https://www.theseus.fi/bitstream/handle/10024/145426/Orasmae_Avery.pdf;jsessionid=54FC4DCAE5EFF4E107BA498AF922E60D?sequence=1

"Dekh Le"- A Women Empowerment Public Service Film [Advertisement]. 2014. Retrieved Jan/Feb 2019, from https://www.youtube.com/watch?v=KUFIaBoSJaM

"Every Drop Counts"—Save Water—Campaign|Ecological Commission—MOSC [Advertisement]. 2017. Retrieved Feb 5, 2019, from https://www.youtube.com/watch?v=qlOM9i8kITw

Aeon, V. Cryptocurrency and the Diffusion of Innovation [Coin Journal], (2018). Retrieved 9 Feb 2019, from https://www.google.com/search?q=diffusion of innovation model&client=firefox-b-d&tbm=isch&source=iu&ictx=1&fir=zbfvKqkz235R0M:,3kTnh63eW_fO6M,/m/0487h_&vet=1&usg=AI4_-kQg522LP3-0WtZaJ-wHjI5zpuFG3A&sa=X&ved=2ahUKEwjU-L613ezgAhVLKo8KHai_BFcQ_B0wEXoECAUQBg#imgrc=h9CLhIVbqh4iEM:&vet=1

Aiello, A. E.; Larson, E. L. An Analysis of 6 Decades of Hygiene-related Advertising: 1940–2000. *Am. J. Inf. Contr.* **2001**, *29* (6), 383–388.

Breast feeding and Foods after Six Months [Advertisement]. 2005. Retrieved 26 Feb 2019, from https://www.youtube.com/watch?v=lgLGIACk2aU

Burke, L.; Logsdon, J. M. How Corporate Social Responsibility Pays Off. *Long Range Plan.* **1996**, *29* (4), 495–502.

Courts, L. B. The Portrayal of the Menstruating Woman in Menstrual Product Advertisements. *Health Care Women Int.* **1993**, *14* (2), 179–191.

Coy, L. Article Summaries for May 2011 Psychosomatic Medicine. *Psychosomat. Med.* **2011**, *73* (4), 287. DOI: 10.1097/psy.0b013e31821f9725.

Crane, A.; McWilliams, A.; Matten, D.; Moon, J.; Siegel, D. S. The Corporate Social Responsibility Agenda. In *The Oxford Handbook of Corporate Social Responsibility*; 2008.

Dorfman, L.; Wallack, L. Advertising Health: The Case for Counter-ads, 1993. Retrieved 1 Jan 2019, from https://www.ncbi.nlm.nih.gov/pmc/articles/PMC1403454/ PMCID: PMC1403454

Droppert, H.; Bennett, S. Corporate Social Responsibility in Global Health: An Exploratory Study of Multinational Pharmaceutical Firms. *Globalization Health* **2015**, *11* (1), 1–8.

Drumwright, M. E. Company Advertising with a Social Dimension: The Role of Noneconomic Criteria. *J. Market.* **1996**, *60* (4), 71–87.

Every Woman's Right—An Initiative by Astral Pipes [Advertisement]. May 21, 2017. Retrieved 5 Feb 2018, from https://www.youtube.com/watch?v=QXCOUQ7ZBko

Framing Women's Health Issues in 21st Century India—A Policy Report [PDF]. May 2016. The George Institute for Global Health India.

Generations of Care #TouchOfCare [Advertisement]. 2017. Retrieved 23 Feb 2019, from https://www.youtube.com/watch?v=7zeeVEKaDLM

Government of India IUCD Campaign by PSI India with English Subtitles [Advertisement]. 2012. Retrieved Jan/Feb 2019, from https://www.youtube.com/watch?v=JUjqq6MH21c

Importance of Exclusive Breastfeeding for Six Months [Advertisement]. 2016. Retrieved Mar 3, 2019, from https://www.youtube.com/watch?v=M2inODafkRo

India Needs a Superhero a Right To Information Public Service Ad from Skylark Productions on Vimeo [Advertisement]. 2014. Retrieved 14 Feb 2019, from https://www.youtube.com/watch?v=6sVeo3G0Gio

India: What Will It Take to Keep Children Healthy? [Advertisement]. 2012. Retrieved 20 March 2019, from https://www.youtube.com/watch?v=8r9-HByrCNg

Indian Stroke Association: Public Service Announcement [Advertisement]. , 2012. Retrieved 1 Mar 2019, from https://www.youtube.com/watch?v=OFtHt6l-7uM

International Women's Day Special | DeepikaPadukone [Advertisement]. 8 Mar 2019. Retrieved Mar 13, 2019, from https://www.youtube.com/watch?v=Z76GjEFtWGc

Jaago Re—RadhikaVaz on the Need for Gender Sensitisation in Schools [Advertisement]. 2017. Retrieved Feb/Mar 2019, from https://www.youtube.com/watch?v=wIQlAomhlxc

Jahdi, K. S.; Acikdilli, G. Marketing Communications and Corporate Social Responsibility (CSR): Marriage of Convenience or Shotgun Wedding? *J. Busi. Ethics* **2009,** *88* (1), 103–113.

KICK—A TVC by NACO Promoting HIV Testing Among Pregnant Women. Public Service Ad on HIV/AIDS [Advertisement]. Nov 30, 2015. Retrieved 11 Feb 2019, from https://www.youtube.com/watch?v=dVMw0VR91R4

Let's Make This World a Better Place by Preventing Gender Biased Sex Selection [Advertisement]. 2017. Retrieved 15 Mar 2019, from https://www.youtube.com/watch?v=OcN6Uu6M_pg

Lexicon. (n.d.). Retrieved from http://lexicon.ft.com/Term?term=corporate-social-responsibility--(CSR)

Lifebuoy Hand Washing Campaign [Advertisement]. 2013. Retrieved Feb 19, 2019, from https://www.youtube.com/watch?v=YImzLDw7SdM

Lifebuoy Help a Child Reach 5—Gondappa [Advertisement]. 2013). Retrieved 13 Mar 2019, from https://www.youtube.com/watch?v=UF7oU_YSbBQ

Love Is love … Gender Sensitization and Its Importance! DishaShaikh|TEDxSIESCOMS [Advertisement]. 2018. Retrieved 19 Feb 2019, from https://www.youtube.com/watch?v=hfsTB_-EnL4

Moon, B. K. *The Global Strategy for Women's, Children's, Adolescent's Health (2016–20130)* [PDF]; World Health Organization: Geneva, 2015. Every Women Every Child.

Moriarty, S.; Mitchell, N. D.; Wells, W. D. *Pearson India Education Services Pvt. Ltd.*, 10th ed., Vol. 1, Ser. 1; Pearson: India, 2016.

MSG Management Study Guide. (n.d.). Retrieved from https://www.managementstudyguide.com/integrated-marketing-communications.htm

Pearson, R. Beyond Women Workers: Gendering CSR. *Third World Quart.* **2007,** *28* (4), 731–749.

Percy, L. *Strategic Integrated Marketing Communication: Theory and Practice*; Butterworth –Heinemann: Oxford, 2008; 2, 5, 82–84, 88–92, 90–92, 103–104, 134–135, 140, 153–155, 225, 245–247, 252, 256–257, 260, 263–264.

Porter, M. E.; Kramer, M. R. *Strategy & Society: The Link between Competitive Advantage and Corporate Social Responsibility* [PDF]. *Harv. Busi. Rev.*, Dec 2006.

POSHAN Abhiyan Exclusive Breastfeeding [Advertisement]. 2018. Retrieved Jan 3, 2019, from https://www.youtube.com/watch?v=xBasjWSChXk

Samsung Technical School—A CSR Initiative—We Care for the Girl Child [Advertisement]. May 29, 2017. Retrieved Mar 10, 2019, from https://www.youtube.com/watch?v=SttFYufPKws

Sex Education in India [Advertisement]. 2014. Retrieved 19 May 2018, from https://www.youtube.com/watch?v=EiIxkOah09E

Snider, J.; Hill, R. P.; Martin, D. Corporate Social Responsibility in the 21st Century: A View from the World's Most Successful Firms. *J. Busi. Ethics* **2003**, *48* (2), 175–187.

Start with the Boys [Advertisement]. Oct 21, 2014. Retrieved Jan 9, 2019, from https://www.youtube.com/watch?v=0Nj99epLFqg

Stop Saying Women Cant [Advertisement]. 2019. Retrieved 12 Mar 2019, from https://www.youtube.com/watch?v=uBFMF0XDka4

Tai, F. M.; Chuang, S. H. Corporate Social Responsibility. *Ibusiness* **2014**, *6* (3), 117.

Tata Tea Jaago Re—Let's Build a Safer Society for Women [Advertisement]. 2017. Retrieved Feb/Mar 2019, from https://www.youtube.com/watch?v=fT8dC7xesgY

Tata Tea—Inequality Gets Learnt. Equality Needs Teaching [Advertisement]. 2017. Retrieved Jan/Feb 2019, from https://www.youtube.com/watch?v=SpPozOvNrKA

Tinarbuko, S. Jan 1, 2008. Retrieved Jan/Feb 2019, from http://ndl.iitkgp.ac.in/document/S1Yn8xfw23-1eyIbiDNbyX3gxizJJw9grA80XQrq6LhcjZktehenID6ITDSyS__y3HKoQ_BHqkJNVMeqdtnMSA4.https://journals.lww.com/healthcaremanagerjournal/pages/articleviewer.aspx?year=2010&issue=10000&article=00007&type=abstract

Velkoff, V. A.;Adlakha, A. *Women's Health in India* [PDF]. U.S. Department of Commerce Economics and Statistics Administration Bureau of the Census, USA, Dec 10, 1998.

Wallack, L. 1993. Retrieved 3 Feb 2019, from http://ndl.iitkgp.ac.in/document/XrZMy_ZEq7rHTgfnb0UXX5cL8u6pICrL57O3WDT-M-8WsX8zEuv-WWlg8mBeqJt2S5Q7pLPO1w-mCsrGcNy37w

Waller, D. S. Consumer Offense Towards the Advertising of Some Gender-related Products. *J. Consumer Satisfaction, Dissatisfaction Complain. Behav* **2007**, *20*, 72–85.

Wofford, D.; MacDonald, S.; Rodehau, C. A Call to Action on Women's Health: Putting Corporate CSR Standards for Workplace Health on the Global Health Agenda. *Globalization Health* **2016**, *12* (1), 68.

Woodruff, K. Alcohol Advertising and Violence Against Women: A Media Advocacy Case Study. *Health Educ. Quart.* **1996**, *23* (3), 330–345.

Zkjadoon. Public Service Advertisement (PSA)—Structure & Examples, Nov 17, 2016. Retrieved from http://www.businessstudynotes.com/marketing/marketing-management/purpose-structure-public-service-advertisement-psa/

CHAPTER 8

Impact of Corporate Social Responsibility (CSR) on Education in India: An Analysis of Post Companies Act, 2013 Era

ABHIJEET BAG[1*] and CHANDRANI DUTTA[2]

[1]*Cooch Behar Panchanan Barma University, Cooch Behar, India*

[2]*Khudiram Bose Central College, Kolkata, India*

Corresponding author. E-mail: abhijeet.bag@gmail.com

ABSTRACT

The chapter briefly traces the evolution of corporate social responsibility (hereinafter referred to as CSR) in India finally culminating in the form of Section 135 of the Companies Act, 2013. Among the various eligible activities, promotion of education, enhancement of the vocational skills, improvement of road safety through mass education, etc. occupy a significant place in Schedule VII of the Companies Act, 2013 as a part of the CSR mandate. Hence, in this chapter, an attempt has been made to analyze the impact of CSR on Education in India for 4 years after implementation of the Companies Act, 2013. The chapter focuses on top three companies in the information technology sector and in the banking sector based on the market capitalization criteria as on August 27th, 2018 as per BSE SENSEX. The chapter tries to classify the CSR activities into interventions addressing the supply side barriers and demand side barriers of education and evaluate the role of each sector in the same. Moreover, the chapter also attempts to conduct an analysis to find whether there exists any sector-oriented influence on different activities of CSR in education in India through statistical test of ANOVA.

8.1   INTRODUCTION

Corporate social responsibility (hereinafter referred to as CSR) is a significant phenomenon in business context as well as in academic context. This term encompasses something more than the mere philanthropic activities undertaken by the corporates. According to World Business Council for Sustainable Development (WBCSD), CSR is a continuous commitment of any business to foster economic development along with the betterment of quality of life of its employees and their families and eventually culminating the same for overall community and social development.[1] CSR is more a strategic management concept where the companies try to address the environmental and social effects of the business. It is a business strategy in which the companies should aim to improve the well-being of all the stakeholders.

The roots of CSR in India lie in the National Voluntary Guidelines (NVG) on social, environmental and economic responsibilities of business by the Ministry of Corporate Affairs (MCA) supported by the Indian Institute of Corporate Affairs (IICA) in July, 2011. These guidelines are a revised form of the earlier guidelines namely CSR Voluntary guidelines, 2009 released by the MCA in December, 2009 applicable on all types of entities across different sectors, locations, sizes, etc. These guidelines are based on triple-bottom line approach whereby companies try to maintain balance between societal expectations, environmental considerations, and other stakeholders' interest in a sustainable manner. The guidelines encompass nine principles and motivate the micro, small, and medium enterprises (MSMEs) to implement the same for ensuring their survival and growth in the long term.[2] In order to extend the objectives of the NVG on social, environmental, and economic responsibilities of business and to meet a larger section of the society, SEBI made it compulsory to include Business Responsibility Report as a part of the annual report. Business Responsibility Report is applicable for the top 100 listed companies in National Stock Exchange (NSE) and Bombay Stock Exchange (BSE) on the basis of market capitalization as on March 31st, 2012.[3] The Department of Public Enterprises issued guidelines for expenditures on CSR

---

[1]*http://www.wbcsd.org/work-program/business-role/previous-work/corporate-social-responsibility. aspx as cited in https://www.pwc.in/assets/pdfs/publications/2013/handbook-on-corporate-social-responsibility-in-india.pdf*
[2]*http://www.mca.gov.in/Ministry/latestnews/National_Voluntary_Guidelines_2011_12jul2011.pdf*
[3]*http://www.sebi.gov.in/cms/sebi_data/attachdocs/1344915990072.pdf*

activities for the Central Public Sector Enterprises (CPSEs) in order to set an example for the private counterparts. The guidelines which came into force from April, 2013 mandate the CPSEs to allocate certain amount based on the Profit After Tax (PAT) of the previous year for CSR projects and Sustainable development activities. If the PAT of the previous year is less than Rs. 100 crores, the concerned CPSE should allocate 3–5% of the PAT of the previous year in the budget for CSR projects and sustainable activities. If the PAT of the previous year ranges from Rs. 100 crores to Rs. 500 crores, the CPSE is mandated to allocate 2–3% of the PAT of the previous year in the budget for CSR projects and sustainable activities. Lastly, the PAT for the preceding year is Rs. 500 crores and above then the budgetary allocation should have range from 1–2% of the PAT of the last year for the projects. [4]

Hence from the above account, it is clearly evident that the journey of CSR is long in India which has now culminated in the form of a Section 135 of the Companies Act, 2013.

8.2   CSR AND COMPANIES ACT, 2013

The Companies Act, 1956, did not have any mandatory provision with regard to CSR in India. Thus, a pathbreaking change was initiated by the Companies Act, 2013 (hereinafter referred to as the Act) by introducing mandatory provision of CSR for the first time in India. The provision may be subdivided into CSR provisions that are uniformly applicable to all companies under section 166(2) of the Act and Section 135 applicable to some specified classes of companies. Section 166(2) requires a director of a company to attain the objectives of the company for the benefit of the members as a whole keeping in mind the best interests of different stakeholder groups like employees, shareholders, community, environment, and the company itself. Section 135(1) of the Act deals with those specified companies on whom mandatory spending of CSR has been imposed. As far as Indian companies are concerned, any company which satisfies any of the following three conditions should spend a designated amount of its profit on CSR activities. The conditions are having a net worth of Rs. 500 crores or more or turnover of Rs. 1000 crores or more during any financial year or net profit of Rs. 5 crores or more during any

[4]http://www.recindia.nic.in/download/DPE_Guidelines_CSR_Sust.pdf

financial year. Rule 3(2) of the Company CSR Rules, 2014 has clarified that any financial year would mean any of the three preceding financial years. This is applicable to all Indian companies irrespective of the fact whether they are private or public or whether they belong to the listed or unlisted category. Another thing that should be considered here is that the turnover and the net profit criteria should be fulfilled at the end of the relevant year and not at any time during the financial year. But the Act and the Rules are silent with a corresponding provision on the net worth criteria. So, it may be inferred from the other two conditions that the net worth criteria will also apply on the financial year ending date. Rule 3(2) also states that once a company is taken under the purview of Section 135(1), it can only be out if the scope of this section if it ceases to be covered under this section for three consecutive financial years. As far as the foreign companies are concerned, foreign company as defined in section 2(42) of the Act will comply with section 135 if it has a branch office or project office in India and it satisfies the eligibility norm as stated in Section 135(1) of the Act. A company needs to spend minimum of 2% of the average net profit of the three preceding financial years on various CSR activities. Schedule VII of the Companies Act enumerates the list of activities permitted under CSR projects of the companies. They range from eradication of hunger, malnutrition, provision of safe drinking water, promotion of gender equality, women empowerment, to promotion of ecological balance, setting up of public libraries, slum area development, financing incubators located in an academic institution, supporting war widows, and dependents and last but not the least promotion of education including special education and improvement of vocational skills among children, women, elderly, and differently abled people and implementation of livelihood enhancement projects. However, activities under promotion of education have been added following an amendment in Schedule VII to incorporate awareness to create road safety measures through education of the masses, consumer protection through their education, setting up nonacademic techno park Technology Business Incubators not located within an academic institution but supported by department of Science and Technology, fostering of research and studies in any area of Schedule VII, etc.[5].

---

[5]*http://www.taxmann.com/commentaries/samples/Volume3_SampleChapters.pdf*

8.3   RIGHT TO EDUCATION AND CURRENT SCENARIO OF EDUCATION IN INDIA

Article 21, inserted under the Constitution (Eighty-sixth Amendment) Act, 2002 provides for free and compulsory education for all children in India falling in the age group of 6–17 years as a fundamental right and the same should be provided by the state in the manner as the state by law decides. As a result of this, Right of Children to Free and Compulsory Education (RTE) Act, 2009 was enacted which states that every child should have access to basic and elementary education in a formal school satisfying some essential criteria and parameters. The Act had come into force with effect from April 1st, 2010. The term "free education" implies that a child who is admitted in a school supported by the appropriate government will not be liable to pay any fees and charges that may prevent him/her from pursuing elementary education. The term "elementary education" indicates that appropriate government and local authorities should ensure admission attendance and completion of the basic education for all children in the age group of 6–14 years. The Act, hence, takes into account admission of a non-admitted child in a system of formal education. The law also provides for the specific roles played by the central government, state government, and parents in this regard and how the responsibilities should be shared among different governments. The law specifies standard norms in the form of pupil-teacher ratio, building and infrastructure, school working days, and teacher working hours to ensure quality education in this regard. The governments should ensure that the pupil-teacher ratio should be maintained in each school and there should not be any imbalance in the rural-urban distribution of teachers. Moreover, it has been mentioned that the teachers should not be engaged in nonacademic work except disaster relief, decennial census, election to local authorities, state legislatures, and parliament. The Act strictly lays down proper training and entry qualifications for the appointment of teachers and prohibits any form of physical and mental abuse of children, private tuitions of teachers, screening procedure for admission, capitation fees, etc. Thus, the Act is in place to ensure holistic development of a child where a child will get an opportunity to grow in talent, personality in absence of any trauma, phobia in a child focused learning environment.[6]

---

[6]*http://mhrd.gov.in/rte*

In the present context, education sector should work on three criteria namely accessibility, equity and quality to overcome the challenges facing the sector. Remarkable improvement is observed in the provision of primary education across gender and social categories as measured through the Gross Enrolment Rate (GER). The GER for elementary education (class I–Class VIII) in the year 1950–1951 was 46.4 for male population and 17.7 for female population. There was a huge disparity in the above figures across gender but thereafter the disparities reduced and now, in the year, 2015–2016, the GER of the male population has rose to 94.5 as contrasted with 99.6 for the female counterparts. The growth in the GER over the time frame is 103.66% for the male and 462.71% for the female. In the secondary level (class IX-X), the GER rose from 57.4 and 45.3 for male and female, respectively, in the year 2004–2005 to 79.2 and 81.0 for male and female, respectively, in the year 2015–2016. The increase in the GER is 37.98% for the male population and the corresponding figure for the female is 78.81%. The statistic for the senior secondary level (class XI–XII) reflects the GER as 30.8 and 24.5 for male and female, respectively, in the year 2004–2005 rising to 56 and 56.4 from male and female population in the year 2015–2016. The GER increased by 81.82% and by 130.20% for the male and female, respectively, over the given time period. The picture of higher education (18 years to 23 years) looks dismal against this backdrop as the GER is 9.3 and 6.7 for male and female in the year 2001–2002 and the corresponding figures are 25.4 and 23.5 for male and female in the year 2015–2016. The growth in the GER is 173.12% for the male and 250.75% for female in this case. Though the growth in the GER is higher in case of female than male and in the year 2015–2016, in all the three levels of education except one, the GER of the female has outnumbered the male but in the field of higher education, the female participation is still less than the male counterparts. The government's initiative in the form of financial and physical incentives for girls and establishment of residential schools in the areas of low literacy have improved the picture of female participation till the secondary level but consideration is required to reduce the gap in the higher education level.

National Achievement Survey, 2015 points out that in the subjects of English, Mathematics, Science, and Social Science, the urban students perform better than the rural students. This is reflected in the mean achievement score in the class X examination in the year 2015. The mean achievement score in English is 244 for rural areas and 263 for urban areas, in Mathematics, it is 247 for rural areas and 256 for urban areas, in Science and Social Science, and they are 247 and 257 for rural and urban counterparts, respectively. One of the main reasons for such unequal results is the lack of accessibility of nearest schools in rural areas especially at the secondary level. As per the National Sample Survey (NSS) Report (71st Round), greater than 12% of the households do not have any secondary school within 5 km of their houses while the corresponding percentage is less than 1% for the urban households. In order to mitigate this gap, the Government of India is providing transport facilities at concessional rate, distributing bicycles to the students, making provision for online courses, and undertaking similar initiatives.

Another issue that requires attention is the shortfall of teachers in the government elementary school against the sanctioned post. The highest shortfall is recorded in the State of Jharkhand. According to the RTE Act, 2009, vacancy in a teaching post in a school should not be more than 10% of its sanctioned strength. Government is taking steps to devise solution to this problem in the form of recruitment of new teachers and transfer of surplus teachers from schools having zero enrolment to the needed schools.

The dropout of the students is a major area of concern in the current scenario and it is more pertinent in the secondary level than primary level. According to the NSS Report (71st Round), lack of interest in education is a significant reason other than financial limitations and engagement in domestic and economic activities that contributes to such dropout of students. A practical solution to the above problem will be in the provision of educational counseling and vocational training for the students. A gender gap is observed in the presence of female teachers for every 100 male teachers in secondary education most importantly and this is also regarded as a cause for dropout of children. Hence, it is needless to say that the reduction in the gender gap will definitely enhance the global competitiveness of the Indian education sector.

Lastly, though the government's expenditure on education has risen from 3.87% of GDP in 2013–2014 to 4.04% of GDP in 2014–2015, a lot remains to be done as all the states have not increased their expenditure on education in the same manner.[7]

---

[7]*http://mhrd.gov.in/sites/upload_files/mhrd/files/statistics/ESAG-2018.pdf*

Hence, from the above account, it is very obvious that now the companies have an opportunity to intervene in the education sector to meet the demand and supply side factors t enable betterment of the sector.

8.4 REVIEW OF LITERATURE

Here, an attempt has been made to review a few works on CSR and education in a chronological manner. The literatures focus on CSR efforts of the companies in various educations oriented activities both before the implementation of the Companies act, 2013.

- **A study conducted by the Tata Strategic Management Group in collaboration with UNICEF and Confederation of Indian Industry (2010)** gives an overview of the RTE Act, 2009 and the three corporate engagement models to ensure effective implementation of CSR strategies especially in the field of education in India. Like, in the first model, the corporate plays the significant role in conceptualization of the initiative that is implemented on its own or with the assistance of a partner entity like an NGO. In the second model as discussed, the companies play a passive role by providing only the financial assistance to the educational activities undertaken by the NGOs, government, and other institutions. The third model depicts how companies design and implement CSR projects of other third party entities like NGOs, other organizations. The study chooses some projects adopted by the companies under each of the three models and discovers some practical challenges faced and responses devised under each project. In the case of the first model, projects like Nanhi Kali Programme of Mahindra and Mahindra group, Satya Bharti School Programme of Bharti Foundation and others are selected as case studies. The article describes Future First Initiative of HSBC and Read India by Pratham Education Foundation to point out the challenges and key learning outcomes of the second model. Finally, to study the effectiveness of the third model, the article analyses Pedagogic Renewal of Chhattisgarh by ICEE and Akshaya Patra Mid-Day Meal Programme. Finally, the study concludes by observing that each of the models plays a crucial role in fulfillment of RTE objectives but the companies should make an optimum utilization of the above models after understanding their critical success factors.

- **Das Gupta (2014)** in a chapter in an edited volume has described the evolution of the concept of CSR and the journey of CSR from social philanthropy to corporate accountability toward its various stakeholders. The author goes on to describe how the perception of CSR is undergoing a change in the Indian context as well where the companies are formulating specific policies, strategies, and goals to support their CSR programmes. The author tries to uphold the criticisms for making mandatory CSR requirements, a reality. He tries to reflect the position of pre Companies Aχτ, 2013 era when there were discussions on a separate monitoring agency to implement the proposed manda-tory CSR framework, the impact on the small- and medium-scale industries, etc. The chapter points out some challenges in the implementation of CSR in India like the absence of community participation, need to build the capacities of the local nongov-ernment organizations (NGOs), and issues of transparency and so on.

- **A study Conducted by Samhita Social Ventures** shows the pattern of spending of top 100 companies as per BSE top 500 lists selected on the basis of their spending on CSR activities at 2% of PAT. The study covers a period of 3 years before the implementation of the Companies Act, 2013 and includes companies classified into various sectors like heavy engineering and manufacturing, banking, IT and finance, healthcare, and FMCG sector. The spending has been analyzed under demand and supply side interventions to remove the barriers from the field of education. The study clearly depicts that building infrastructure and providing scholarships are the two major areas of intervention among the companies across different sectors.

8.5 OBJECTIVES OF STUDY

The present study is conducted to attain the following objectives:

1. To study the impact of Section 135 of the Companies Act, 2013 on the education in India.

2. To analyze the CSR initiatives of the companies of different sectors in terms of demand side interventions and supply side interventions to remove the barriers of education.
3. To study whether the sectors cast any significant impact on the pattern of interventions of the companies to meet the challenges of demand and supply side barriers.

8.6   RESEARCH METHODOLOGY

The present study is empirical in nature. The study is based on secondary data collected from articles, journals, official websites of the companies, MHRD, etc. The study focuses on two sectors namely information technology sector and the banking sector. The analysis is done on the top three companies namely WIPRO, Infosys, TCS, Kotak Mahindra Bank, SBI, and HDFC Bank of these two sectors based on the market capitalization criteria on August 27th, 2018 as per BSE SENSEX. Since the study wants to study the impact of Section 135 on the education sector in India, the analysis is done for a period of for 4 years after implementation of the Companies Act, 2013, that is, from 2014–2015 to 2017–2018. The initiatives of the companies are classified first into demand and supply side interventions based on the study conducted by Samhita Social Ventures on educational initiatives of the top 100 companies as per BSE 500 list prior to the implementation of the Companies Act, 2013. The supply side interventions address mainly two aspects namely issues related to accessibility and issues related to quality and include in them activities like infrastructure and donation of learning material, remedial education, learning methods, school administration and management, building capacity of the providers of education, etc. The demand side interventions address mainly sociocultural norms and practices and family level circumstances and include in them creation of parental and community awareness, skill development, school-based nutrition and health, cash or kind assistance to the students, etc. Moreover, the chapter will try to evaluate the impact of the sector on the pattern of the CSR activities in education using statistical tool of ANOVA.

8.7   EMPIRICAL ANALYSIS

TABLE 8.1   Company Wise Expenditure of Total CSR and Contribution Toward Education.

Year		2014–2015	2015–2016	2016–2017	2017–2018
Currency units					
Kotak Mahindra Bank	CSR activities (Rs. Crores)	12.0	16.4	17.3	26.4
	Total on education (Rs. Crores)	6.6	10.4	12.0	14.7
	Percentage	54.8	63.1	69.1	55.6
State Bank of India (SBI)	CSR activities (Rs. Crores)	115.8	143.9	89.8	113.0
	Total on education (Rs. Crores)	41.2	19.5	3.6	10.9
	Percentage	35.6	13.5	4.0	9.6
HDFC Bank	CSR activities (Rs. Crores)	118.6	194.8	305.4	374.0
	Total on education (Rs. Crores)	16.2	10.7	7.5	7.9
	Percentage	13.7	5.5	2.4	2.1
WIPRO	CSR activities (Rs. Crores)	132.7	156.0	176.4	183.3
	Total on education (Rs. Crores)	92.8	109.8	129.1	135.0
	Percentage	69.9	70.4	73.2	73.6
INFOSYS	CSR activities (Rs. Crores)	239.5	202.3	289.4	312.6
	Total on education (Rs. Crores)	65.4	43.6	61.7	16.3
	Percentage	27.3	21.6	21.3	5.2
TATA Consultancy Services (TCS)	CSR activities (Rs. Crores)	218.4	294.2	379.7	400.0
	Total on education (Rs. Crores)	34.4	78.1	90.6	91.0
	Percentage	15.7	26.5	23.9	22.8

Source: Self-computed.

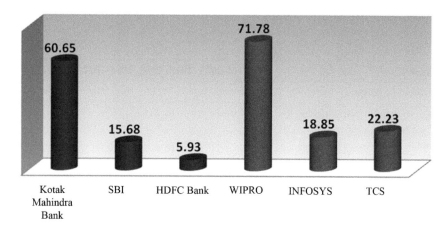

FIGURE 8.1   Average contribution toward education among all CSR activities from 2014–2015 to 2017–2018 (%).
Source: Self-computed.

The given figure states that the IT companies contributed the most toward education among CSR activities. Among the banks, Kotak Mahindra Bank is the highest contributor toward education while WIPRO is that of the highest among the selected IT companies from 2014–15 to 2017–2018. Moreover, though, the average contribution of SBI in education sector was not unfair as regards the contribution of other companies but its trend of growth of contribution over the years was really pathetic by means of massive decrease in contribution over the recent years (Table 8.1).

TABLE 8.2   Sector-Wise CSR Contribution Toward Demand and Supply for Education.

Year	Demand (%)					Comparison	Sector	Supply (%)					Comparison
	CK	SD	UD	H	Total			ID	LM	RE	DT	Total	
2014–2015	4	16	44	17	81	↑	Bank	19	0	0	0	19	↓
	2	58	2	0	62	↑	IT	25	13	0	0	38	↓
2015–2016	0	3	47	17	67	↑	Bank	33	0	0	0	33	↓
	27	34	3	5	70	↑	IT	19	0	1	10	30	↓

TABLE 8.2 *(Continued)*

Year	Demand (%)					Comparison	Sector	Supply (%)					Comparison
	CK	SD	UD	H	Total			ID	LM	RE	DT	Total	
2016–2017	0	0	48	17	65	↑	Bank	34	0	0	1	35	↓
	0	67	1	2	71	↑	IT	3	0	8	18	29	↓
2017–2018	1	0	17	17	35	↑	Bank	34	31	0	1	65	↓
	0	53	1	0	54	↑	IT	15	0	22	9	46	↓

SUPPLY

LM	Learning method
DT	Development of trainers
RE	Remedial education
ID	Infrastructure development

Demand

UD	Underprivileged development
SD	Skill development
CK	Cash and kind
H	Health

Source: Self-computed.

As regards demand supply conditions under education in all the sectors, it has been analyzed that the demand for contribution in all the sectors of education is much higher than that of supply. This signifies that both the banking sector and the IT sector are unable to meet the massive demand for contribution in education. Though the supply of contributions by both the banking and IT sectors increased immensely in recent years, yet such increase was unable to satisfy the requirement of education.

TABLE 8.3 ANOVA Test.

ANOVA: Single factor

Summary

Groups	Count	Sum	Average	Variance
Banking sector	4	109.72633	27.431583	27.527413
IT sector	4	150.46524	37.616309	6.9617482

TABLE 8.3   *(Continued)*

Result of ANOVA

Source of variation	SS	df	MS	F	P-value	F critical Value
Between groups	207.45731	1	207.45731	12.03029	0.0133287	5.9873776
Within groups	103.46748	6	17.244581			
Total	310.92479	7				

Source: Self-computed.

From the above table, it has been observed that the mean level of contri-bution reported by IT sector (37.32) is higher than that of banking sector (27.43). But are these differences statistically significant? According to the result, the value of F is 12.03 which is greater than the F critical value, that is, 5.98 at 95% level of confidence with a *p*-value less than 5%, that is, 0.013. Therefore, the null hypothesis cannot be accepted (signifying no significant differences among the means of the two groups). Hence, the alternative hypothesis is accepted, that is, there exists differences among the two sectors and IT sector contributes more toward education as compared to banking sector.

8.8   CONCLUSION

CSR is a movement that focuses on creating awareness among business organizations regarding the effect of their business on the society at large, including not only all its stakeholders but also the whole ecological environment. It emphasizes on satisfying the overall needs of the society for its sustainable development keeping intact the natural aestheticism of this biological environment. As regards to the present study, it has been observed that the demand for contribution of the business organizations toward CSR activities, particularly in education, is increasing at an alarming rate. The banking and IT companies have taken enough initia-tives to feed the hunger of education but that also not been able to move up to the fullest. But the IT companies have shown highlighting performances toward contribution for education than that of the banking companies. It is really a pathetic situation for a developing economy like India, where a major nationalized bank like SBI has been unable to show satisfactory performance for the betterment of the society in terms of educating the underprivileged society. So, not only all banks and IT companies must join hands but also all business organizations must move forward in providing services to the best of their ability. This initiative should not be taken for granted as regards fulfilling the criteria of Companies Act 2013 but be taken as a self-initiative using all their core competencies for a significant economic growth of Indian economy.

8.9   LIMITATIONS OF STUDY

The present study suffers from certain limitations discussed below:

➢   This study is focused on the contribution for education only among all other CSR activities.

➢   Only the performance of few banks and few IT companies has been analyzed as regards to contribution for CSR activities.

➢   The evaluation of performances of the two selected sectors has been based on 4 years data only.

KEYWORDS

- **corporate social responsibility**
- **promotion of education**
- **demand side barriers**
- **supply side barriers**

REFERENCES

1. Das Gupta, A. Implementing Corporate Social Responsibility in India: Issues and the Beyond. In *Implementing Corporate Social Responsibility, Indian Perspectives*; Ray, S., Raju, S. S., Eds.; 2014; p 35. <http://www.springer.com/978-81-322-1652-0>
2. Samhita Social Ventures. Mapping Education Initiatives of 100 Companies with the Largest CSR Budgets. <https://drive.google.com/file/d/0B1xABlImO5ITRWJjclJB bmJ1VTQ/view>
3. Tata Strategic Management Group, UNICEF, CII. Best Practices of CSR in the field of Education in India, 2010. http://www.bhartifoundation.org/uploads/bhartifoundation/ files/1487307948-csr-in-the-field-of-education-unicef-on-bharti-foundation.pdf

4. http://www.sebi.gov.in/cms/sebi_data/attachdocs/1344915990072.pdf
5. http://mhrd.gov.in/rte
6. http://mhrd.gov.in/sites/upload_files/mhrd/files/statistics/ESAG-2018.pdf
7. http://www.mca.gov.in/Ministry/latestnews/National_Voluntary_Guidelines_2011_ 12jul2011.pdf
8. http://www.recindia.nic.in/download/DPE_Guidelines_CSR_Sust.pdf
9. http://www.taxmann.com/commentaries/samples/Volume3_SampleChapters.pdf
10. https://www.pwc.in/assets/pdfs/publications/2013/handbook-on-corporate-social-responsibility-in-india.pdf

CHAPTER 9

Role of Indian Post Offices on Women Empowerment: A Study on Social Responsibility Perspective

SOURAV KUMAR DAS

School of Business and Economics, Adamas University, West Bengal, India.

E-mail: ssd.sourav@gmail.com

ABSTRACT

In the present scenario of enlightening women empowerment and removal of gender inequality to boost up socioeconomic development in a sustainable way, woman agents play a crucial role in terms of financial inclusion of the Indian Post Offices. They provide door-to-door services to the people, especially old ones in rural areas and minimize the work load of the account holders. Under this background, the objective of the study is to know the role of agents of the post offices who are working for the betterment of local people. The study is based on both primary and secondary data. The study finds that the woman agents are struggling with their jobs and are receiving meager financial compensation. Even though several actions are taken by the governments as part of social responsibilities, still they have not taken any necessary action in the Indian Post Offices sector to boost up the women empowerment move.

9.1 INTRODUCTION

Various financial institutions like commercial banks, cooperative banks, post offices, LIFE Insurance Corporation of India provide savings opportunities for the public. Apart from these, post offices are also acting as financial institutions and provide a vast range of financial services. Post office savings bank is one of the largest banks in India. In order to mobilize small savings of the general public, small savings agents (both men and women) are appointed by the district collectors at the district level. Among such agents, woman agents, that is, Mahila Pradhan Kheriya Bachat Yojana Agents (MPKBY agents) play an important role through promotion of sale of recurring deposits as well as sale of other deposits. Empowering the underprivileged female citizens has got a revolutionary change in the Indian postal sector by means of these MPKBY agents. Recently, these woman agents face several problems due to a drastic decline in commission in other deposits. Not only this, the Central Government is taking many steps that provides huge disincentive to work for schemes to the existing agents. This in turn hampers the "Power" of women in the developing Indian economy that ultimately hinders the progress of financial inclusion as well as creates a hindrance in the development of Indian Post Offices from the social responsibility fulfillment perspective.

9.2   LITERATURE REVIEW

Tamilkodi (1983) mentioned that small savings schemes provide a range of benefits for general public, even including their children. Further, she stated that certain initiatives must be taken to make the procedures of availing such facilities easier so as to cater to the needs of illiterate and socially and economically backward populace of the nation.

Karthikeyan (2001) in his study "Small Investors' Perception on Post Office Saving Schemes" analyzed and stated that *there was significant difference among the four age groups, in the level of awareness for Kisan Vikas Patra (KVP), National Savings Schemes (NSS), and Deposit Scheme for Retired Employees (DSRE), and the overall score confirmed that the level of awareness among investors in the old age group were higher than in those of the young age group. No difference was observed between male and female investors except for the NSS and KVP. Out of the factors analyzed, necessities of life and tax benefits were the two major ones that influence the investors both in semi-urban and urban areas.*

Richa (2004) in her study focused that among all financial institutions, post office would be the most attractive institution for both for medium and small savers. As per Ministry of Finance, the attractiveness for post office schemes was due to higher interest rates as against what the banks provide.

Ganapathi (2010) mentioned that several small savings schemes were present that could not only cater to the needs of small investors but is also tax saving for people in high tax brackets. There is also a dire need for effective advertisements for the post office savings schemes so that the poor illiterate persons could also know the benefits of such schemes, both in terms of returns and also safety and security purposes of their small savings.

Malakar (2013) in his research paper "Role of Indian Post in Financial Inclusion" analyzed the role of Indian Post Offices in promoting financial inclusion and the challenges faced by them in providing banking services. He suggested that proper training and innovative technologies must be incorporated in the Indian Postal system for its sustainable development.

Samal (2013) in his study "Future of India Post" stated that India Postal Service should take necessary steps due to the presence of organized or unorganized courier facilities of mail service and also to cater to the needs of more demanding customers. He focused on several points like introduction of new products and innovation of existing products for fast mail service, like E-Post, E-Payment, Express Parcel Post, etc. He also stated that around 240 million savings accounts operate and the outstanding balances of all 8 NSS has increased to Rs.5,828,329.6 million as of 31.03.2010 and 14,415 departmental post offices out of 25,563 were computerized till March 31, 2010.

9.3 OBJECTIVES OF THE STUDY

The objectives of the study are:

- ❖ To give a brief idea about the administration of Indian Post Office and various schemes in operation.
- ❖ To overview the role of women empowerment as a part of social responsibility for financial inclusion.
- ❖ To figure out a brief profile of woman agents working within the post offices.
- ❖ To analyze how the woman agents of the post offices are helping in financial inclusion in the context of social responsibility.

9.4   RESEARCH METHODOLOGY

9.4.1   SELECTION OF SAMPLE

Two post offices, viz., Baruipur head post office from South 24 Parganas and Howrah head post office from Howrah district, have been selected for the study. Around 64 and 56 woman agents are involved with the financial activities of the post offices of these two districts, respectively. All these woman agents have been considered for the study.

9.4.2   DATA COLLECTION

This study is based on both secondary and primary sources of information. The secondary data have been collected mainly from the internet sources from the websites of Department of Posts, Government of India, etc. Primary data have been collected, by means of structured questionnaire, from entire 120 woman agents (56 from Howrah HO and 64 from Baruipur HO).

9.4.3   STATISTICAL TOOLS USED

Data so collected, particularly, the monthly deposits, monthly income, and family income of the agents are first considered for normality testing. The Shapiro-Wilk and Kolmogorov-Smirnov test values show that null hypothesis is accepted for all these variables and the data sets follow normal distribution. SPSS software has been used to get the results. To test the profile of the surveyed woman agents, Chi-square test has been used. Simple regression analysis has been done at two stages taking two regression models for showing their role in financial inclusion. All the tests are carried out at 5% level of significance.

9.5   DATA FINDINGS AND ANALYSIS

9.5.1   OVERVIEW OF INDIAN POST OFFICE ADMINISTRATION

In 1688, the first post office was established in India by the East India Company in Bombay followed by Calcutta and Madras. The East India

Company established the first post office department in Calcutta in 1774 and Madras in 1778 and Bombay in 1792. It has the vast network of branches with a distinct outreach in rural areas. The total number of post offices increased from 23,344 in 1947 to 154,910 as on March 31, 2016. Out of such post offices, 89.70% post offices are in rural areas.

The Department of Posts, under the Ministry of Communications, Government of India, has a minister of state with independent charge by the Secretary of the Department of posts and the Director General Postal services. The Chairperson and six members look the matters relating to personnel management, postal services, technology induction and implementation, postal life insurance, human resources development, and banking. The whole nation is divided into 23 postal circles where each circle is headed by a Chief Postmaster General. Each postal circle is segregated into several regions that are headed by a Postmaster General.

There are so many attractive schemes provided for the general people. The various savings schemes of Indian Post Offices are savings account scheme with a minimum balance of Rs.50, recurring deposit scheme with a minimum deposit of Rs.10 and multiples of Rs.5, time deposit account with the minimum deposit of Rs.200 for 5 years, monthly income schemes of a period of 5 years, National Savings Certificate with minimum of Rs.100 and no maximum limit, Public Provident scheme with minimum deposit of Rs.500 per year and maximum Rs.70,000 and Postal Life Insurance.

9.5.2   WOMEN EMPOWERMENT AS PART OF SOCIAL RESPONSIBILITY

Raising the power of women creates an enthusiasm among them for developing self-esteem, self empowerment, and personality enhancement. Women empowerment ultimately leads to breaking off the traditional barriers of suppress and religious false beliefs, and creating inspiration for performing every job at the best. This empowering of women, particularly to the underprivileged females, has become a crucial social responsibility in recent times. Several private companies like Hindustan Unilever, P & G, Avon have conducted several projects for their income generations that uplift their standard of living. Even the central government along with the regulatory bodies has taken several initiatives like mandatory performance of Corporate Social Responsibility activities every year (as per Companies

Act 2013). Nowadays, women are considered as economic agents in performing activities in dynamic ways. Thus, not only as entrepreneurs or as service holders in different companies, females also work at the Indian Post Offices at agents for promoting and providing financial services at door steps. It has become a crucial issue for Indian Post Offices that even though the woman agents are performing better in terms of promoting financial inclusion, still the Indian Post Offices are not performing better social responsibility for the upliftment of standard of living of the under privileged women populace.

9.5.3   BRIEF PROFILE OF WOMAN AGENTS

Three types of agents, viz., Standardized Agency System (SAS), MPKBY Agents, and Public Provident Fund (PPF) are engaged for post offices services in India. Higher secondary passed women can act with all the financial services under MPKBY. They are recruited through written tests and interview and are appointed through Block Development Offices in respected areas. They only get commission at a rate of 4% on recurring deposits for 5 years and 0.5% on collection of other deposits (earlier it was 1%) for one time only. However, they do not get commission in respect of deposits for senior citizens.

Recently, it has been observed in some post offices that, the agents can make the post office transaction only 12 days in a month and one policy transaction per day. The demographic profile of the surveyed woman agents of the selected two head post offices are shown below.

TABLE 9.1   Demographic Profile of the Respondents.

Age of the surveyed population		
Category	Howrah HO	Baruipur HO
	Frequency	Frequency
Below 30	10	Nil
31–60	32	50
Above 60	14	14
Educational qualification of the surveyed population		
Category	Howrah HO	Baruipur HO
	Frequency	Frequency

TABLE 9.1 *(Continued)*

Age of the surveyed population		
Category	**Howrah HO**	**Baruipur HO**
	Frequency	**Frequency**
Higher secondary	25	23
Graduate	27	33
Post graduate	4	8
Marital status of the surveyed population		
Category	Howrah HO	Baruipur HO
	Frequency	Frequency
Unmarried	11	10
Married	36	49
Widow	9	5
Family size of the surveyed population		
Category	Howrah HO	Baruipur HO
	Frequency	Frequency
Less than 2	2	7
2–4	51	53
More than 4	3	4
Family income level of the surveyed population		
Category	Howrah HO	Baruipur HO
	Frequency	Frequency
Below Rs.15,000	11	Nil
Rs.15,000–25,000	26	7
Above Rs.25,000	19	53

Source: Computed by authors.

The demographic profile shows that most of the woman agents are within the age group of 31 to 60 of both the post offices. Most of them are graduate and married. Their family incomes are in the range of Rs.15,000 to Rs.25,000, and more than Rs.25,000 in Howrah and Baruipur, respectively.

In order to determine whether there is a systematic association between the variables, Chi-Square Analysis is conducted. To conduct this test, two null hypotheses are:

H_{01}: The demographic factors of the respondents of Howrah head post office has no influence over the problem faced while working.

H_{02}: The demographic factors of the respondents of Baruipur head post office has no influence over the problem faced while working.

The test statistics are shown in Table 9.2A and Table 9.2B.

TABLE 9.2A   Chi-Square Test Statistics of Howrah HO.

Chi-Square	Age	Educational qualification	Marital status	Family income	Family size
value	14.714	17.393	24.250	17.214	40.071
Df	2	2	2	40	4
Sig.	.001	.000	.000	.999	.000

Source: Computed by authors.

TABLE 9.2B   Chi-Square Test Statistics of Baruipur HO.

Chi-Square	Age	Educational qualification	Marital status	Family income	Family size
value	20.250	14.844	54.406	39.312	33.125
Df	1	2	2	28	3
Sig.	.000	.001	.000	.076	.000

Source: Computed by authors.

The null hypothesis (H_0) is rejected at 5% level of significance. Table 9.2A highlights that the chi-square value of age, educational qualification, and marital status and family size are highly significant (sig. value below 0.05) except family income, which lead to the rejection of H_{01} for all the parameters except family income. This mentions that the age, educational qualification, marital status, and family size of the woman agents of Howrah H.O affect their working-related problems to a great extent but their family income has no significant effect at all on their work.

Table 9.2B reflects that the chi-square value of age, educational quali-fication, marital status, and family size of Baruipur H.O are also highly significant except family income which leads to rejection of H_{02}. So, it can be stated that, the family income of the woman agents does not create any problem while working.

9.5.4   ROLE OF WOMAN AGENTS IN FINANCIAL INCLUSION

Recently, post office is going more popular as a financial institution. Only woman agents can act for the services of recurring deposits in the process of post office financial services. Apart from the inclusion in recurring deposits, the agents are also involved with the other schemes with other common agents.

One way ANOVA, t-test have been used to find the role of woman agents in financial inclusion is shown below.

Most of the respondents of Howrah HO have their income ranging between Rs.10,000–Rs.15,000 and that of Baruipur HO is Rs.15,000–Rs.20,000 (Figure 9.1).

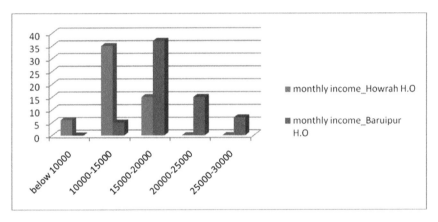

FIGURE 9.1   Monthly income of respondents of Howrah HO and Baruipur HO (in Rs.). *Source*: Primary data survey.

So, it can be concluded that the monthly income of agents of Baruipur H.O is higher than that of Howrah HO.

Figure 9.2 states that the monthly deposits at Baruipur HO are higher than that of Howrah HO.

Two-stage regression analyses are prepared to test how the woman agents are performing in financial inclusion. The simple regression equation is written as $Y_i = b_0 + b_1 X_i + u_i$.

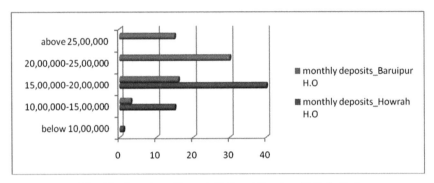

FIGURE 9.2   Monthly deposits at Howrah H.O and Baruipur H.O (in Rs.).
Source: Primary data survey.

Stage 1: To examine how far the variation in monthly income of the agents can be explained by the variation in their working hours. Here, the simple regression model is Monthly income$_i$ = constant + (regression coefficient × working hours$_i$) + error term. The results are shown in Table 9.3.

TABLE 9.3A   Model Summary of Regression Model of Stage 1.

Model	R	R square	Adjusted R square	Std. error of the estimate
1	.802[a]	.644	.641	3122.655

[a]Predictors: (Constant), working hours.
Source: Computed by authors.

The correlation between working hours and monthly income is 0.802 and the value of R^2 is 0.644. R^2 tells that working hours can explain for 64.40% of the variation in monthly income of the agents.

TABLE 9.3B   ANOVA Summary of regression model of Stage 1[b].

Model		Sum of squares	df	Mean square	F	Sig.
1	Regression	2077421694.386	1	2077421694.386	213.048	.000[a]
	Residual	1150615305.614	118	9750977.166		
	Total	3228037000.000	119			

[a]Predictors: (Constant), working hours.
[b]Dependent variable: Monthly income.
Source: Computed by authors.

Again, to test the goodness of fit, F-test is also done. It is found that F-stat is 213.048 with a *p*-value of less than 1%. So, it can be concluded with more than 99% level of confidence that the regression model has a fine predictive power in measuring the variation in monthly income.

TABLE 9.3C   Coefficient Values of Regression Model of Stage 1[a].

Model		Unstandardized coefficients		Standardized coefficients	T	Sig.
		B	Std. error	Beta		
1	(Constant)	−4099.212	1476.396		−2.776	.006
	working hours	191.813	13.141	.802	14.596	.000

[a]Dependent variable: Monthly income.
Source: Computed by authors.

From Table 9.3C, it can be mentioned that coefficient of working hours is highly significant (Sig. value less than 1%). This indicates that working hours play a significant role in predicting monthly income of the agents.

Stage 2: The regression model Monthly deposits$_1$ = constant + (regression coefficient × working hours$_1$) + error term, is used to examine the variation of monthly deposits with the variation of working hours, as shown in Table 9.4.

TABLE 9.4A   Model Summary of Regression Model of Stage 2.

Model	R	R square	Adjusted R square	Std. error of the estimate
1	.796[a]	.633	.630	321392.808

[a]Predictors: (Constant), working hours.
Source: Computed by authors.

It can be concluded that 63.30% of the variation in monthly deposits can be well explained by working hours.

TABLE 9.4B   ANOVA Summary of Regression Model of Stage 2[b].

Model		Sum of squares	Df	Mean square	F	Sig.
1	Regression	21049380390263.950	1	21049380390263.950	203.783	.000(a)
	Residual	12188613735652.720	118	103293336742.820		
	Total	33237994125916.680	119			

[a]Predictors: (Constant), working hours.
[b]Dependent variable: Monthly deposits of customers.
Source: Computed by authors.

From Table 9.4B, it can be stated that F-stat is 203.783 and it is also highly significant with more than 99% level of confidence. Hence, it has a good explanatory power in measuring the variation in monthly deposits.

TABLE 9.4C   Coefficients Values of Regression Model of Stage 2[a].

Model		Unstandardized coefficients		Standardized coefficients	t	Sig.
		B	Std. Error	Beta		
1	(Constant)	−314492.499	151955.015		−2.070	.041
	Working hours	19307.938	1352.547	.796	14.275	.000

[a]Dependent variable: Monthly deposits of customers.
Source: Computed by authors.

From Table 9.4C, it can be stated that coefficient of working hours is highly significant (Sig. value less than 1%). This concludes that working hours play a significant role in explaining monthly deposits of the agents. There is a positive relation in increase or decrease of monthly income and monthly deposits of the woman agents.

9.6   SUMMARY AND CONCLUSION

During post liberalization period, financial sectors like banking sector has taken a leading role for country's economic growth. At the same time, Indian Post Offices also had given the financial services to all sections of people in the society. Indian people, especially the Indian villagers are very much aware of the post office as a banker, which may claim as the pioneer of financial inclusion in India. There is no doubt of the fact that the woman agents of the post offices can lead the path of financial inclusion through their smooth networking system. From the analysis, it is observed that:

➤ A reasonable amount of deposits coming through the woman agents devoting 4–5 h services daily on an average.
➤ There is positive relationship between working hours with the monthly deposits by agents.

> ➤ The earnings of the agents also depend on their working hours, personal effort, family support, etc.

Apart from doing the great role in financial inclusion of the Indian Post Offices, the woman agents are also facing some challenges that hinder the progress of women empowerment, highlighting on the social irresponsibility of the Indian Post Offices. To increase the effectiveness of their role, a few suggestions may be made as follows:

- ❖ Most of the post offices are not well equipped with basic infrastructure. Within this set up, the woman agents are setting their arrangements and helping in financial inclusion. So, there is a strong need for a well-modified infrastructure.
- ❖ Staff members of the post offices are not sufficient to give proper services to the agents so that their time of waiting within the post offices may be minimized.
- ❖ Due to lack of communication between head post offices and sub-post offices, the agents generally suffer in some cases while depositing and also updating the books of the customers. So, an innovative and technologically updated media must be introduced for effective communication at any time.
- ❖ The commission rate in some cases and deposits have been unfortunately reduced by the Central government. This is not a motivating factor of the woman agents at all.
- ❖ There is an urgent requirement of proper training system to bring the innovative ideas of the woman agents.

The chapter suffers from some limitations, viz., small sample size, short study period, only a handful of women agents, etc. increasing the size of the above may lead to different and more reliable results. But it cannot be denied that the present chapter provides an indication as to how the woman agents are helping the Indian Post Offices in mobilizing financial resources from rural people in two districts of West Bengal. The same may be true in case of other head post offices in different districts in West Bengal and also in other states of India. To make a more reliable conclusion in this context, a more systematic research with a wider time frame and resources is necessary.

KEYWORDS

- **post offices**
- **socioeconomic development**
- **financial inclusion**
- **woman agents**
- **social responsibility**

REFERENCES

Ganapathi, R. Investors Attitude Towards Post Office Deposits Schemes. *BVIMR Manag. Edge* **2010**, *3*(2), 26–45.

Jain, D.; Kothari, K. Investor Attitude Towards Post Office Deposits Schemes - Empirical Study in Udaipur district, Rajasthan. *IJMT* **2012**, *2*(7).

Karthikeyan, B. Small Investors' Perception on Post Office Small Savings Schemes', Unpublished Thesis, Madras University, Tamil Nadu, India, 2001.

Kothari, C. R. *Research Methodology - Methods and Techniques,* 2nd ed.; New Age International Publishers: New Delhi, 2004.

Malakar, D. Role of Indian Post in Financial Inclusion. *IOSR J. Humanit. Soc. Sci. (JHSS)* **2013**, *6*(4), 4–7.

Samal, B. Future of India Post, 2013. http://sapost.blogspot.in/2013/05/future-of-india-post-written-by-by.html

Tamilkodi, A. P. P. Small Savings Schemes in Tamil Nadu: A Trend Study (1970–80), Unpublished Thesis, University of Madras, Tamil Nadu, 1983.

CHAPTER 10

Corporate Social Responsibility, Firm Reputation, and Reputational Risks: A Case of the Banking Sector in Ghana

GEORGE KOFI AMOAKO[1*], EFFIE KWANSEMA ANSAH[2], REBECCA BAAH-OFORI[3], and GLADYS NARKI KUMI SOM[4]

[1]*Marketing Department, Faculty of Management, University of Professional Studies, P.O. Box LG 149 Legon Accra, Ghana*

[2]*Accra Institute of Technology, P. O. Box AN-19782, Accra-North, Ghana*

[3]*Faculty of Information Technology and Communication, University of Professional Studies, P.O. Box LG 149 Legon Accra, Ghana*

[4]*Central Business School, Central University Accra Ghana, P.O. Box 2305 Tema, Greater Accra, Ghana*

Corresponding author. E-mail: gkamoako@gmail.com

ABSTRACT

Leveraging on tools for enhancing financial performance, increasing market shares, and other areas of competitiveness have turned out to be very significant in the present competitive world of business. Particularly, within the current milieu of swelling international competitiveness and business best practices, Carroll (2015) stresses that global dimensions of corporate social responsibility (CSR) have in no way supplanted domestic business concerns. Several studies indicate that CSR programs could be utilized as a tool to enhance financial performance and consequently, enhance an organization's corporate reputation as well as buffer its reputational risks. CSR has evolved from economic, social, and environmental dimensions. The idea of CSR has progressively generated interest within corporate institutions, governments and other stakeholders, and has led to broader discussions on its definition between researchers (Carroll, 2004; Dahlsrud, 2006; Robins, 2005). Founded on a review of existent research on CSR, Vilanova et al. (2009) designed a new model on how CSR influences the financial performance of an organization as well as other aspects of its competitiveness. Precisely, they demonstrate that CSR positively influences reputation which in turn enhances performance. The goal of this study is to review or determine whether there is a positive link between CSR, corporate reputation and reputational risks using the Banking sector in Ghana as a case study. A sample of very reputable banking institutions in Ghana has been used in this review. The review supported a positive connection between CSR, corporate reputation, and reputational risks in Vilanova et al.'s (2009) model in relation to CSR and scope of performance. However, a firm that is socially responsible does not necessarily serve as defense mechanism to encounter reputational risks.

10.1   INTRODUCTION

Finding tools to sustain and enhance the financial performance as well as the general performance of organizational competitiveness is very vital in the present competitive international economy. Also, the actions of companies have rippling effects on the economy and/or society in general; hence, corporate social responsibility (CSR) has gained significance among stakeholders of organizations (Lundberg and Ek, 2018). As a result, CSR's effects on firm reputation and reputational risks have garnered much attention in recent years. Several studies have established a positive connection between CSR and financial performance. Vilanova et al. (2009) have designed a model for CSR's connection to an organization's competitiveness including its financial performance. Precisely, they indicate a positive link between CSR and corporate reputation that in turn, is positively connected to different aspects of organizational competitiveness.

The objective of this study is to test the proposed connections in Vilanova et al.'s (2009) model. In other words, a review would be carried out to test the proposed positive connection between CSR and corporate reputation. This chapter examines whether CSR projects enhance corporate reputation and reduce reputational risks. A sample of very high ranking banks customers (students) in Ghana has been sampled for this study. The study discovered that CSR is positively connected with corporate reputation, but it does not necessarily reduce reputational risks.

This review affirms that there is a positive connection between CSR and corporate reputation in Vilanova et al.'s (2009) framework. This implies that organizations that are perceived as socially responsible enhance their reputation. This outcome ought to be of interest to stakeholders who design strategies and engage in conducts that lead to or maintain CSR activities. Usually, the projected benefits that come from an enhanced reputation are utilized to promote CSR projects. This study empirically records a positive connection between CSR and reputation. In addition, the outcomes could build individual stakeholder's trust in investing in businesses with unrivalled CSR initiatives.

10.1.1 THEORIES TO ASSESS AND EXPLAIN CSR

10.1.1.1 STAKEHOLDER THEORIES

The Stakeholder Theory of the firm is utilized as a premise to assess the groups to which an organization ought to cater for. Most stakeholder studies indicate that companies should be comprehended within the context of their stakeholder relationships (Berman and Johnson-Cramer, 2017). According to Freeman (1999), organizations could be defined as a series of connections of partners that the supervisors of the firm endeavor to manage. Freeman defines stakeholders as any group of people or person who can influence or is impacted by the attainment of an institution's goals (Freeman, 1999). Stakeholders are generally categorized under primary and secondary stakeholders. Clarkson (1995) postulates that primary stakeholders are persons whose continuous contribution is integral for the survival of an organization. They include owners and investors, workers, clients and suppliers, as well as public stakeholders such as the government and societies that make available infrastructure and markets, set laws and guidelines that have to be followed, and collect taxes and obligations. Secondary stakeholders are people who impact or are impacted by the organization; however, they are not involved directly in dealings with the organization and are not crucial for its existence.

10.1.1.2   SOCIAL CONTRACTS THEORY

Gray et al. (1996) posits that society is "a series of social contracts between members of society and society itself." With regard to CSR, firms do not act responsibly because it is in their commercial interest, but they do because it is partly how society indirectly expects them to function. Donaldson and Dunfee (1999) created the Integrated Social Contracts Theory as a method for supervisors to make decisions in an ethical context. They distinguish between macro social contracts and micro social contracts. Hence, a macro social contract in communities, for instance, it is a community's expectation that a firm offers some help to the community and the particular type of engagement is the micro social contract.

10.1.1.3   LEGITIMACY THEORY

According to Suchman (1995), legitimacy is a widespread perception or supposition that the actions of an organization are necessary, good, or suitable for some social customs, values, and beliefs. Suchman (1995) reviews existent literature on legitimacy management comprising theories such as the strategic tradition of resource dependence theory (Pfeffer and Salancik, 1978) and institutional traditions (DiMaggio and Powell, 1983). In his analysis, he categorizes three kinds of organizational legitimacy, i.e., pragmatic, moral, cognitive legitimacy.

Similarly, he indicates three major issues with legitimacy management—obtaining, keeping and fixing legitimacy. Furthermore, Suchman posits that legitimacy management is highly dependent on communication. Hence, in any effort to include legitimacy theory, it is essential to analyze certain types of corporate communication.

Consequently, in order to assess the utilization of CSR by businesses as possibly driven by some type of belief as indicated in the social contracts theory, examined with certain stakeholder analysis so as to provide improved reputation or legitimacy to the organization. However, this is not the only method for assessing the utilization of CSR. Nevertheless, the division into principles, practices, and results is a technique to evaluate performance in that field.

10.1.2   DEFINING CORPORATE/FIRM REPUTATION

There are different definitions for corporate reputation in the literature. Gotsi and Wilson discuss different perspectives and indicate that, overall, corporate reputation ought to be seen as "a stakeholder's overall evaluation of a company over time" (2001, p. 29). Reputation is a communally collective impression, an agreement in relation to how an organization will conduct itself in any given circumstance (Bromley, 2002; Sandberg, 2002). It is dependent on some communally held beliefs about an organization's capacity and readiness to fulfill the interests of different stakeholders (Fombrun, 1996).

10.2   BUILDING OF CORPORATE REPUTATION

Corporate reputation is a broad based-stakeholder notion that is revealed in the perceptions that stakeholders have of a firm (Smidts et al., 2001). Findings indicate that reputations with diverse stakeholders interact. Especially, reputation with workers has an effect on a community and clients' perceived reputation of an organization (Carmeli, 2005). Institutions in taking care of their Corporate Reputation must not just consider their relationship with stakeholders, but likewise, manage how individual stakeholder's perception affects each other (Dutton et al., 1994). Reputation is viewed as an important, intangible resource. Reputational assets could appeal to consumers, produce business interest, enhance financial performance, draw top-personnel talent, grow profits on assets, ensure competitive advantage, and draw good feedback from financial analysts (Carmeli and Tishler, 2005; Davies et al., 2003; Fomrun and Gardberg, 2000; Fombrun and van Riel, 2004).

Since reputations can be assessed, some form of comparison is needed. Stakeholders usually analyze what their knowledge of a firm by comparing it to certain standards to decide whether or not it meets their expectations of how a firm ought to conduct itself. The inability to meet their expectations or a gap between their expectations and the firm's conduct should be a concern for the firm (Reichart, 2003). Reputations are largely dependent on stakeholders' evaluation of a firm's capacity to cater for their expectations.

10.3   CSR AND REPUTATIONAL RISK

Reputational risk is the danger or threat against the good name or position of an organization or corporation. Reputational risk could happen as result of different situations: arise as a consequence of the activities of the organization; it could indirectly occur as a result of the conduct of the organization's staff; or tangentially through other external stakeholders including shareholders or suppliers. As well as possessing good administration practices and transparency, businesses additionally have to be socially responsible and environmentally mindful to prevent reputational risk. Reputational risk is a concealed threat that could put the existence of even huge and best-run organizations. It can usually wipe out millions or billions of dollars in market shares or lost revenues and could sometimes lead to a change at the highest levels of management. The major challenge with reputational risk is that it could actually occur out of the blue with no warning. Furthermore, it could happen as a result of the conduct of bad workers, for example, the huge trading losses revealed by some of the world's largest financial institutions occasionally.

10.3.1   DETERMINANTS OF REPUTATIONAL RISK

The degree to which an organization is exposed to reputational risk is dependent on three things. First, it depends on whether the organizations reputation surpasses its actual conduct. Second, to what extent external beliefs and expectations change, which could broaden or (less likely) close this gap. The final factor is the quality of its internal coordination, which could likewise have an impact on the gap.

10.3.2   REPUTATION-REALITY GAP

Successfully handling reputational risk starts with knowing that reputation is a matter of perception. An organization's general reputation is a component of its reputation among its different stakeholders (stockholders, clients, suppliers, workers, regulators, lawmakers, NGOs, and the communities in which the organization runs) in specific classes (product quality, corporate governance, worker relations, client support, intellectual capital, financial performance, and treatment of environmental and social challenges). A solid positive reputation among stakeholders in several classes will lead to a general robust positive reputation for the entire organization.

Reputation is different from the real conduct of the organization and could be better or worse. When the reputation of an organization is more positive than its fundamental reality, this gap is a potential threat. In the end, the inability of an organization to match its supposed reputation would be exposed, and its reputation would decrease until it more closely looks like the reality on the grounds. In order to bridge reputation-reality gaps, an organization should either enhance its capacity to fulfill expectations or decrease expectations by promising less. When expectations are not met, boycotts are an indication of this. During the 1990s, the business press gave the impression that customer boycotts work and that they were growing in number. The Economist, for instance, indicated that pressure groups were attacking American organizations, politicizing business, and frequently giving officials very outrageous ultimatums. Customer boycotts were becoming widespread because they obtain results.

10.3.3   *CHANGING BELIEFS AND EXPECTATIONS*

The changing convictions and expectations of partners are an additional key determinant of reputational risk. When expectations are changing and an organization's behavior remains the same, the reputation-reality gap expands and risks increase. There are several examples of business practices that were previously acceptable to stakeholders, which are no longer accepted to be good or ethical. Before the 1990s, aggressive takeovers in Japan were practically non-existent; this was partially attributable to the cross-holding of shares by the top groups of corporations called the Keiretsu. This was a practice that weakened the power of other investors. As the keiretsu structure weakened in the 1990s, stockholder rights and takeovers have increased. Furthermore, there were some business practices that were accepted in the USA, which are no longer accepted such as brokerage organizations utilizing their research functions to trade venture-banking contracts; insurance underwriters' incentive payments to brokers that made them to charge and structure coverage to serve the interests of underwriters instead of the interests of customers; the selection of the friends of CEOs to serve on the boards of companies as independent directors, income control, and smoothing of incomes.

Additionally, reputation is essential in equity markets. The Social Investment Forum posits that in 2001 almost two billion dollars were put into managed funds subject to social and environmental screening, an increment of 40% from the amount that was invested in 1999. The systems to measure the social and environmental performance of organizations, as well as counsel on its ethical and social obligations, are a multimillion pound business in the UK alone. The majority of consultancy services are linked to accounting practices providing services in the area together with more dedicated consultancies. In addition to CSR impacts on corporate reputation (either positive or negative), there are other arguments in relation to CSR that come from the indirect influence of criticism on poor corporate social performance. They include decreased staff confidence and management time spent replying to NGOs.

10.3.4   WEAK INTERNAL COORDINATION

Another key cause of reputational risk is poor coordination of the decisions taken by different sectors and teams in an organization. In the event that a group creates expectations that another group in unable to meet, the organization's reputation could be hurt. A typical example is the marketing section of a software firm that organizes a huge promotional campaign for new software before developers have identified and fixed all its bugs. As a result, the firm is compelled to choose between introducing an imperfect software or disappointing its customers to introduce it at a later date. Similarly, the timing of unconnected decisions could place a firm's reputation at risk, particularly in the event that it leads a stakeholder team to make negative conclusions. This was experienced by American Airlines in 2003 as it attempted to fight off insolvency. While the company negotiated a significant reduction in pays with its unions, its board accepted that top management keeps its bonuses and a large payment to a trust fund intended to shield executive pensions in case of insolvency. Yet, the organization did not inform its unions; this enraged the unions when they discovered what the company had done. Consequently, they revisited the concessions package they had accepted. Also, poor internal coordination impedes an organization's capacity to identify the changing beliefs and expectations of its stakeholders.

10.3.5   THE DYNAMICS OF THE CONCEPT OF CSR IN CONTEMPORARY TIMES

CSR is an idea that has developed in economic, social and environmental dimensions. The idea has progressively created interest among industries and governments as well as other stakeholders. Likewise, it has encouraged a comprehensive assessment of its definition among some researchers (Carroll, 2004; Dahlsrud, 2006; Robins, 2005). Furthermore, CSR continues to receive attention due to the efforts by international institutions (especially UNGC), governments (for instance, China's green growth strategy), and civil society groups. These initiatives have led to better labor ethics, boosted the utilization of renewable energy and put in place practical anti-corruption measures through transparency in disclosures (UNGC, 2012). Some international organizations that engage in different businesses (MNCs) have engaged in CSR activities that are geared toward promoting sustainable and inclusive business practices to enhance work conditions and improve their corporate reputation globally. Therefore, as the concept of CSR has been developed primarily in western nations, particularly in the USA, the historical advancement of CSR has gained great attention from policymakers and investors globally.

10.3.6   CSR PRACTICE AS A SOCIAL AND BUSINESS RESOURCE

In later part of the 19th century, organizations raised concerns in relation to the welfare of their workers and their effect generally on society. The advent of labor movements as well as the spread of slums as a result of the industrial revolution led industries to offer social welfare on a limited scale for its workforce such as building of hospitals and bath houses as well as the provision of food coupons (Carroll, 2008). At the same time, individual business humanitarians became popular in the USA (e.g., John D. Rockefeller and Cornelius Vanderbilt). Despite the fact that the concept of philanthropy was not at the time very grounded, the benefits provided by these donors were acknowledged by local communities and different social groups (Sharfman, 1994). The values that encouraged these initiatives were mostly religious and led by groups like the Young Men's Christian Association (YMCA) (Carroll, 2008). Carroll (2008) depicts business charity during this time as leading the advancement of

CSR. CSR developed during the 1950s. According to Bowen (1953), CSR is the responsibilities of business owners to follow their policies to make decisions or to pursue initiatives that are in line with the norms and values of the society within which they run their organizations. He contended that businessmen are liable for the consequences of their conducts in a circle that is larger than their corporate financial performance, which signifies the presence and significance of corporate social performance.

CSR focuses on how stakeholders of an organization are treated ethically or in a socially responsible way. Stakeholders can be found both inside the organization and externally. Therefore, being socially responsible could increase the human development of stakeholders both internally and externally. Organizations are increasingly focusing on analyzing their social responsibilities. For instance, according to Business in the Community (2000), it has the goal of producing materials and resources with regard to how organizations ought to measure and record their effect on the community (Business Impact, 2000). The World Business Council for Sustainable Development (WBCSD, 1999) attempts to create a strong comprehension of CSR as well as a matrix of CSR indicators. WBCSD postulates that CSR is the moral conduct of an organization toward society that is management's actions in relation to its connection with other stakeholders that have a real interest in the organization.

In the 21st century, however, the focus has shifted to the implementation of CSR activities as well as an assessment of its impact. Nevertheless, the advancement of the CSR concept is consistently studied. Schwartz and Carroll (2003) decrease Carroll's four classifications of corporate responsibilities (that is economic, legal, ethical, and philanthropic) to a three stage method, which are economic, legal, and ethical. Similarly, the International Labour Organization (ILO) (2007) redefined CSR as a way organization assesses how their operations affect society. Also, CSR values are incorporated into an organization's internal procedures and communication with stakeholders on a purely voluntary basis. Recently, the European Commission (2011) proposed a simpler definition for CSR as the obligation of organizations due to the effects their activities have on society, which show that organizations ought to have a system established to blend their CSR programs into their operations and key strategies in their interactions with stakeholders.

CSR ensures that organizations are able to give back to the communities within which they operate. This is done by assuming responsibility for the effects an organization's activities have on the communities they operate in. One of the benefits of implementing CSR is that it could enhance the organization's reputation (Lin et al., 2016). Also, improved stakeholder opinions present a valuable asset that would result in better financial performance (Walker and Mercado, 2015). CSR is not just good citizenship because it leads organizations to willingly go beyond their legal duties to enhance society's quality of life (Martin, 2008). The focus of socially responsible organizations is not only profit maximization. As CSR initiatives are not just centered on profit maximization, they are still to some extent controversial. Some individuals contend that CSR projects increase costs, affect performance, and compete with value-maximizing programs. Others contend that these extra CSR activities support the performance of an organization and aid value-maximizing programs. CSR initiatives enhance trust and relationships with stakeholders, which could in due course result in increased returns. A socially responsible organization might encounter less labor challenges, less complaints from inhabitants of the community, and less environmental issues from the government. Also, socially responsible organizations might have enhanced relationships with their stockholders, bankers, and government officials. For instance, Barnett and Salomon (2006) propose that growing numbers of investors currently value the manner in which organizations cater for their social responsibilities. The above assertions indicate that an organization's performance greatly benefits from its CSR initiatives. Several studies have analyzed the connection between CSR and financial performance (Chand and Fraser, 2006; McWilliams and Siegel, 2001) and proposed that financial performance is actually a major factor why organizations adopt CSR. Most of these studies affirm that there is a positive connection between CSR and financial performance while it improves on corporate reputation (Barnett and Salomon, 2006; McWilliams and Siegel, 2001). Recently, Vilanova et al. (2009) created a model to demonstrate *how* CSR programs are linked to financial performance as well as other aspects of an organization's competitiveness. They postulate that corporate reputation forms part of the framework that connects CSR and competitiveness. The implementation of a CSR strategy affects the image and reputation of an organization, which in turn has an effect on its competitiveness. As indicated by the model, CSR highly impacts reputation, and reputation is a major factor of an organization's competitiveness (Vilanova et al., 2009, p. 60). In this light, CSR affects an organization's competitiveness primarily through reputation; reputation connects CSR and performance (Vilanova et al., 2009, p. 63). Strategic management theory proposes that a great reputation could produce competitive advantages for organizations (Fombrun, 1996; Roberts and Dowling, 2002; Podolny, 1993). Reputation could turn into an undeniably important resource in rough economic times and cushion financial performance in different ways protecting reputable organizations from the full effect of difficult economic times (Dowling, 2001). Likewise, reputation could shield revenues (Fombrun, 1996) from economic recessions. Clients esteem relations with high-reputation organizations and might pay a premium price for the products of high-reputation organizations particularly in unstable markets and economies (Shapiro, 1983). Furthermore, great reputation could aid the creation of cost advantages (Podolny, 1993, pp. 838–841) and is linked to organizational effectiveness (Stuebs and Sun, 2009, 2010). Good reputation could enhance trust and relationships with different stakeholders, which could result in decreased costs and enhanced effectiveness. Podolny (1993, pp. 838–841) cites some cost decreases that could be the outcome of enhanced reputation. As good reputation draws consumers, promotional costs for bringing business are lesser. Good reputation enhances stakeholder relationships and trust as well as reduces the cost of transactions. Similarly, a good reputation could reduce financial costs. Last, a good reputation could reduce labor costs (Frank, 1985) and enhance labor productivity and effectiveness (Stuebs and Sun, 2010).

10.4   METHODOLOGY

A thorough review was done utilizing available literature and findings of other researchers. The literature used focused on CSR, corporate reputation, and reputational risk. This study examined the relationship among CSR, firm reputation and reputational risk among university student bank customers in Ghana. Students were chosen because most Ghanaian university students actively use bank services; each university student is required to open a bank account as a part of the admission process. Moreover, some students run their own businesses, which require an active bank account. In addition, students generally need bank accounts to receive their allowance from their guardians or parents. Data for this study were gathered from undergraduates at the Central University Business School. The majority of students who participated in the study were between the ages of 20 to 40 years, and earned an income from a job. A team of data collectors was placed at the entrance of Business School; hence, most students who entered the college within that period were approached and asked if they would like to participate in the survey after they had been briefed on the objectives of the study. Those who met the criteria and agreed to participate either answered the questionnaire right away or took it with them to complete it later. They later dropped it into a collection box at the College's front office. A total of 370 questionnaires were distributed; 290 were returned from which 279 had fully been completed and were useful for the study.

The concepts that analyzed were CSR, corporate reputation, and reputational risk. The measurement of these constructs was done using a Likert-type with seven-point scale, beginning from "1" – strongly disagree and "7" – strongly agree. These variables were assessed utilizing the exploratory factor analysis, confirmatory factor analysis, unidimensionality, and construct validity. Structured equation modeling was utilized to test if CSR significantly influences corporate reputation and reputational risk.

TABLE 10.1 Background Information.

Variables	Frequency	Percent
Gender		
Male	123	51.2
Female	117	48.8
Age group		
<21 years	4	1.7
21–30 years	138	57.5
31–40 years	86	35.8
41–50 years	10	4.2
51–60 years	2	0.8
Marital status		
Married	89	37.1
Single	149	62.1
Divorced	2	0.8

TABLE 10.1   *(Continued)*

Variables	Frequency	Percent
Annual income		
<GHC1000	82	34.2
GHC1000–GHC1499	60	25.0
GHC1500–GHC2000	55	22.9
>GHC2000	43	17.9
Total	240	100.0

10.4.1   *DATA ANALYSIS*

10.4.1.1   *EXPLORATORY FACTOR ANALYSIS*

The structure and dimension of the CSR, corporate reputation, and reputational risk constructs were analyzed utilizing Exploratory Factor Analysis (EFA) with Varimax rotation and reliability analysis. The EFA initially produced four factors. After analyzing the pattern matrix of the EFA, all the factors maintained some communalities and factor loadings more than 0.5. Cronbach's alpha for the five-item CSR variables was 0.80; for the four-items, corporate reputation variables were 0.81; for the two-item, reputational risk variables were 0.65 and for the two-item, knowledge of other banks variables were merely 0.28. Due to the low reliability of the fourth factor, it was subsequently deleted before the confirmatory factor analysis was done. The EFA results are shown in the Appendix.

	EFA results				
Coding	Variables and items	EFA factor loadings			
CSR	*Corporate social responsibility*	CSR	CR	RR	OB
CSR1	I consider my bank to be reputable due to its CSR activities	0.793			
CSR2	The CSR activities of my bank influenced my choice of the bank	0.780			
CSR3	The more CSR activities undertaken by my bankers, the higher my perception of its reputation	0.724			
CSR4	The CSR of banks reduces risk of transactions	0.710			
CSR5	I know some CSR activities undertaken by my bank	0.503			

CR	*Corporate reputation*	
CR1	I trust my bank because of its high reputation	0.846
CR2	My bank is highly reputable compared to other banks	0.812
CR3	I will recommend my bank to my relatives and friends	0.789
CR4	My bank has done enough in relation to CSR	0.583
RR	*Reputational risk*	
RR1	The management experience of my bank did not influence my choice	0.833
RR2	The history of my bank did not influence my choice	0.811
OB	*Other banks*	
OB1	I do not transact business with other banks because of risks	0.826
OB2	I am not aware of the CSR activities of other banks	0.615

Correlation matrix for the initial pool of the research construct items generated

	CSR1	CSR2	CSR3	CSR4	CSR5	CR1	CR2	CR3	CR4	RR1	RR2	OB1	OB2
CSR1	1.00	0.65	0.56	0.45	0.52	0.41	0.34	0.42	0.48	−0.04	−0.07	0.11	−0.07
CSR2	0.65	1.00	0.45	0.41	0.48	0.26	0.23	0.30	0.38	−0.11	−0.10	0.16	−0.02
CSR3	0.56	0.45	1.00	0.40	0.30	0.29	0.30	0.25	0.34	0.03	−0.01	0.02	0.04
CSR4	0.45	0.41	0.40	1.00	0.19	0.23	0.13	0.21	0.24	0.12	−0.01	0.18	0.04
CSR5	0.52	0.48	0.30	0.19	1.00	0.30	0.31	0.37	0.40	−0.03	−0.08	0.18	−0.04
CR1	0.41	0.26	0.29	0.23	0.30	1.00	0.60	0.67	0.41	−0.05	0.01	0.12	−0.05
CR2	0.34	0.23	0.30	0.13	0.31	0.60	1.00	0.48	0.49	−0.01	0.05	0.04	−0.01
CR3	0.42	0.30	0.25	0.21	0.37	0.67	0.48	1.00	0.42	−0.07	−0.04	0.14	0.02
CR4	0.48	0.38	0.34	0.24	0.40	0.41	0.49	0.42	1.00	−0.05	−0.06	0.15	0.01
RR1	−0.04	−0.11	0.03	0.12	−0.03	−0.05	−0.01	−0.07	−0.05	1.00	0.48	0.12	0.19
RR2	−0.07	−0.10	−0.01	−0.01	−0.08	0.01	0.05	−0.04	−0.06	0.48	1.00	0.15	0.14
OB1	0.11	0.16	0.02	0.18	0.18	0.12	0.04	0.14	0.15	0.12	0.15	1.00	0.17
OB2	−0.07	−0.02	0.04	0.04	−0.04	−0.05	−0.01	0.02	0.01	0.19	0.14	0.17	1.00

10.4.1.2   CONFIRMATORY FACTOR ANALYSIS

The objective of this chapter is to retain items that have high loadings to maintain face validity as the change indices indicate that several items have a lot in common with one other than the specified model permits. Hence, consistent with existent literature and utilizing CFA, malicious items were sequentially removed until the standardized loadings and the fit indices showed that no enhancement could be achieved through item removal.

The measurement model was estimated utilizing LISREL (8.8). The initial model had poor fit indexes ($\chi^2 = 89.23$, df $= 42$, CFI $= 0.96$, RMSEA $= 0.07$, AGFI $= 0.90$, and model AIC $= 137.23$). The modification indexes indicated that certain items have significant cross loadings. These items are CSR5 and CR4. Therefore, they were sequentially removed and then, the measurement model was rerun after each deletion. The fit indices showed that the modified model gives an outstanding fit to the data (Hu and Bentler, 1999) ($\chi^2 = 32.27$, df $= 25$, CFI $= 0.99$, RMSEA $= 0.03$, AGFI $= 0.95$, and model AIC $= 72.27$). This model has better fit indexes and is preferred for two reasons:

First, the AIC for this (72.27) is lesser than the AIC for the saturated model (137.23). Second, the AGFI for this model (0.95) is more than the AGFI for the saturated model (0.90). Hence, the modified model is used for our discussion in the next sections (see Tables 10.2 and 10.3).

10.4.1.3 UNIDIMENSIONALITY AND CONSTRUCT VALIDITY – FACE VALIDITY

The scales utilized have internal consistency as demonstrated by the high-level composite reliability (Gerbing and Anderson, 1988).

TABLE 10.2 CSR, Corporate Reputation, and Reputational Risk Measurements and Validity.

Code	Variables and items	Factor loading	Composite reliability	Average variance extracted
CSR	*Corporate social responsibility*		0.79	0.50
CSR1	I consider my bank to be reputable due to its CSR activities	0.89		
CSR2	The CSR activities of my bank influenced my choice of the bank	0.72		
CSR3	The more CSR activities undertaken by my bank, the higher my perception of its reputation	0.64		
CSR4	The CSR activities of banks reduce risk of transactions	0.53		
CR	*Corporate reputation*		0.82	0.60

TABLE 10.2   *(Continued)*

Code	Variables and items	Factor loading	Composite reliability	Average variance extracted
CR1	I trust my bank because of its high reputation	0.88		
CR2	My bank is highly reputable compared to other banks	0.67		
CR3	I will recommend my bank to my relatives and friends	0.76		
RR	*Reputational risk*		0.72	0.59
RR1	The management experience of my bank did not influence my choice	0.50		
RR2	The history of my bank did not influence my choice	0.96		

Note: Items deleted during confirmatory factor analysis:
CSR5, CR4.

TABLE 10.3   Correlation Matrix and Reliability Analysis.

Key variables	Mean	SD	1	2	3
1. Corporate social responsibility	4.40	1.39	1.00		
2. Corporate reputation	5.21	1.29	0.52*	1.00	
3. Reputational risk	4.00	1.76	−0.05	−0.04	1.00

Note: *Correlation is significant at 0.01 level.

CFA results indicate that the measures are reliable and valid (Fornell and Larcker, 1981; Gerbing and Anderson, 1988).

- *Convergent validity*: In order to determine the convergent validity, the precise construct items must share a high percentage of variances in common. Based on Table 10.2, the convergent validity, which is demonstrated below;

  1. All item loadings are significant.
  2. The comparatively high average variances extracted (AVE) (CSR = 50%, CR = 60%, RR = 59%).
  3. Composite reliability (CR) is greater than 0.7. (CSR = 0.79, CR = 0.82, RR = 0.72), which affirms the measure's reliability.

The correlation between the indicators is high, which indicates internal consistency and, hence, the construct's unidimensionality (Gerbing and Anderson, 1988).

- *Discriminant validity*: It is vital to show that each construct is different from other constructs and captures certain phenomena that the other measures do not. Discriminant validity is measured by comparing the shared variance (squared correlation) between each pair of constructs against the lowest of the AVEs for these two constructs (Fornell and Larcker, 1981). In this study, the discriminant validity is determined through

  1. The absence of significant cross loadings that are not indicated by the measurement model (i.e., congeneric measures). Similarly, the absence of significant cross loading is shows a construct's unidimensionality (Gerbing and Anderson, 1988).
  2. Also, all variances extracted (AVE) values (Table 10.2) are greater than the square of each of the inter construct correlation values presented in Table 10.3. This shows that the factors have a lot in common with the construct they are linked to than the other constructs. Hence, the three-construct model indicates discriminant validity.

10.4.1.4   STRUCTURAL EQUATION MODELING: HYPOTHESES TESTING

Assessment tests to determine whether CSR significantly influences corporate reputation and reputational risk showed that it does. The outcomes for structural equation model analysis revealed that CSR practices significantly influence corporate reputation ($p < 0.05$): the more banks practice CSR, the more their reputation is enhanced. CSR, however, did not significantly influence reputational risk. This indicates that CSR practice does not necessarily lead to reduction in reputational risk.

Figure 10.2 (Regression weights) shows the t-values for the path diagram.

Figure 10.1 shows the path diagram for CSR, corporate reputation, and reputational risk.

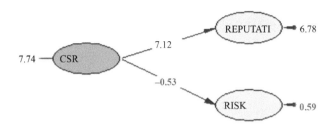

Chi - Square = 32.27, df = 25, P-value = 0.15030, RMSEA = 0.035

FIGURE 10.1   Path diagram for CSR, corporate reputation, and reputational risk.

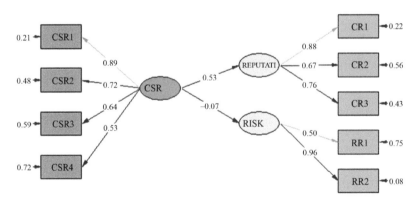

Chi-Square = 32.27, df = 25, P-value = 0.15030, RMSEA = 0.035

FIGURE 10.2   Standardized solutions (regression weight).

10.4.2   MANAGERIAL IMPLICATIONS

The connection between CSR, corporate reputation, and reputational risk are intertwined. Corporate managers need to assess the right approach in their implementation of CSR strategies. This would go a long way to leverage on its positive influence on the reputation of the firm and its products and services.

Also, for a firm to remain competitive enough in this global market place, it needs to devise strategic communication channels to deal with reputational risk if it does occur. CSR's supposed positive influence on corporate reputation, and corporate reputation's supposed positive influence on reputational risk are usually utilized as reasons to validate and push CSR projects. The more banks practice CSR, the more their reputation is enhanced. CSR, however, does not significantly influence reputational risk per the findings of this study. This indicates that CSR practice does not necessarily lead to reduction in reputational risk in the banking sector of Ghana.

10.5   CONCLUSION

This chapter's goal is to assess the effects of CSR on corporate reputation, and its effects on reputational risk. The effect of CSR on reputational risk is created through brand performance. If an organization wants to improve on its performance through its brand or image, its managers should make efforts to enhance the firm's reputation and prevent it from being undermined. A firm's reputation is established in the long term; however, it can be easily hurt or destroyed. The results of the analysis demonstrate that there is a significant positive connection between CSR and corporate reputation. Furthermore, it suggests that organizations that are more socially responsible have better corporate reputations. This further adds to recent CSR research as it validates the proposed relationship in Vilanova et al. (2009). This outcome has significant implications when combined with other findings of earlier studies on CSR. Past CSR researches indicate, overall, a positive connection between CSR and financial performance (Beurden and Gössling, 2008). This study shows that in addition to enhancing financial performance, it enhances reputation. An organization could perform better (enhanced financial performance) by performing better (enhanced CSR and reputation). The structural equation model demonstrated that CSR practices lead to positive corporate reputation; however, it does not significantly lead to reduction in the reputational risk of banks in Ghana.

KEYWORDS

- **corporate social responsibility**
- **firm reputation**
- **reputational risk**
- **banking sector**
- **Ghana**

REFERENCES

Ali, I.; Ali, J. F. *Corporate Social Responsibility, Corporate Reputation and Employee Engagement*, 2011. MPRA Paper No. 33891. Retrieved from: http://mpra.ub.uni-muenchen.de/33891/

Andriof, J.; Waddock, S. *Unfolding Stakeholder Engagement, in S. Sutherland Rahman*, 2002

Barnett, M. L.; Salomon, R. M. Beyond Dichotomy: The Curvilinear Relationship between Social Responsibility and Financial Performance. *Strategic Manage. Rev.* **2006,** *27* (11), 1101–1156.

Barron, D.; Rolfe, M. *Measuring Reputation: Corporate Appeal, Political Influence and Regulation*; Oxford University Press: Oxford, 2011.

Berman, S. L.; Johnson-Cramer, M. E. Stakeholder Theory. Seeing the Field Through the Forest, 2017. https://doi.org/10.1177/0007650316680039 (accessed Mar 12, 2018).

Bowen, H. R. *Social Responsibilities of the Businessman*; Harper & Row: New York, 1953.

Bromley, D. B. Comparing Corporate Reputations: League Tables, Quotients, Benchmarks, or Case Studies? *Corp. Reput. Rev.* **2002,** *5,* 35–50.

Carmeli, A. Perceived External Prestige, Affective Commitment, and Citizenship Behaviors'. *Org. Studies* **2005,** *26* (3), 443–464

Carmeli, A.; Tishler, A. Perceived Organizational Reputation and Organizational Performance: An Empirical Investigation of Industrial Enterprises. *Corp. Reput. Rev.* **2005,** *8* (1), 13–30.

Carroll, A. B. A History of Corporate Social Responsibility: Concepts and Practices. In *The Oxford Handbook of Corporate Social Responsibility*; Andrew, C., others, Eds.; Oxford University Press: Oxford, 2008; pp 19–46.

Carroll, A. B. A Three-dimensional Conceptual Model of Corporate Performance. *Acad. Manage. Rev.* **1979,** *4* (4), 497–505.

Carroll, A. B. Corporate Social Responsibility: A Historical Perspective. In The *Accountable Corporation*; Epstein, M. J., Hanson, K. O., Eds.; Vol. 3; Praeger Publisher: Westport, CT, 2006; pp 3–30.

Carroll, A. B. Corporate Social Responsibility (CSR) is on a Sustainable Trajectory. *J. Def. Manage.* **2015,** *5,* 132. DOI: 10.4172/2167-034.1000132

Carroll, A. B. The Pyramid of Corporate Social Responsibility: Toward the Moral Management of Organizational Stakeholders. *Busi. Horizons*, July/Aug 1991, pp 39–48.

Carroll, C. E. *How the Mass Media Influence Perceptions of Corporate Reputation*: Exploring Agenda-setting Effects within Business Mews Coverage; Dissertation, The University of Texas, Austin, TX, 2004.

CCPA. *Corporate Community Involvement: Establishing a Business Case*; Centre for Corporate Public Affairs: Melbourne, 2000.

Chand, M.; Fraser, S. The Relationship between Corporate Social Performance and Corporate Financial Performance: Industry Type as a Boundary Condition. *Busi. Rev.* **2006,** *5* (1): 240–245.

Clark. T. *The Stakeholder Corporation: A Business Philosophy for the Information Age*; Long Range Planning Publication, 1998.

Clarke, J. *Corporate Social Reporting*: An Ethical Practice? In Gowthorpe, C., 1998.

Clarkson, M. B. E. A Stakeholder Framework for Analyzing and Evaluating Corporate Social Performance. *Acad. Manage. Rev.* **1995,** *20* (1), 92–117.

Dahlsrud, A. *How Corporate Social Responsibility Is Defined: An Analysis of 37 Definitions. Corp. Soc. Respons. Environ. Manage.* **2006.** DOI: 10.1002/csr.132. http://onlinelibrary.wiley.com/doi/10.1002/csr.132/abstract.

Davies, G.; Chun, R.; da Silva, R. V.; Roper, S. *Corporate Reputation and Competitiveness.* Routledge: New York, 2003.

DiMaggio, P. J.; Powell, W. W. The Iron Cage Revisited; Institutional Isomorphism and Collective rationality in Organizational Fields. *Am. Sociol. Rev.* **1983,** *48*, 147–160.

Donaldson, T. Making Stakeholder Theory Whole. *Acad. Manage. Rev.* **1999,** *24*, 237–241.

Dowling, G.R. *Creating Corporate Reputations*; Oxford University Press: Oxford, 2001.

Dutton, J. E.; Dukerich, J. M.; Harquail, C. V. Organizational Images and Member Identification. *Admin. Sci. Quart.* **1994,** *39*, 239–263.

European Commission. Communication from the Commission to the European Parliament, the Council, the European Economic and Social Committee and the Committee of the Regions—A Renewed EU Strategy 2011–2014 for Corporate Social Responsibility, 2011.

Fombrun, C. J. Building Corporate Reputation through CSR Initiatives: Evolving standards. *Corp. Reput. Rev.* **2005,** *8* (1), 7–11.

Fomrun, C. J.; Gardberg, N. Who's Top in Corporate Reputation. *Corp. Reput. Rev.* **2000,** *3* (1), 13–17.

Freeman, R. E. Divergent Stakeholder Theory. *Acad. Manage. Rev.* **1999,** *24*, 233–236.

Gotsi, M.; Wilson, A. M. Corporate Reputation: Seeking a Definition. *Corp. Commun.* **2001,** *6*, 24–30.

Griffin, A. *The Long-term Value of Reputation to Business*. Regester Larkin Reputation Strategy and Management, 2010. http://www.regesterlarkin.com/uploads/the_longterm_value_ofreputation_to_business.pdf

Lin, H.; Zeng, S.; Wang, L.; Zou, H.; Ma, H. How Does Environmental Irresponsibility Impair Corporate Reputation? A Multi-Method Investigation. *Corp. Soc. Respons. Environ. Manage.* **2016,** *23*, 413–423. https://doi.org/10.1002/csr.1387

Lundberg, J.; EK, D. *CSR Reporting in the Banking Industry*. Working Paper Jonkoping University, 2018.

Martin, J. D. *Shareholder Value Maximization: Is There a Role for Corporate Social Responsibility?* Working Paper Baylor University, 2008

Neda, V. Corporate Reputation and Social Responsibility: An Analysis of Large Companies in Croatia. *Int. Busi. Econ. Res. J.* **2011,** *10* (8), 85–96.

Porter, M. E.; Kramer, M. R. Strategy and Society: The Link between Competitive Advantage and Corporate Social Responsibility. *Harv. Busi. Rev.* **2006,** *84* (12), 78–92.

Sandberg, K. Kicking the Tires of Corporate Reputation. *Harv. Manage. Commun. Lett.* **2002,** *5*, 3–4.

Schwartz, M. S.; Carroll, A. B. Corporate Social Responsibility: A Three-domain Approach. *Busi. Ethics Quart.* Oct 2003, pp 503–530.

Servaes, H.; Tamayo, A. The Impact of Corporate Social Responsibility on Firm Value: The Role of Customer Awareness. *Manage. Sci.* **2013,** *59* (5), 1045–1061.

Sharfman, M. Changing Institutional Rules: The Evolution of Corporate Philanthropy, 1883–1953. *Busi. Soc.* **1994,** *33* (3) (Dec), 236–269.

Smidts, A.; Pruyn, T. H.; Van Riel, C. B. M. The Impact of Employee Communication and Perceived External Prestige on Organizational Identification. *Acad. Manage. J.* **2001,** *44* (5), 1051–1062.

Stuebs, M. T.; Sun, L. Corporate Reputation and Technical Efficiency: Evidence from the Chemical and Business Services Industries. *J. Appl. Busi. Res.* **2009,** *25* (5), 21–29.

Stuebs, M. T.; Sun, L. Business Reputation and Labor Efficiency, Productivity and Cost. *J. Busi. Ethics* **2010,** Forthcoming.

Walker, M.; Mercado, H. The Resource-Worthiness of Environmental Responsibility: A Resource-Based Perspective. *Corp. Soc. Respons. Environ. Manage.* **2015,** *22*, 208–221. https://doi.org/10.1002/csr.1339

An Empirical Study on the Perception Variation Regarding CSR Expenditures and Different Purposes for Spending among Selected Companies

SHOUNAK DAS* and SUMI KARMAKAR

Department of Commerce, University of Calcutta, Calcutta, India

Corresponding author. E-mail: snhdas@yahoo.in

ABSTRACT

Corporate social responsibility (CSR) is not a fanfare, it is an important responsibility on the part of every organization to do something for the social, ecological, and economic welfare of their environment, from where they are taking resources for survival. It has been observed over the past few years that many companies legally responsible to spend for CSR activities are not doing as per. The fulfilling of social responsibility is the main determinant for availing of social license to operate in future successfully. It has been observed in the study that different companies under consideration of research, take CSR expenditures in different ways. It has been in that way classified under Carroll's "Pyramid of Responsibilities." The perception variation regarding CSR has a good impact on the distribution of actual CSR spending around prescribed CSR spending and also has a moderate impact on actual CSR spending. The purpose for which CSR expenditures are done also varies widely and the importance is given to various types of expenditure is an important factor in deciding the purpose of expenditure by the companies. The issue of CSR is not taken seriously by most of the companies as visible from their disclosure and spending pattern. The central government realizing this issue has amended the Companies Act

2013 in 2019 to include penal provisions for the companies and officials for non-adhering the CSR rules. The most important remedy to solve this problem is to develop filling for CSR among the companies culturally, like as developed by some companies.

11.1   BACKGROUND

With the tremendous growth of industries in the recent years, it became mandatory for such activities that would protect the society at large from the different impacts of the growing industries/organizations.

CSR is an approach to contribute toward the sustainable development by providing social, economic, and environmental benefits to the stakeholders at large. CSR is often referred to as the "Triple Bottom Line", that is, People, Planet, and Profit. The companies must work toward balancing the economic and social objectives, so as to ensure the social license to operate in the long term success.

The 1950s saw the start of the modern era of CSR when it was commonly known to be SR or Social Responsibility. In 1953, Howard Bowen published his book "Social Responsibilities of Businessman" and coined the phrase "Corporate Social Responsibility's" and is perhaps considered as the "Father of CSR".

The government of India is the first country in the world to make spending for CSR expenditure mandatory for specific categories of companies, fulfilling certain specific conditions. The Companies Act 2013 made it mandatory for some companies to spend a certain prescribed amounts for CSR with effect from 2104–2015 financial years.

Ministry of Corporate affairs has notified Sec 135, Schedule VII of the companies Act and Companies (Corporate Social Responsibility Policy) Rules, 2014; which has come into effect from 1st April 2104.

Section 135 of the Companies Act 2013 provides that mandatory yearly CSR spending of 2% of the average net profit for preceding 3 years will be applicable for the following companies, (1) net worth of the company to be Rs 500 crore or more, (2) turnover of the company Rs 1000 crore or more, (3) net profit of the company Rs 5 crore or more. Again, as per the CSR rules, the provisions of the CSR are not only applicable to Indian Companies, but also applicable to branch and project offices of a foreign company in India.

It has been observed over the years that in spite of the legal obligations there is wide variation among companies regarding perception for CSR spending and for that spread of actual spending around the prescribed spending very wide. Considering this problem, the specific area of the Companies Act 2013 governing CSR expenditure has been amended and put into effect from 2019 July onward.

As per amendment of the Companies Act 2013 regarding CSR provisions, the most important inclusion is the penal provision for nonadherence of the CSR provisions as applicable.

In case of default, the company shall be punishable with fine which shall not be less than fifty thousand rupees but which may extend to twenty-five lakh rupees and every officer of such company who is in default, shall be punishable with imprisonment for a term which may extend to three years or with fine which shall not be less than fifty thousand rupees but which may extend to five lakh rupees, or with both.

Over the years, it has also been observed that purpose for which the CSR sending's done varies widely in terms of absolute spending. Possible reasons for it might be perception variation regarding different purposes; impacted by feasibility, company interest, government pressure, etc.

So, in-depth study regarding perceptual variation regarding CSR expenditure and its impact on the deficit or excess in CSR expenditure and actual CSR expenditure, along with variation in the purpose for which it has been spent needs more research focus.

11.2 LITERATURE REVIEW

The CSR topic has an exhaustive literature that has evolved due to the continuous efforts of researchers, practitioners, and thinkers. Wood (1991) opines that "The basic idea of corporate social responsibility is that business and society are interwoven rather than distinct entities." Cannon (1992) also discussed the evolution of corporate social responsibility over the years. According to him "The primary role of business is to produce goods and services that society wants and needs; however, there is interdependence between business and society in the need for a stable environment with an educated workforce." Carroll's (1979, 1991) defined CSR as follows "Corporate social responsibility encompasses the economic, legal, ethical, and discretionary (philanthropic) expectations that society has of organizations at a given point of time."

"Corporate Social Responsibility In India : An Overview" (2017) by S. Vijay Kumar concludes with the impact of the CSR provisions in India and the rate of CSR spending by different pharmaceutical companies, Banking and Finance Sector Companies, Public Sector Enterprise. "CSR performance: The Story Of Banks in India" (2011) by Suresh Chandra Bihari and Sudeepta Pradhan focus on the CSR activities of major Indian banks and the impact of CSR on performance; more specifically on the Profit After Tax (PAT) of such banks like ICICI, HDFC, IDBI, PNB, Bank of Baroda, Union Bank Of India, Oriental Bank Of Commerce, and the image of such banks have been analyzed. "Emergence And Significance Of CSR in Current Business Scenario" (2015) by K. Priyadrashini and P. Jeyabharathy gave looked into an overview of the corporate social responsible activities by Indian companies, the government's enforcements and to throw light on the times of Indian survey on CSR. Another study titled "A Study On Corporate Social Responsibility And Usage Of Plastic Bags In Small and Medium Size Retail Business In Madurai" (2015) by Kumaran Thayumanavan focused on investigation of small and medium sized retailer's attitude toward the distribution of Plastic bags in Madurai district, the conceptual understanding of the retailers' of CSR. "Corporate Social Responsibility In India: Issues and Challenges" (2015) by Ch. Venkat Rajam examined the attitude and practice of business ethics by different companies and gives an overview of the issues and challenges faced by the corporate to implement CSR.

Based on the extensive review of literature, it has been observed by the researchers that the literature lacks any empirical study regarding the perception variation with respect to CSR expenditures and its impact on actual and deficit or excess in CSR spending and on other hand the variation in spending under different heads due to variation in perception. Hence, the researchers considered this as an important research gap.

11.3   OBECTIVES OF THE STUDY

1. To see how CSR expenditure is being considered by different companies by applying Four Layered Pyramid of Responsibilities of Carroll.
2. To conclude on variation in mean (deficit)/excess in CSR spending among few selected companies.

3. To conclude on variation in mean actual CSR spending among few selected companies.

4. To know what are the different activities for which CSR expenditures are done and whether there is any inequality in spending for different activities and its trend.

5. To conclude on variation in mean CSR spending under different heads of expenditure for top 100 companies as per survey of KPMG India.

11.4   METHODOLOGY FOLLOWED

1. CSR spending pattern, how far it has been actually spent and for what purpose it has been spent and their disclosure; all this information is collected and computed based on company specific documents, various reports, articles, and research publications. These information has been collected and computed for past 10 years (till 2017–2018) for Tata Steel, Tata Motors, Ambuja Cements, Indian Oil Corporation Ltd, NHPC Ltd., ICICI Bank, ITC Ltd., AXIS Bank and BHEL and are analyzed to conclude how these companies consider CSR expenditure. It has been classified into four categories as per Four Layered Pyramid of Responsibilities Model by Carroll. Classification has also been represented diagrammatically. The basis for selection of the companies is the availability of adequate data regarding CSR expenditure and representative of various sectors as much as it is possible.

2. Data regarding actual CSR expenditure and Prescribed CSR expenditure have been collected and there from (deficit)/excess in CSR spending for Tata Motors, Indian Oil Corporation Ltd and ICIC Bank for 4 years from 2014–2015 to 2017–2018 has been computed and presented in tabular form. Single factor ANOV has been conducted to identify whether variation in mean (deficit)/ excess in CSR spending among above companies statistically significant or not.

3. Data regarding actual CSR expenditure have been collected for Tata Motors, Indian Oil Corporation Ltd and ICIC Bank for 4 years from 2014–2015 to 2017–2018 and presented in tabular form. Single factor ANOV has been conducted to identify whether

variation in mean actual CSR spending among above companies statistically significant or not.

4. Category-wise actual CSR expenditure activities for top 100 listed companies as per survey of KPMG India (2018) for 4 years from 2014–2015 to 2017–2018 have been collected. It has been categorized into eight types of activities (represented diagrammatically). It has been analyzed to conclude on what are the different activities for which CSR expenditures are done and whether there is any inequality in spending for different activities and its trend.

5. Category-wise CSR expenditure activities for top 100 listed companies as per survey of KPMG India (2018) for 4 years from 2014–2015 to 2017–2018 have been collected. Single factor ANOV has been conducted to identify whether variation in mean CSR spending under different heads of expenditure for top 100 companies statistically significant or not.

11.5   PRESENTATION OF DATA AND ANALYSIS

The four-layered pyramid of responsibilities model was organized by Carroll as shown in Figure 11.1.

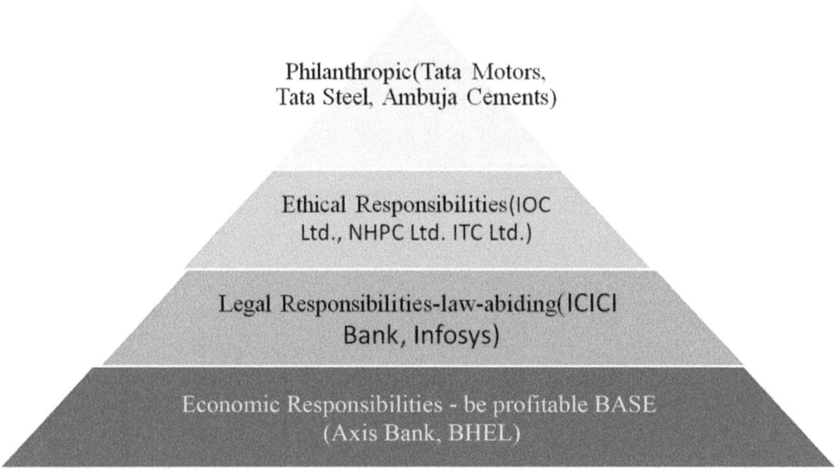

Philanthropic(Tata Motors, Tata Steel, Ambuja Cements)

Ethical Responsibilities(IOC Ltd., NHPC Ltd. ITC Ltd.)

Legal Responsibilities-law-abiding(ICICI Bank, Infosys)

Economic Responsibilities - be profitable BASE (Axis Bank, BHEL)

FIGURE 11.1   The four-layered pyramid of responsibilities model.

Source: Pyramid of Responsibilities by Carroll, 1991

Analysis:

Tata Steel, Tata Motors and Ambuja Cements consider CSR expenditure as their philanthropic duty and they spend it not for abiding any rules, but for ensuring overall social development irrespective of social cost they incurred. The years when they suffer loss; they spend for CSR activities. IOC Ltd., NHPC Ltd., and ITC Ltd. spend CSR as their ethical responsibility and they also do not go by the principle of law abiding for CSR expenditures. They spent for CSR expenditure to mitigate social cost they incurred.

ICICI Bank and Infosys consider CSR expenditure as a legal duty and hence try to spend as per prescribed limit and do not spend for CSR activity considering the social cost they incurred. Companies fall under the economic responsibilities consider profit as the sole motive behind their existence and some companies who are legally out of CSR sphere are polluting the society and who are legally under the CSR sphere try to avoid it.

TABLE 11.1 Annual (deficit) or Excess CSR Spending over Prescribed Limits in (Cr).

Year / Companies	2014–2015	2015–2016	2016–2017	2017–2018
Tata Motors	18.62	20.57	25.94	21.44
IOC Ltd.	(19.61)	15.18	1.32	3.11
ICICI Bank	(16.00)	(40.00)	(18)	.10

Source: Computed by author.

Ho: There is no significant difference in mean (deficit) or excess in CSR expenditure among the three companies.

Analysis:

ANOVA: Single factor

Groups	Count	Sum	Average	Variance
Tata Motors	4	86.57	21.6425	9.598425
IOC Ltd.	4	0	0	208.7997
ICICI Bank	4	−73.9	−18.475	271.5692

Summary					
Source of variation	SS	df	MS	F	P-value	F crit
Between groups	3225.516	2	1612.758158	9.874689	0.005374	4.256495
Within groups	1469.902	9	163.3224194			
Total	4695.418	11				

From the above table, it has been observed that value of *F* is 9.874689 which is higher than the *F* critical value, which is 4.256495 at 95% level of confidence with a *P*-value of 0.005374, which is less than 5%; hence, the Null hypothesis is being rejected and there lies significant difference among the mean (deficit) or excess in CSR expenditure among the three companies. It has been observed that mean deficit reported by ICICI Bank (−18.475) is maximum followed by IOC Ltd. (0) and TATA MOTORS (21.6425). There exist significant difference in mean (deficit) or excess at least between two companies and it is obviously due to perception regarding CSR spending, impacted by their thought process and embedded in organizational culture.

TABLE 11.2 Actual CSR Expenditure in Cr.

Year / Companies	2014–2015	2015–2016	2016–2017	2017–2018
Tata Motors	18.62	20.57	25.94	21.44
IOC Ltd.	113.79	156.68	213.99	331.05
ICICI Bank	156.00	172.00	182.00	170.30

Source: csrbox.

H_0: There is no significant difference in mean actual CSR spending among the three different companies.

Analysis:

ANOVA: Single factor				
Groups	Count	Sum	Average	Variance
Tata Motors	4	86.57	21.6425	9.598425
IOC Ltd.	4	815.51	203.8775	8872.823
ICICI Bank	4	680.3	170.075	114.6892

Summary

Source of variation	SS	Df	MS	F	P-value	F crit
Between groups	75179.22	2	37589.61	12.53389	0.002503	4.256495
Within groups	26991.33	9	2999.037			
Total	102170.5	11				

From the above table, it has been observed that value of F is 12.53389, which is higher than the F critical value which is 4.256495 at 95% level of confidence with a P value of 0.002503, which is less than 5%; hence, the Null hypothesis is being rejected and there lies significant difference in the mean actual CSR spending among the three different companies. It has been observed that mean actual CSR spending reported by IOC Ltd. (203.8775) is maximum followed by ICICI Bank (170.075) and Tata Motors (21.6425). There exist significant difference in actual CSR spending at least between two companies and it is mainly due to higher prescribed CSR spending, but if the difference exists between IOC Ltd. and ICICI Bank; the difference is both due to perception regarding actual CSR spending and higher prescribed CSR spending. Perception is impacted by thought process.

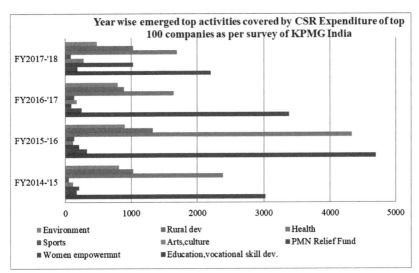

FIGURE 11.2   CSR expenditure activities for top 100 listed companies (as per market capital) as per India's CSR reporting survey (2018) in cr.

Source: India's CSR reporting survey (2018) of KPMG India

Analysis:

Education and Skill Development is the most important activity in all the 4 years under consideration. The CSR spending is very high for it than other activities except health issues for all the years. The expenditure for it increased initially, but then a downward trend is visible. The health is the second most important activity for CSR spending. The expenditure for it increased initially then it falls and a stable trend is visible. The next two activities for which a moderate amount of CSR expenditure is being incurred is Rural Development and Environment CSR spending pattern for Rural Development is highly fluctuating and for Environment it is more or less stable. Spending for the rest of the four activities are more or less stable, except a high increase in expenditure for PMN Relief Fund visible in 2017–2018 and spending amount are very meager in comparison to four top CSR spending activities.

There is a high variation in importance given to various activities by companies for CSR spending as visible from above spending pattern. India being a poor country it is very good that a good portion of CSR spending has been spent for health and education. But Rural Development and environmental issues are also very important for a country like India, expenditures for those activities are not so high and activities like Woman Empowerment and sports are extremely neglected. Spending for Cultural activities and PMN Relief Fund is satisfactory. It has been also observed that in all the 4 years under consideration the top four CSR spending activities and bottom four CSR spending activities remain same.

TABLE 11.3 Year-wise CSR Spending Classification of top 100 Listed Companies (as per Market Capitalization) as per India's CSR Reporting Survey (2018) in Cr.

Year / Expenditures	2014–2015	2015–2016	2016–2017	2017–2018
Environment	812.31	901.8	797	483
Sports	53.56	134.76	133	80
Women Empowerment	172.63	331.5	244	185
Rural development	1031	1327.57	889	1029
Arts & culture	113.62	114.9	168	279
Education	3021.47	4689.81	3384	2202
Health	2382.27	4330.21	1641	1691
PMN relief fund	211	206	90	1029

Source: India's CSR reporting survey (2018) of KPMG India.

H_0: There are no significant differences in mean CSR spending under different heads of expenditure.

Analysis:

ANOVA: Single factor				
Groups	**Count**	**Sum**	**Average**	**Variance**
Environment	4	2994.11	748.5275	33471.7
Sports	4	401.32	100.33	1617.832
Women Empowerment	4	933.13	233.2825	5257.156
Rural development	4	4276.57	1069.143	34100.79
Arts & culture	4	675.52	168.88	6031.566
Education	4	13297.28	3324.32	1073148
Health	4	10044.48	2511.12	1585132
PMN relief fund	4	1536	384	188024.7

Summary						
Source of variation	**SS**	**df**	**MS**	**F**	**P-value**	**F crit**
Between groups	40740193	7	5820028	15.90832	0.000000	2.422629
Within groups	8780352	24	365848			
Total	49520545	31				

From the above table, it has been observed that value of F is 15.90832, which is higher than the F critical value which is 2.422629 at 95% level of confidence with a P-value of 0.00; hence. the Null hypothesis is being rejected and there lies significant difference in the mean CSR spending under different heads of expenditure. It has been observed that mean CSR spending for Education is highest (3324.32), followed by Health (2511.12), Rural Development (1069.143), Environment (748.5275), PMN Relief Fund (384), Women Empowerment (233.2825), Arts & Culture (168.88) and Sports (100.33). The statically significant difference in spending is due to importance given to some specific heads of income by the companies. As health, education, and rural development are in very pathetic condition in India, these sectors receive special importance. Women Empowerment, Environment and sports are also much neglected sectors in India, but still it does not get enough importance due to perception variation among companies.

11.6   CONCLUSION

1. Different companies take CSR expenditure in different pulse, to Tata Motors, Tata Steel and Ambuja Cements it is their philanthropic duty. To IOC Ltd., NHPC Ltd., and ITC Ltd. it is an ethical duty. In case of ICICI Bank and Infosys, the spending for CSR is a legal obligation. Finally, AXIS Bank and BHEL consider profit as the only motive; they not at all recognize CSR spending as an important thing culturally.
2. There lies a significant difference between the mean (deficit) or excess in CSR expenditure among the three companies under consideration and the root cause is the difference in perception concerning CSR expenditure.
3. There lies a significant difference in the mean actual CSR spending among the three different companies under consideration. The main cause is either difference in prescribed pending and difference in perception, both or due to difference in prescribed pending only.
4. CSR expenditures are basically done under health, education, rural development, and environment heads. Rests of the areas have meager expenditure under CSR activities. This concept is true for all the years under consideration.
5. There lies a significant difference in the mean CSR spending under different heads of expenditure. The reason is perception variation regarding items for which it has to be spent, impacted by various factors like government pressures, organizational culture, and interest, feasibility, etc.

11.7   RECOMMENDATIONS

1. More awareness on the part of governments and civil society needs to be spread for recognizing the companies that social motive is equally important like profit motive; for long-term sustenance of any business and business should make believe it from their core that doing CSR is a part of their ethical duty as a social being, not a mere legal obligation.

2. Inequality in spending under CSR activities for different purposes needs to be reduced and for this, government has to develop a separate guidelines or rules regarding this and an adequate awareness on the part of both the government and general public needs to be spread and voiced for company understanding and recognition of importance of spending more amount for neglected areas. It should be done by both increasing the allocation for CSR activities and also doing it in more balanced way.

11.8   LIMITATIONS AND FUTURE RESEARCH SCOPES

The study is basically based on secondary data and considered few companies and years. The more extensive and in-depth study can be done by taking more companies and years, specifically to understand the impact of new regulation on the deficit or excess by applying different other statistical tools and also to know about perception variation in different respects related to CSR. More sophisticated tools can be utilized to understand the sector-specific variation in perception regarding various aspects of CSR and impact of CSR regulations. Primary data can be utilized to understand empirically perception variation among companies regarding CSR and its various aspects.

KEYWORDS

- **corporate social responsibility**
- **social license**
- **ecological**
- **perception variation**
- **penal provisions**

REFERENCES

Annual Reports of the Companies, Ministry of Corporate Affairs, Government of India.
Balasubramanian, N. K. CSR as an Instrument Of Global Competitiveness. *IIMB Manage. Rev.* **2003,** 61–72.

Bihari, S. C.; Pradhan, S. CSR and Performance: The Story of Banks in India. *J. Trans. Manage*. **2011**, *16*, 20–35.

Cannon, T. *Corporate Responsibility*, 1st ed.; Pitman Publishing: London, 1992.

Companies Act, 2013—Challenges and Opportunities for Corporate Growth, Global Publication, 2014.

Corporate Social Responsibility Report. . Cisco. 2019.

Corporate Social Responsibility Reporting. *China USA Business Review*, 2012, Vol. 11, . No.11.

Crane, A.; Mathen, D.(. *Corporate Social Responsibility*; Vol. I, II, III; Sage: London, 2007.

CSR Report. Polyplastic CO., Ltd., 2019

CSRbox Official Website.

Fatma, M.; Rahman, Z. Consumer Perspective on CSR Literature Review and Future Agenda. *Manage. Res, Rev.* **2015**, *38* (2).

http://en.wikipedia.org/wiki/Corporate_social_responsibility.

http://home.kpmg.

http://www.bhel.com/.

http://www.icicibank.com.

http://www.iocl.com.

http://www.itcportal.com.

http://www.nhpcindia.com/.

http://www.tatamotors.com.

https://economictimes.indiatimes.com/

https://indianexpress.com/.

https://timesofindia.indiatimes.com.

https://www.ambujacement.com/.

https://www.axisbank.com/.

https://www.cisco.com/c/en_in/index.html.

https://www.hindustantimes.com.

https://www.infosys.com/.

https://www.polyplastics.com/en/.

https://www.tatasteel.com/.

https://www.telegraphindia.com/.

https://www.thehindu.com.

https://www.thestatesman.com/.

Kumar, S. V. Corporate Social Responsibility in India: An Overview. *J. Asian Busi. Manage*. **2017**, 9 (1), 53–67.

Maigan, I. Ferrell, O. Corporate Social Responsibility and Marketing. An Integrative Framework. *J. Acad. Market. Sci.* **2001**, *32* (1), 3–19.

Muniapan, B.; Das, M. Corporate Social Responsibility: A Philosophical Approach from an Ancient Indian Perspective. *Int. J. Indian Culture Busi. Manage*. **2008**, 1 (4). 408–420.

Nalband, N. A.; Kelabi, S. A. Redesigning Carroll's CSR Pyramid Model. *J. Adv. Manage. Sci*. **2014**, 2 (3), 236–239.

Report of the High Level Committee on Corporate Social Responsibility, Ministry of Corporate Affairs. 2018.

Singh, A.; Verma, P. From Philanthropy to Mandatory CSR: A Journey Towards Mandatory Corporate Social Responsibility in India. *Eur. J. Busi. Manage.* **2014,** *6* (14), 146–152.

Singla, A.; Sagar, P. . Trust and Corporate Responsibility: Lessons from India. *J. Commun. Manag.* **2004,** . *8* (3), 282–290.

Srivastava, A. K.; Nehi, G.; Mishra, V.; Pandey, S. Corporate Social Responsibility: A Case Study of TATA Group. *IOSR J. Busi. Manag.* **2012,** *3*, 17–27.

Tewari, R.; Pathak, T. Sustainable CSR for Micro, Small and Medium Enterprises. *J. Manag Public Policy* **2014,** *6* (1), 34–44.

Wheeler, D.; Colbert, B.; Freeman, R. E., . Focusing on Value of Corporate Social Responsibility, Sustainability and a Stakeholder Approach in a Network World. *J. Gen. Manag.* **2003,** *28* (3), 1–28.

Wood, D. J.. Corporate Social Performance Revisited. *Acad. Manage Rev.* **1991,** *16*, 691–718.

www.csr-weltweit.de

www.forbesindia.com

Corporate Social Responsibility: Impact and Outcome Approach, Emerging Challenges

NAND L. DHAMEJA* and FERHAT MOHSIN

FMS Manav Rachna International Institute of Research and Studies (MRIIS), Faridabad, India

Corresponding author. E-mail: nanddhameja@yahoo.co.in

ABSTRACT

Corporate social responsibility refers to the business responsibility to the community in response to environmental, social, ethical, and economic concerns. The study relates to the concept and practices of CSR, changing the structure of such spending, and raises certain issues and challenges arising from such practices. The paper is divided into four parts. The first part presents examples of certain distortions relating to socio-economic inequality, lagging human development indicators, pollution, and environment degeneration necessitating the need for CSR, it raises issues like:

- Who is responsible for all these distortions? How can these be mitigated?
- What are the approaches for such mitigation and contribution practices, in India and abroad?
- What issues and challenges arise from such practices?

CSR involves the relocation of resources from private to public bodies for environmental and social benefits to integrate with the organizational core business. This is the subject matter of part two and presents, in brief, the meaning and significance of CSR for the organizations and employees.

There have been different approaches toward CSR contribution, such contributions are voluntary in Western countries, and India is the only country where such contribution as a certain percentage of profit is mandatorily required. The third part presents the contribution practices of business houses and agencies in India and abroad..

In India, for the fiscal year 2017, an actual contribution by the top 92 companies, for which data were available, was Rs. 6810 crore, (against the total prescribed contribution of Rs.7388 crore) and these included 15 public sector units (PSUs) accounting for Rs. 1996 crore, that is, about 29% of the total Education and healthcare were the main attraction for CSR contribution. Top ten corporations' share of contribution was nearly 50% of the total which amounted to total contribution of approximately Rs. 18,000 crore.

The last part traces the changing practice of CSR spending as it has moved corporate social activity from the fringes to the forefront or board-rooms and is in many cases linked to impact. It leads to certain issues as:

- As every business uses national resources, should not the contribution be in relation to resources utilized rather than profit?
- Why CSR contribution be restricted to incorporated enterprises? Should every enterprise, whether incorporated or not, commercial or not, profit-making or not, be required to contribute for the resources deployed?
- Social and economic distortions, referred to above, are caused by all residents, should there be not a system to make individuals contribute toward CSR. As such CSR should be better to called "Citizen Social Responsibility".
- There should be a system to identify enterprises having good CSR, just as there are identification mark VEG (GREEN) or Non-VEG (RED) for eatables, or "ISI" or "Hall Mark" or Agmark to reflect respective purity; or for that matter every cigarette packet mandatorily carries health hazard requirement, that is, "Smoking is Injurious for Health".
- Responsibility should not only to contribute and spend, but should also indicate "impact" and "outcome" of such spending to reflect its effectiveness. As mentioned earlier, some companies have started following the approach of reflecting impact or outcome.
- Last, as contribution toward CSR is by handful of companies, and that too in many cases, their contribution is higher that mandatorily

required, will such law not have dampening effect and such higher contribution be incentivized.

Corporate social responsibility is business responsibility in response to environmental, social, ethical, and economic concerns. The study relates to the concept and practices of CSR, changing the structure of such spending, and raises certain issues and challenges arising from such practices. The paper is divided into four parts. The first part presents certain distortions relating to socio-economic inequality, lagging human development indicators, pollution, and environmental degenerations necessitating the need for CSR. Since CSR involves the relocation of resources from private to public bodies for environmental and social benefits to integrate with the organizational core business; this is the subject matter of part two and presents, in brief, the meaning and significance of CSR for organizations and employees. Part three lists three different approaches toward CSR contribution discusses the mandatory system of CSR contribution in India and presents the practices of contribution by various business houses and agencies abroad and India. The changing practice of CSR spending, as it has moved corporate social activity from the fringes to the forefront or boardrooms, or its linkage to impact and also certain issues arising therefrom are the subject matter of part four. Summary and conclusions are presented at the end.

Economies are developing but there are certain distortions relating to socio-economic inequality, lagging human development indicators, environment degeneration. Various socio-economic parameters impinging growth of an economy, in particular, developing economy, include:

- Spending on Research & Development in India as a percentage of GDP is only 0.6 of which two-third is spent by government. For China, the corresponding percentages are 1.83 and 10; and for USA are 2.8 and 10[19]
- As regards medical care,[13] India has very scanty medical services as for every 1000 people, there were only 1.7 trained allopathic doctors and nurses to compared 2.5 as recommended by WHO guidelines.
- Bed density in India in 2002 was 0.67 per 1000 population with the global average of 2.6 and WHO benchmark of 3.5. India requires about 6–7 lakh of additional beds over the next 5–6 years requiring an investment of US $ 25–30 billion.

- Private spending on medical care in India is about three-fourth and only a fraction is covered by insurance.
- As regards higher education, India has about 800 universities and about 6 lakh colleges; general enrolment ratio (GER) for higher education is only 25, while for China and other countries, the GER is more than twice this figure.
- In the list of world top 500 higher education institutions, India has only nine institutions, the corresponding figures for China is 22.
- Similarly, as regards, research impact reflected by Published Research Metrics (1996–2007), there were only 12.64 million citations with an H-Index of 521 for India, the corresponding figures for China were 39.24 million and 712, respectively.[19]
- Pollution in any form like noise, water, and air has become a serious issue in developing countries after WW II due to rapid industrialization and lack of regulations, and it is the root cause of many diseases that kill and disable living organism.
- Air pollution has significant health impacts that have increasingly been becoming major environmental challenges. Burning of crop residue is one reason for worsening of air quality in Punjab, Haryana, Uttar Pradesh, and Delhi NCR and financial assistance for agricultural mechanization has been a step toward improvement of air quality. As an example, to control air pollution, government took a decision to leapfrog from BS-IV to BS-VI fuels.[15]

  Continuing unabated deforestation, mining, and construction has been adversely hurting the ecology of Western Ghat covering states namely, Gujrat, Maharashtra, Goa, Karnataka, Tamil Nadu, and Kerala; and a large area over 56,825 km^2 of "ecologically sensitive area" could not be saved from constant environmental degradation.[22]

  Cigarette butts are among the most abundant types of human produced garbage in oceans as plastic based filter made of cellulose acetate has been found to affect sea birds and sea turtles.[4] Oil spills, chemical manufacturing, diamond mining, agriculture, and fishing are other examples having detrimental effects on environment.[7]

  Increasing population is demographic advantage, but as a result of geographical diversity and increasing dependency ratio from 100: 193 in 1991 to 100: 223 in 2001 to expected 100: 300 in 2040, is quite alarming.[18]

From above socio-economic aberrations, one may ask,

- Who is responsible for all these?
- How can these be mitigated?
- What are the approaches for such mitigation?
- What have been the practices in India and abroad in carrying out activities toward philanthropy or development of society and what has been the changing scenario of such practices?
- What are the issues and challenges for such practices in future?

Before we attempt to address the above issues, and discuss contributions by certain business organizations or others toward economic and social development, let us briefly discuss the meaning and significance of CSR.

12.1   CSR MEANING AND SIGNIFICANCE

CSR has been defined differently by various authorities. Definition by UNIDO is all inclusive and it goes as

"CSR is a management concept whereby companies integrate social and environmental concerns in their business operations and interactions with their stakeholders. CSR is generally understood as being the way through which a company achieves a balance of economic, environmental, and social imperatives (Triple-Bottom-Line Approach) while at the same time addressing the expectations of shareholders. In this sense it is important to draw a distinction between CSR, which can be strategic business concept and charity sponsorships or philanthropy. Even though the latter can also make a valuable contribution to poverty reduction, will directly enhance the reputation of a company and strengthen its brand, the concept of CSR clearly goes beyond that."[21]

As against the above, Business Dictionary defines CSR as "A company's sense of responsibility towards the community and environment (both ecological and social) in which it operates. Companies express this citizenship (1) through their waste and pollution reduction processes, (2) by contributing educational and social programmes and (3) by earning adequate returns on the employed resources"[6]

CSR termed as "Triple-Bottom-Line" (TBL) approach helps companies to promote its commercial interests along with its responsibilities towards the society. CSR is broader than the acts of charities or philanthropic activity as it (the former) is a part of business strategy; to address socio-economic and environmental issues to achieve Sustainable Development Goals (SDGs) in the long run.[21]

In other words, private individuals or agencies work for the betterment of society by undertaking various activities or functions so as to mitigate social evils, though government always remains as a facilitator.[7]

Corporations are benefitted from CSR as:

- It improves public image and also relationship with consumers;
- It helps to attract and retain productive employees;
- It also becomes attractive to investors.

Employees are also benefitted from CSR as:

- Workplace environment becomes positive, productive, and instill strong culture among employees;
- Brings in creativity by developing leadership qualities among employees;
- Encourages professional and personal growth.

12.2   CSR APPROACHES

Countries have adopted different CSR approaches[7,20]; even in European countries adoption of CSR is very heterogeneous; the normal practice is to disclose. CSR approaches followed could be categorized under three broad heads as:

- CSR as Corporate Philanthropy
- CSR as Value Creation
- CSR as Risk Management

12.3   CSR ENACTMENTS IN INDIA

Certainly, there have been philanthropic contributions by various agencies and business houses. Approaches of such contributions vary among coun-tries. Such contributions are voluntary in Western countries while India is the only country where such contribution is mandatory for certain profit-able business organizations. As per the law enacted in April 2014, certain profitable companies are required to contribute toward CSR equivalent to 2% of average profit of the last 3 years.

CSR activities can be carried out in any one of the following three ways:

- through a registered Trust or Society set up under its direct administrative control or
- by outsourcing the CSR tasks to a non-for-profit enterprises engaged in CSR activities for at least 3 years, or
- in collaboration with fellow companies having some arrangements based on the CSR rules.

Rule for carrying out CSR activities:

- CSR will not include personal or family activity.
- Administrative and operational expenses of business cannot be included as CSR activity.
- Contribution to political organizations cannot be a part of CSR activity.
- CSR activities should be carried out in Indian territory.
- CSR Committee comprising of at least three directors, of which one shall be independent director, shall be responsible for carrying out the CSR activities of listed companies; while for unlisted companies or private companies, CSR Committee shall have at least two directors, independent director on the Committee is not mandatorily required.
- CSR Report shall be published every year as per the format prescribed. The Report shall include details like, CSR policy, details of funds utilized, and explanation for non-utilization of funds, if any. These must also be displayed on the official website of the company.
- Up to 5% of CSR spending can be deployed for capacity building exercise.

As against the above, there is view that objective of a business enterprise is to maximize profit in the interest of its shareholders, and it should not be expected to contribute toward CSR as the business enterprise does not have expertise in CSR. In the words of economist Milton Friedman,[10] "there is one and only one social responsibility of business—to use its resources and engage in activities designed to increase its profits...".

Milton Friedman argued that corporations do not have the skills and expertise on social activities like, how to alleviate poverty, educate the uneducated, and empower women.

As against the above-mentioned alarming socio-economic parameters impacting nation's development, there are ample examples of business houses world over contributing toward the development of societies.

Business houses contributions toward society abroad:

- In a recent example, Alibaba's Jac Ma, China's richest man, has announced his plan to step down from the Chinese e-commerce giant worth $420 billion on September 13th, his 54th birthday to pursue philanthropy in education.
- Walmart Foundation, besides small donations in the communities where it operated, has over 990 of charitable organizations that have plans to invest for skill development and career readiness.
- Most of the major universities like Harvard, Stanford, Yale, and Oxford have been set up by philanthropic funds. They raise funds from several sources and are aggressively seeking philanthropic funds. They use bait such as naming important buildings after major donors after offering donors honorary degrees and so on.

As an example, Stanford University was founded in 1885 by California Senator Leland and his wife Jane Stanford in the memory of their only child Leland Stanford Jr. who died of typhoid fever at the age of 13 years. They donated a large fortune including the 8180-acre Palo Alto stock farm to set up university with the objective, "to promote the public welfare by exercising an influence on behalf of humanity and civilization."

Similarly, Satya Nadella, CEO Microsoft said,

Everywhere we operate, we focus on contributing to local communities in positive ways helping to spark growth, competitiveness and economic opportunity for all.

Microsoft, a multinational company, has the mission to empower every person and every organization on the planet and to get technology and skill for digital economy; to ensure that technology benefits reach individual; and to bring broadband connectivity to Americans, in particular the rural communities.

12.3.1   CSR CONTRIBUTIONS AND ITS DISCLOSURE IN THE US

CSR, as stated earlier, is voluntary in European and USA,[5] though there is a disclosure of such contribution. Disclosure in USA is as:

- 95% of world largest 259 companies published their Annual CSR reports.
- 65% of Fortune 500 companies offered matching gift programs.
- $17.8 billion were contributed toward CSR by corporations during 2017.
- 55% of consumers were willing to pay more for products from socially responsible companies.

Similarly, a study[9] by the Reputation Institute (RI), a Boston-based reputation-management consulting firm, on the basis of a survey of consumers' perceptions covering company governance, positive influence on society, and treatment of employees, for 170,000 respondents in 15 countries, has accorded *Rep Trak Pulse* (The *Rep Trak Pulse* reflects issues like how people evaluate companies in general, or has the company become more critical, or does it behaves ethically, conducts business fairly, operates transparently, protects the environment, and supports worthy causes). Top 10 most responsible companies in the descending order of Rep Trak Pulse system points, listed in the study are as:

	1	2	3	4	5	6	7	8	9	10
Company	Lego	Microsoft	Googles	Wait Disney Co.	BMW Group	Intel	Robert Bosch	Cisco Systems	Rolls-Royce Aero-space	Colgate-Palmolive
Rep Trak Points (in %)	74.4	74.1	73.9	73.5	71.5	71.1	71.0	71.0	70.7	70.4

12.3.2   PHILANTHROPIC ACTIVITIES UNDERTAKEN BY BUSINESS HOUSES IN INDIA

In India, large-scale philanthropic activities were undertaken by business houses to build some of India's finest institutions. For example, Sir Ratan Tata Trust (SRTT) established in 1919, and The Sir Dorabji Tata Trust established in 1932, provide grants and partner with organizations that engage in innovative and sustainable initiatives in the areas of education, health, civil society, and governance. Tata Sons spent about Rs. 750 crore during 2015–2016 on various philanthropic activities and Institutions.

Similarly, Birla companies have contributed to non-government organizations (NGOs) and to their own trusts to run various educational, healthcare institutions, Birla Institute of Technology and Sciences, Pilani, set up in 1964 by G. D. Birla is an example. G. D. Birla founder of Birla Group, espoused the concept of *"trusteeship"*; which entails that the wealth generated by the company, is to be held as in a trust for our multiple stakeholders, for the larger good of society, and that is CSR

The philosophy of *"Trusteeship"* has been followed over generations in Birla Group. Accordingly, the concept of *"sustainable livelihood,"* which transcended *cheque book philanthropy* was weaved in by the successor, *Aditya Birla*. In his view, it was unwise to keep on giving endlessly. Instead, he felt that channelizing resources to ensure that people have the wherewithal to make both ends meet, would be more productive. To quote, Aditya Birla, *"Give a hungry man fish for a day, he will eat it and the next day, he would be hungry again. Instead, if you taught him how to fish, he would be able to feed himself and his family for a lifetime."* The successor Kumar Mangalam Birla, institutionalized the concept further represented by economic success.

As regards contribution toward CSR activities, the Birla Group spends in excess of Rs. 250 crore annually,[1] covering 20 hospitals and 56 schools, spread-out 5000 villages reaching out 7.5 million people annually, of which 60% are below poverty line and belong to scheduled casts and scheduled tribes. For the CSR spending, the focus area is rural development, to help build model villages covering activities in five key areas namely, education, health & family welfare, social causes, infrastructure development and sustainable livelihood.

In terms of amount spent on CSR, as per Ministry of Corporate Affairs since the enactment of CSR rules in 2014, Rs. 9554 crore was spent during 2014–2015, and this increased to Rs. 13,625 crore by 7983 companies for the year 2015–2016. However, 187 companies defaulted in spending during 2014–2015 and were subjected to penal action.[3]

CSR spending in 2017, as stated by Saurabh Kumar[16] in his blog on Corporate Social Responsibility, has improved as 33% companies have spent more than 2% of net profit, that is, more than the mandated spending; and defaulters of CSR spending have reduced from 44% in 2016 to 36% in 2017; however, more than one-third of the companies have not complied with the CSR rules and release of data. Analysis of CSR spending for top 100 companies[17] listed on National Stock Exchange (NSE) indicates that:

- there is not much change in their CSR spending,
- education and health care attract most of the monies,
- Maharashtra has the maximum inflow of CSR spends.
- For 2017, an actual spend for the top 92 companies, for which data were available, was Rs. 6810 crore, these included 15 public sector units (PSEs) accounting for Rs. 1996 crore, that is, about 29% of the total.

Fifty percent of the total of CSR spending was by top 10 companies, that is, Rs. 3307 crore. According to Abhishek Humbad, founder and chief executive officer of Goodera, the overall CSR spending has reduced by 10% that of the last year, due to (1) companies' profits have grown at lower rate, and (2) 16% of companies reduced their overall CSR spending, though their profits increased.

Public sector focus: In case of public sector enterprises (PSEs), CSR spending reduced by 9% during 2017, though the prescribed spend grew by 1%. To improve, spending should be to invest in fewer but strategic projects instead of taking up more projects. "On an average, while private companies take up 14 projects, the corresponding number for PSEs is 26, which leads to thinning of resources and lack of adequate focus on projects under PSEs." However, NTPC which ranked no. 6 in the spend tally, spent almost half of its CSR budget on hunger, healthcare, and poverty alleviation projects; also, its CSR activities were primarily in the neighborhood villages of its units.

According to Ranjan Kumar Mohapatra, director human resources, Indian Oil Corp. Ltd (IOCL),[8] public sector entities are generally at "an advantage" when carrying out CSR activities since they do not need to obsess over profit. CSR has moved corporate social activity from the fringes to the forefront or boardrooms. CSR activities are not a new thing, IOC has been involved with various state government projects and initiatives especially in healthcare, education, and skilling since its inception in 1964 and CSR is a subset of sustainable development. Of late the focus is converting waste to energy and plants each of a capacity of 5 tons/day have been set up at Varanasi and Faridabad. Specialized technical education is the another area of IOC focus, and Institute of Chemical Technology

(ICT)–IOC is being set up at Bhubaneswar in collaboration with ICT Mumbai and students will be able to pursue integrated MTech courses in chemical engineering, executive MTech, and PhD programs.

Nearly half of the top 10 CSR spenders spent during 2017, more than 2% of their profits, that is, more than the prescribed limit. In that respect, Tata Steel Ltd, which ranked at No. 9, led the tally with a spending of almost 67% above its prescribed limit. According to Biren Ramesh Bhutta, Chief CSR Officer, Tata Steel, 2% of profit was not a cut-off limit, rather we look for high-impact activities to bring in social change, and this is built into the DNA of our company. He believed that the need for the day was that more companies in India should carry out effective CSR practices. To quote Biren Ramesh Bhutta, "There are two compelling reasons: if you as a business want to survive for 100 years, you have to do right by the society you work in and if you want to grow, you cannot do so by leaving a large section of the society so behind."

Besides Tata Steel Ltd., other top contributors included RIL, ONGC, TCS, HDFC, Infosys, NTPC, and ITC. It may be mentioned that as against the actual spending of Rs. 6810 crore on CSR during 2017, the figures for the years 2016 and 2015 were Rs. 6188 crore and Rs. 6151 crore, respectively. The prescribed CSR contribution for the corresponding 3 years were Rs. 7388 crore, Rs. 6799 crore and Rs. 6151 crore, respectively. This is reflected by the following Exhibit I.

12.4   EXHIBIT I

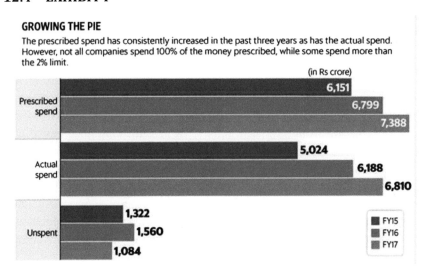

GROWING THE PIE

The prescribed spend has consistently increased in the past three years as has the actual spend. However, not all companies spend 100% of the money prescribed, while some spend more than the 2% limit.

(in Rs crore)

Looking at the developments in CSR spending since 2014, the year it was mandated in India, following observations can be made:

- The actual CSR spending as percent of the mandated spending has increased over 3 years from 82% in 2015 to 91% in 2016, to 92% for the year 2017. However, the rate of increase of CSR spending has reduced from 23% during 2016 to 10% during 2017.
- CSR Spending has moved beyond the compliance, with focus on creating a long-term impact for the beneficiaries. In this respect, Humbad of Good era said, "Many companies are proactively conducting extensive monitoring and evaluation, and impact assessment for their projects and reporting these through CSR specific detailed reports." Similarly, processes and governance have been focused for CSR spending by Infosys. In the words of Sudha Murty, Chairperson of Infosys Foundation, "These have been tightened. Third-party impact assessment has been introduced and is periodically reviewed for improvement. Reach has been expanded to other states where Infosys Foundation does not have a presence."
- There have been certain changes in CSR spending over the years. "The first two years, there was struggle to get clarity on how existing work should be aligned to CSR and how initiatives have to be taken that are in conformity to the CSR schedule. In the third year (i.e. 2017), we found an improvement in quality of proposals that are being developed and an increased interest to develop flagship programmes that will give the companies greater visibility," says Niraj Seth, EY India.
- CSR spending in public sector is also focused on impact assessment. For example, IOC has taken many structural as well as procedural interventions to strengthen the CSR process, has framed a CSR Policy and Guidelines to streamline the execution, monitoring, evaluation, and impact assessment of its activities; CSR activities are mostly now being executed in project mode and unit-level CSR panels have been constituted to conceive, implement and monitor CSR projects; according to Kali Krishna, chief general manager (corporate communications).
- Thought process, as regards CSR spending, is going beyond spend allocation, according to Jayaram of KPMG. To quote Jayaram, "We see more detailed discussion around impact and very structured process for monitoring and evaluation."
- Companies have looked at the impact assessment of CSR spending during the last 3 years. In that respect, Sukthankar of HDFC Bank states as, "This is our third year of CSR learning: While working

in a specific geography, even though we may have started with one project or one specific activity, when we identified other areas of intervention that could make things better for the community, we saw value in a more holistic approach."

- Again, in that respect, according to Ambasta of ITC, "After a slow start, companies have set their CSR policy, focus areas and implementation mechanism in place. Most companies over the last three years are bound to have increased their CSR spends till they at least touch the 2% target. This has and will positively impact as well as address the developmental challenges that our country faces, including reduction in inequality."

Reliance Industries Limited (RIL)[14] carries out its CSR activities under the aegis of Reliance Foundation (RF). The key philosophy of all the social development initiatives of RIL is based on three core commitments of Scale, Impact, and Sustainability. The Reliance Foundation focuses on the social initiatives with a three-pronged strategy:

- to have direct engagement with the community;
- through collaborations and partnerships at state and local government and also with non-government agencies;
- through Jio Infocomm by leveraging the power of information technology.

During 2017–2018, RIL's CSR initiatives focused on the following seven areas with a total expenditure of Rs. 771 crore, which was above the required limit (the average PAT for the 3 years was Rs. 36,075 + 29,901 + 25,171 = 91,147; average Rs. 30382). The CSR spending on seven areas for the year 2017–2018 presented below indicates that about 90% of total spending was on three areas namely, education, rural transformation and health, and of this education accounted for a lion share of 48% of the total.

	Amount spent (Rs. crore)	In percentages
Education	373	48.4
Rural transformation	195	25
Health	148	18
Sports for development	50	
Disaster response	4	
Arts, culture & heritage	1	
Urban renewal	–	
Total	771	

Source: Annual Report 2017–2018 (pp 164–165).

12.4.1   ISSUES FOR CONSIDERATION

As discussed above, various socio-economic parameters impinging nation development arise on corporations' working—whether profit making or not. As such, CSR contribution should be linked to resources deployed rather than the profit earned. CSR contribution in relation to profit is rather inequitable as it amounts to taxing efficiency by requiring profit making companies to contribute.

According to P R Ramesh,[12] Chairman of auditing, financial advisory and risk management firm, Deloitte India, "It is an obligation of every organisation to give back to the community because businesses use resources of the community and they don't exist in isolation." As such, CSR contribution should not only by profit making companies, but CSR expenditure also should be a percentage of revenue and not just profit.

Further, it is not only the incorporated enterprises, but also unincorporated enterprises, or even the individuals should be made responsible to contribute toward CSR. As such CSR should not be corporate social responsibility, but rather it should be *Citizen Social Responsibility.*

Contribution toward CSR is by a handful of companies, as discussed earlier, top 10 companies contributed about half of the total contribution for the year 2017, and such companies had been contributing even before the enactment in 2014. As such, how far the objective of the enactment to bring a change in the attitude of corporates to give back to the society, has been achieved; and is there not a need to have a relook on the mandatorily requirement and also the procedure and methodology of such contribution. Since there are companies which contribute more than the required amount, should it not be incentivized? For example, Mindtree Ltd, the Bengaluru-based information technology (IT) outsourcing company got the shareholders' approval to spend up to 10% of net profit on social cause. As such, with $88.4 million profit last year, the company plans to spend over 6.5% of its profit on social causes, which includes 2% spend on CSR and the 4.5% grants to academic institution, that is, set up a Mindtree AI (artificial intelligence) Chair at Stanford University.[11]

As there is a requirement to have a distinct mark, *"Veg" or "non-veg food" by "Red" or "Green mark"*; *Hallmark* for silver and gold jewellery, *ISI* mark for industrial products, and *Agmark* for agricultural products certifying their respective purity[2]; and on every cigarette packet, there is a mandatory *Health Hazard Requirement*, similarly, a system to reflect or otherwise observance or erosion of social values be institutionalized. Examples of GAP, the San Francisco-based clothing company, Nike and many other companies which faced widespread consumer backlash on their reported abusive labor practices, highlight the need to institutionalize such system rather than to leave it to the market forces.

Last, responsibility should not only be to spend, but also to indicate its *"impact" and "outcome,"* though some companies are already carrying out extensive monitoring and evaluation, and impact assessment of CSR spending initiated. In this regard, P R Ramesh[12] raised the point that responsibility should not be about CSR spending toward social works or about *"outlays."* but rather it should be about *"outcomes"* of the spending, and the "impact measurement metrics system" be in place that will facilitate incentivization of CSR spending.

12.5 SUMMARY AND CONCLUSIONS

CSR is an age-old concept and every enterprise has an obligation to give back to the community as it uses nation resources. Working of an enterprise causes certain distortions resulting in environmental degeneration impacting nation's growth. No doubt business houses contribute to address to the issue of economic and environmental degeneration, such contribution involves relocation of resources from private to public bodies. India is the only country where such contribution is mandatory for certain profitable business enterprises. Analysis of CSR spending by top 100 NSE listed companies indicate that not much has changed; that the contribution by top 10 companies account for half of the total contribution; education and healthcare account for the highest share, and that Maharashtra is having the maximum CSR contribution.

The study concludes that:

- Every enterprise should have the obligation to give back to the community for the resources deployed, so CSR should be linked to the revenue, the practice of mandatory relating to profit amounts to taxing of efficiency; and every enterprise whether profit making or not, should be required to contribute.
- Further, it is not only the incorporated enterprise, but also unincorporated enterprises, or even the individuals should be made responsible to contribute. As such CSR should better be known as *Citizen Social Responsibility.*

- The enactment in 2014 was with an objective to bring a change in the attitude of corporates to give back to the society, as a contribution so far is by a handful of the companies which otherwise had been contributing, there is a need to have a relook on the mandatory requirement and also the procedure and methodology of such contribution; as there are companies which contribute even more than the required amount, such contributions should be incentivized.
- System that reflects or otherwise observance or erosion of social values be institutionalized similar to that by a distinct mark, as *"veg" or "non-veg" by "red" or "green" mark; Hall mark logo for jewellery, ISI mark for industrial products and Agmark for agricultural products*; or for a cigarette packet, a mandatory *"Health Hazard Requirement."* Such system should be institutionalized and not be left to market forces as in the cases of GAP, San Francisco-based clothing company, and Nike which faced consumer backlash on their reported abusive labor practice.
- Last, CSR should not only be to spend, but emphasis also should be to have a system for extensive monitoring and evaluation and impact assessment for CSR projects, as is being practiced by some companies.

KEYWORDS

- **aberrations**
- **mitigation approach**
- **resource allocation**
- **contribution practices**

REFERENCES

1. Birla Group. Annual Report, 2017–2018.
2. Bureau of Indian Standard (BIS) is the national standard organization in India and it has laid down Hall mark logo for jewellery, ISI mark for industrial products and Agmark for agricultural as an indicator of their respective purity.
3. Corporate Trend. *Economic Times*, 18 Dec 2017.

4. Cigarette Butts One of the Biggest Ocean Pollutants. *Times of India*, 4 Sept 2018, p 15.

5. CSR Contributions and Its Disclosure in the US. *Double the Donation Research* https://doublethedonation.com/tips/matching-grant-resources/matching-gift-statistics/Matching Gift and Corporate Giving Statistics (updated Aug 2018)

6. CSR Defined in Business Dictionary as Reported in Wikipedia

7. Nand, D. Corporate Social Responsibility Initiatives: Practices and Issues. *Indian J. Public Admin.* **2016,** *LXIII* (4), 761–780.

8. Zagar, H. PSUs Need to Join Forces to Deliver Big-ticket Social Projects. *Live Mint*, 27 Aug 2018.

9. Karsten Strauss Forbes Staff. The 10 Companies with the Best CSR Reputations in 2017. https://www.forbes.com/sites/karstenstrauss/2017/09/13/the-10-companies-with-the-best-csr-reputations-in-2017/#601

10. Friedman, M. *Capitalism and Freedom*; The University of Chicago Press: Chicago, 1962; p 60637.

11. Mindtree Move to Spend 10 Percent Profit on CSR Spurs Investors Debate. Live Mint, 8 Aug 2018.

12. Manku, M. CSR Expenditure Should Be a Percentage of Revenue, Not Profit. *Mint*, 15 Apr 2015.

13. Mitra, P.; Vaidya, M. India Healthcare: Inspiring Possibilities Challenging Journey. McKinney & Co. and Confederation of Indian Industries (CII) December, 2012.

14. Reliance Industries Limited. Annual Report 2017–18; pp 164–179.

15. Sharma, S. Air Quality in North India to Be Better this Winter Than 2017. *Hindustan Times*, 27 Aug 2018.

16. Kumar, S. Corporate Responsibility under Companies Act, blog,ipleaders.in/csr-laws-in India, 28 June 2018.

17. Chowdhry, S. How Companies are Spending on CSR Projects? *Live Mint*, 17 Oct 2017.

18. Ajai, S. World Population Day: Is India Moving Towards Being an Ageing Economy? India May Become Old Before It Has a Chance to Become Rich. *Mint*, 11 July 2018.

19. Kundu, T. Learning from China's Rise in Higher Education. *Mint*, 6 Aug 2018. H index, or Hiresch index measures the research impact of a scientist or an institution or a journal. A scientific contributor with an index of h has published h papers, each of which has been cited in other papers at least h times.

20. Tilcsik, A.; Marquis, C. Punctuated Generosity: How Mega-events and Natural Disasters Affect Corporate Philanthropy in U.S. Communities. *Admin Sci. Quart* **2013,** *58* (1), 111–148, as Reported in Wikipedia, Corporate Social Responsibility.

21. United Nations Industrial Development Organization. https://www.unido.org/our-focus/advancing-economic-competitiveness/competitive-trade-capacities-and-corporate-responsibility/corporate-social-responsibility-market-integration/what-csr (Mar 13, 2018). http:///www.unido.org/what-wew-do/trade/csr/what-is csr-htm/#pp1{g1}/0/,

22. Mohan, W. Failure to Stop Degradation of Western Ghat Worsened Kerala. *Times of India*, 27 Aug 2018.

Index